ST/ESA/STAT/SER.M/4/Rev.3.1

DEPARTMENT OF ECONOMIC AND SOCIAL AFFAIRS
STATISTICS DIVISION

STATISTICAL PAPERS   SERIES M No. 4 REV.3.1

International Standard Industrial Classification of All Economic Activities (ISIC)

Revision 3.1

United Nations • New York, 2004

NOTE

Symbols of United Nations documents are composed of capital letters combined with figures. Mention of such a symbol indicates a reference to a United Nations document.

ST/ESA/STAT/SER.M/4/Rev.3.1

UNITED NATIONS PUBLICATION
Sales No. E.03.XVII.4

ISBN 92-1-161456-2

Enquiries should be directed to:
SALES SECTION
PUBLISHING DIVISION
UNITED NATIONS
NEW YORK, NY 10017

Preface

The International Standard Industrial Classification of all Economic Activities (ISIC) is the international reference classification of productive economic activities. Its main purpose is to provide a set of activity categories that can be utilized for the production of statistics according to such activities.

Since the adoption of the original version of ISIC in 1948, the majority of countries around the world have used ISIC or developed national classifications derived from ISIC. ISIC has therefore been providing guidance for countries in developing national activity classifications and has become an important tool for comparing statistical data on economic activities at the international level.

The final draft of revision 3.1 of ISIC was considered and welcomed by the Statistical Commission at its thirty-third session in March 2002.[1] It now replaces the third revision of the classification,[2] which has been in use since 1989.

---

[1] See *Official Records of the Economic and Social Council, 2002, Supplement No.4* (E/2002/24), para. 54 (a).
[2] Statistical Papers, No.4, Rev.3 (United Nations publication, Sales No. E.90.XVII.11).

Summary of contents

Table of contents

Part one

Introduction to ISIC

I. Historical background and revision

A. Historical background

1. The original version of the International Standard Industrial Classification of All Economic Activities (ISIC)[1] was adopted in 1948. In that connection, the Economic and Social Council adopted resolution 149 A (VII) of 27 August 1948, which read:

"The Economic and Social Council,

"Taking note of the recommendation of the Statistical Commission regarding the need for international comparability of economic statistics, and,

"Taking note of the International Standard Industrial Classification of All Economic Activities which the Statistical Commission has developed with the advice and assistance of Member Governments,

"Recommends that all Member Governments make use of the International Standard Industrial Classification of Economic Activities either by:

" (a)   Adopting this system of classification as a national standard, or

" (b)   Rearranging their statistical data in accordance with this system for purposes of international comparability".

2.   Wide use has been made of ISIC both nationally and internationally in classifying data according to kind of economic activity in the fields of economic statistics, population, production, employment, national income and others. A number of countries have utilized ISIC as the basis for developing their national industrial classification. Substantial comparability has been attained between the industrial classifications of many other countries and ISIC by ensuring, as far as practicable, that the categories at detailed levels of national classifications fitted into only one category of ISIC. An increasing number of countries have adapted their national activity classifications or can provide statistical series according to ISIC. The United Nations, the International Labour Organization (ILO), the Food and Agriculture Organization of the United Nations (FAO), the United Nations Educational, Scientific and Cultural Organization (UNESCO), the United Nations Industrial Development Organization (UNIDO) and other international bodies use ISIC when publishing and analysing statistical data.

3.   Experience in the use of ISIC has revealed the need for periodic review of the structure and definition of its categories and underlying principles. Changes take place in the organization of economic activities and new types of economic activities become important. New analytical requirements develop for data classified according to kind of economic activity. The continuing experience in the use of ISIC and the corresponding national classifications reveal aspects that should be amplified, clarified or improved in other ways. For these reasons, the Statistical Commission initiated reviews and revisions of ISIC in 1956, 1965 and again in 1979. In each instance, the Commission emphasized the need to maintain as much comparability between the revised and preceding versions of ISIC as was possible while introducing the alterations, modifications and other improvements.

4.   The first revision of ISIC[2] was issued in 1958, after having been considered by the Statistical Commission at its tenth session. The second revision[3] was issued in 1968 after proposals for the revision had been considered and approved by the Commission at its fifteenth session in 1968. The third revision of ISIC[4] was considered and approved by the Commission at its twenty-fifth session in 1989 and issued in 1990.

5.   Unlike previous revisions, the third revision of ISIC required harmonization with other activity classifications and with classifications of goods and services. This requirement added considerable complexity and constraints that had not applied in earlier revisions of ISIC. As ISIC occupies a central position in the international comparison and analysis of a wide range of statistics, a great deal of attention was devoted to ensuring that ISIC would be compatible with the economic structure, and the statistical practice and needs of the different countries in the world. Although the general structure of the classification was not changed significantly, a greater level of detail was introduced, especially in the part dealing with service activities, reflecting the growth of this sector of the economy in most countries of the world. The harmonization with other classifications improved the usefulness of ISIC for many analytical and descriptive purposes, for instance, within the context of the extended elaboration of services in the Central Product Classification (CPC).

B. The 2002 update to Revision 3

6.   In the 10 years since the publication of the third revision of ISIC, the economic structure in many countries of the world has changed at an unprecedented rate. The emergence of new technologies and new divisions of labour between organizations has created new types of activities and new forms of industries. This poses a challenge for providers as well as users of statistical data. In response to the growing demands of providers and users of data, the Expert Group on International Economic and Social Classifications, at its fourth meeting in 1999, recommended that an update of the third revision of ISIC be undertaken to better reflect changed structures and analytical requirements.

7.   In this update to ISIC, Rev.3, the structure of the classification and the boundaries of its building blocks remain largely unchanged. Attention has been paid to providing explanatory notes in extended detail, allowing for more accurate interpretation of the content and boundaries of individual classes. New activities that have emerged over the previous 10 years are reflected in the new explanatory notes, allowing for easier, more consistent and thus less ambiguous application of ISIC.

8.   The definition of alternate aggregations for analytical use has been reviewed and updated. While some of the aggregations previously published in the ISIC manual have now been replaced by defined aggregations in other specialized frameworks, new needs for aggregations have emerged. The creation of an "Information sector" was requested by many countries in order to better reflect its importance for national economic activities related to the production and dissemination of information, as well as the interest of analysts in this evolving area. In order to minimize the impact of the creation of this new category, following requests by most countries to preserve the existing structure of ISIC while reflecting change of the economic reality, it was decided to create the information sector in an alternate structure. Experiences with the implementation and use of this alternate structure will be evaluated for inclusion in the regular structure of the classification in future revisions. The definition of an alternate aggregation for the informal sector is in pursuance of the need experienced by many countries to have an internationally agreed definition for data collection and analysis in this area, which is extremely important for a large number of countries.

9.   As requested by the Statistical Commission at its thirtieth session in 1999, future work on ISIC will be guided by the need for convergence between existing activity classifications at the international and multinational levels.[5] This has been reflected in the creation and review of alternate aggregations and, to some degree, in the extended definition of individual classes, drawing on research work already done for other classifications.

II. The underlying principles of the Classification

A. Purpose and nature of the Classification

1. General considerations

10.   In the study of economic phenomena, taking all elements into account simultaneously is not always possible. For purposes of analysis, certain elements need to be chosen and grouped according to particular characteristics. Thus, all economic processes that are to be described in the form of statistics require systematic classification. Classifications are, so to speak, the system of languages used in communication about, and statistical processing of, the phenomena concerned. They divide the universe of statistical data into categories that are as homogeneous as possible with respect to those characteristics that are the objects of the statistics in question.

11.   ISIC is intended to be a standard classification of productive economic activities. Its main purpose is to provide a set of activity categories that can be utilized for the collection and presentation of statistics according to such activities. Therefore, ISIC aims to present this set of activity categories in such a way that entities can be classified according to the economic activity they carry out. Defining the categories of ISIC is as much as possible linked with the way the economic process is organized in units and the way in which this process is described in economic statistics.

12.   In this context, it would be best if there were as many categories in ISIC as there are possible activities or if each production unit carried out only one activity. In this case, a unit could be clearly classified in a certain category. However, for practical reasons, ISIC can have only a limited number of categories. Carrying out only one activity may often be in conflict with the organization of activities and, as a result, in bookkeeping practices. In addition, some types of data, such as financial data, are often available only for units performing several activities, which consequently are not homogeneous in respect of economic activity. Another aspect of homogeneity is the distribution in geographical areas, particularly important for regional statistics. Although the geographical aspect has, in principle, little to do with the activity classification, it does affect the formation of statistical units. Therefore, the homogeneity of units relates to both activity and location.

13.   The requirements for homogeneity and data availability are sometimes in conflict with each other because the smaller or the more homogeneous the unit, the less the data are possibly available. It is suggested (see sect. D of the present chap.) that this problem be solved by using different units for different statistics, defined in such a way that each larger unit consists of a number of complete smaller units. As a result, comparisons can be made between the various statistics even when they use different units.

14.   The detail required in the classification of data by kind of economic activity differs from country to country. Differences in the geographical and historical circumstances and in the degrees of industrial development and organization of economic activities result in differences in the degree of elaboration with which various countries find it necessary or feasible to classify their data according to

kind of economic activity. The level of detail for purposes of international comparison is generally lower than that available for national analysis. In chapter III, it will be explained how ISIC can be used or adapted for national purposes.

2. Differences from other types of classifications

15.   ISIC is a classification according to kind of economic activity, and not a classification of goods and services. The activity carried out by a unit is the type of production in which it engages. This is the characteristic of the unit according to which it will be grouped with other units to form industries. An industry is defined as the set of all production units engaged primarily in the same or similar kinds of productive economic activity.

16.   As it is not possible, even in principle, to establish a one-to-one correspondence between activities and products, ISIC is not designed to measure product data at any detailed level. For this purpose a separate classification was developed, namely, the Central Product Classification (CPC). Although each category in CPC is accompanied by a reference to the ISIC class where the goods or services are mainly produced (criterion of industrial origin), classification of products is based on the intrinsic characteristics of the goods or the nature of the services rendered (see also chap. IV, sect. B).

17.   ISIC does not draw distinctions according to kind of ownership, type of legal organization or mode of operation because such criteria do not relate to the characteristics of the activity itself. Units engaged in the same kind of economic activity are classified in the same category of ISIC, irrespective of whether they are (part of) incorporated enterprises, individual proprietors or government, and whether or not the parent enterprise consists of more than one establishment. Similarly, manufacturing units are classified according to the principal kind of economic activity in which they engage, whether the work is performed by power-driven machinery or by hand, or whether it is done in a factory or in a household. Modern versus traditional is not a criterion for ISIC, although the distinction may be useful in some statistics. Also, ISIC does not distinguish between formal and informal or between legal and illegal production. Classifications according to kind of legal ownership, kind of organization or mode of operation may be constructed independently of the classification according to kind of economic activity. Cross-classification with ISIC can provide useful extra information.

18.   In general, ISIC does not differentiate between market and non-market activities. However, it should be emphasized that this distinction continues to be an important feature of the System of National Accounts (1993 SNA).[6] A breakdown of economic activities according to this principle is useful in any case where data on value added are collected for activities that take place on both a market and a non-market basis. This criterion should then be cross-classified with the categories of ISIC. Non-market services are most frequently provided by government organizations or non-profit organizations in the field of education, health, social work etc.

19.   This revision of ISIC includes categories for the undifferentiated production of goods and services by households for own use. These categories cover, however, only a portion of households, as households with clearly identifiable activities (market or non-market) are classified in other parts of ISIC. These categories have been created for special purposes, such as labour-force surveys, to cover households that it would be otherwise difficult or impossible to assign to other ISIC categories.

B. Principal, secondary and ancillary activities

20.   When discussing economic productive activities, the expression "activity" is to be understood as a process, that is to say, the combination of actions that result in a certain type of products. In other words, an activity can be said to take place when resources such as equipment, labour, manufacturing techniques or products are combined to produce specific goods or services. Thus, an activity is characterized by an input of resources, a production process and an output of products. By convention, one single activity is defined as a process resulting in a homogeneous type of products. In this context, a homogeneous type of products are understood to fall within a category, the production of the members of which is characteristic of a class (the most detailed category) of the activity classification.

21.   One activity as defined here may consist of one simple process, for example, weaving, but may also cover a whole range of sub-processes, each of which is mentioned in different categories of the classification. For example, the manufacturing of a car is considered one activity even though its integrated production process includes sub-activities such as casting, forging, welding, assembling, painting etc. Moreover, if manufacturing of specific parts, such as engines, gearboxes, furniture or instruments, is organized as an integral part of the same manufacturing process, the whole combination of processes is regarded as one activity.

22.   Also, when an enterprise produces end products, the production processes of which fall within different categories of the activity classification, the enterprise is supposed to carry out only one principal activity if these production processes are highly interrelated or integrated. If, for instance, pumps and gearboxes are produced and the casting for both products is carried out by the same employees with the same machines, one of the two processes should be considered a secondary activity; which one is to be so considered should be determined on the basis of the value added (see sect. E of this chap.).

23.   On the other hand, when two or more products of a homogeneous type are produced next to each other, but have production processes that are not interrelated, that is to say, the processes are completely independent with respect to the organization of the production, then these processes may be seen as different activities that are similar, however, with respect to the activity classification. If, for example, pens and pencils are produced in the same enterprise, using, however, different inputs and different production techniques, the enterprise may be considered to carry out two activities even though they both fall within the same category of the classification. This does not imply that, as a consequence, different production units must be distinguished.

24.   Distinction should be made between principal and secondary activities on the one hand and ancillary activities on the other. The output of principal and secondary activities, which are consequently principal and secondary products, is produced for sale on the market, for provision free of charge or for other uses that are not prescribed in advance, for example, they may be stocked for future sale or for further processing. Ancillary activities are undertaken in order to facilitate the principal or secondary activities of the entity.

25.   The principal activity of an economic entity is the activity that contributes most to the value added of the entity, or the activity the value added of which exceeds that of any other activity of the entity. It is not necessary that the principal activity account for 50 per cent or more of the total value added of an entity. The products resulting from a principal activity are either principal products or by-products. The latter are products that are necessarily produced together with the principal products, for example, hides produced when producing meat by slaughtering animals. In section E of this chapter, it will be explained how, in practice, the principal activity of a statistical unit should be determined when classifying according to ISIC.

26.   A secondary activity is each separate activity that produces products eventually for third parties and that is not a principal activity of the entity in question. The outputs of secondary activities are necessarily secondary products. Most economic entities produce at least some secondary products.

27.   Principal and secondary activities cannot be carried out without the support of a number of ancillary activities such as bookkeeping, transportation, storage, purchasing, sales promotion, cleaning, repair and maintenance, security etc. At least some of these activities are found in every economic entity. Thus, ancillary activities are those that exist to support the main productive activities of an entity by providing non-durable goods or services entirely or primarily for the use of that entity.

28.   There are a number of characteristics of ancillary activities that can generally be observed in practice and that help to identify them as ancillary. The output is always intended for intermediate consumption within the same entity and is therefore usually not recorded separately. Although most ancillary activities produce services, some goods-producing activities may, by exception, be regarded as ancillary; the goods thus produced, however, may not become a physical part of the output of the main activity (examples are tools, scaffolding etc.). Ancillary activities are usually fairly small-scale compared with the principal activity they support.

29.   Since processes are generally not viable without the support of a certain number of ancillary activities, the latter should not be separated to form separate entities even though the ancillary activities may be carried out in a separate legal entity or in a separate location and even though separate records may be available (see also sect. D of this chapter). Also, the ancillary activity should not count in determining the activity code of the entity to which the ancillary activities belong. The value of the ancillary activities should be allocated to the principal and secondary activities of the unit they serve. If no exact information on their distribution is available, they should be proportioned according to the value added of the principal and secondary activities. The clearest examples of entities carrying out ancillary activities are central administrative offices or "head offices". Other examples are sales departments, warehouses, garages, repair shops, electricity power plants and accounting or computer departments that primarily serve their parent units.

30.   Under the definition given in paragraph 27 above, the following activities are not to be considered ancillary (therefore, in all these cases, if separate data are available in respect to the activities, separate units should be distinguished and they should be classified by their own activities):
    (a)   Producing goods or doing work that is part of fixed capital formation. The type of units most affected are those doing construction work on the account of their parent unit. This approach is in accordance with the classification in ISIC of own-account construction units for which data are available, to the construction industry;
    (b)   Activities the output of which, although used as intermediate consumption by the principal or secondary activity, is for the greater part sold on the market;
    (c)   Producing goods that become a physical part of the output of the principal or secondary activity, for example, the production of boxes, tin cans or the like by a department of an enterprise, as packaging for its own products;
    (d)   Research and development. These activities are not universal and they do not provide services that are consumed in the course of current production.

31.   Where ancillary activities are organized in support of two or more entities of a multi-unit enterprise, they may constitute a central ancillary entity. In such cases, and similarly when there is a strong interest in covering some activities entirely regardless of whether they are carried out independently or by ancillary entities (for example, computer activities), it could be expedient to make

supplementary tabulations. Ancillary entities could for this purpose be classified according to their own activity besides their classification to the activity of their parent unit. For classification of separate units carrying out ancillary activities, see paragraph 96 below.

C. Principles used in constructing the Classification

1. Criteria in respect of divisions and groups

32. The main criteria employed in delineating divisions and groups (the two- and three-digit categories, respectively) of ISIC concern the characteristics of the activities of producing units which are strategic in determining the degree of similarity in the structure of the units and certain relationships in an economy. The major aspects of the activities considered were (a) the character of the goods and services produced, (b) the uses to which the goods and services were put and (c) the inputs, the process and the technology of production. In delineating the divisions of ISIC, attention was also given to the range of kinds of activity frequently carried out under the same ownership or control and to potential differences in scale and organization of activities and in capital requirements and finance that exist between enterprises. Additional criteria used in establishing divisions and groups were the pattern of categories at various levels of classification in national classifications.

33. In the case of the character of the goods and services produced, account was taken of the physical composition and stage of fabrication of the items and the needs served by them. Distinguishing categories of ISIC in terms of nature of goods and services produced furnishes the basis for grouping producing units according to similarities in, and links between, the raw materials consumed and the sources of demand and markets for the items.

34. The criteria relating to the economic transactors (for example, non-financial enterprises, financial institutions, government, households etc.) and to the types of transactions (for example, intermediate and final consumption, capital formation etc.) reinforce the considerations in respect of the stage of fabrication of, and the needs served by, these items. Applying these criteria in establishing divisions and groups enhances substantially the value of ISIC in distinguishing producing units according to sources of demand and markets for their output and in tracing ties among the producing units, and between them and the rest of the economy. These criteria were also employed in ordering classes within groups and groups within divisions. This improved the hierarchical structure of data arranged according to ISIC.

35. The weights assigned to the types of criteria described above varied from one category to another. In a number of instances, for example, food manufacturing, the textile, clothing and leather industries, the production of machinery and equipment and the service industries, the various aspects of activities are so highly correlated that the problem of assigning weights to the criteria did not arise. In the case of intermediate products, physical composition and stage of fabrication of the items were often given the greatest weight. In the case of goods with complicated production processes, the end use, technology and organization of production of the items were frequently given priority over the physical composition of the goods.

2. Criteria in respect of the classes

36. The criteria concerning the manner in which activities are combined in, and allocated among, establishments were central in the definition of classes (four-digit categories) of ISIC. They were intended to ensure that it will be practical most of the time to use the classes of ISIC for the industrial

classification of establishments, and that the units falling into each class will be as similar in respect of the kinds of activity in which they engage, as is feasible. The classes of ISIC are defined so that as far as possible the following two conditions are satisfied:

(a)   The production of the category of goods and services that characterizes a given class accounts for the bulk of the output of the units classified to that class;

(b)   The class contains the units that produce most of the category of goods and services that characterize it.

37.   The first condition is required in order that establishments, or similar units, may be classified according to kind of economic activity uniquely and easily and in order that the units included in a given class will be as similar to each other as is feasible. For a more detailed explanation of these homogeneity ratios, see chapter III, section F (paras. 127-132).

38.   The two conditions set limits to the detail of classification that may be achieved in the classes of ISIC. These classes must be defined in respect of combinations of activities in which establishments customarily engage in various countries of the world. Establishments may, in practice, carry out a number of different activities; and the range of these activities will differ from one unit to another even though they engage in the same general kind of economic activity. These differences will exist in the case of establishments within one country and will be more pronounced in the case of establishments in different countries. It should be emphasized that the fact that the organization of production differs from country to country makes it likely that the classes of ISIC do not reflect the structure in each individual country.

39.   Another major consideration in forming categories in ISIC was the relative importance of the activities to be included. In general, separate classes are provided for kinds of activity that are prevalent in most countries, or that are of particular importance in the world economy. The introduction of certain categories at the class and other levels of classification for purposes of attaining international comparability in the industrial classification of data has also affected the balance of ISIC.

D. Statistical units

1. General remarks

40.   Economic statistics describe the activities of economic transactors and the transactions that take place between them. In the real world, economic entities engaged in the production of goods and services vary in their legal, accounting, organizational and operating structures. To create statistics that are consistent across entities and internationally comparable, it is necessary to define and delineate standard statistical units to serve as units of observation for their collection and compilation. Comparability of statistics is greatly enhanced when the units about which statistics are compiled are similarly defined and classified.

41.   Economic entities have numerous characteristics and a variety of data are required about them that may be classified in many ways, among the most important of which are by institutional sector, by activity and by geographical region. The need to classify statistical units by these characteristics requires that they be as homogeneous as possible with respect to institutional sector, economic activity or location, and this plays an important role in their definition.

42.   Economic statistics are required by different users for various types of analysis. The System of National Accounts (SNA) is a principal user and it has particular requirements, but there are also other users including policy analysts, business analysts, and businesses themselves that use economic data for

studying industrial performance, productivity, market share and other issues. As different units within an economic entity are suitable for the compilation of different types of data, the type of data that are required is yet another factor in the definition and delineation of statistical units.

(a) Legal entities

43.   Most societies provide for the legal recognition of economic entities, under laws that enable them to define and register themselves as legal entities. Legal entities are recognized by law or society, independently of the persons or institutions that own them. The characteristics of a legal entity are the following: they own goods or assets, they incur liabilities, and they enter into contracts.

44.   An example of a legal entity is a corporation that owns or manages the property of the organization, enters into contracts, receives and disposes of its income, and maintains an independent, complete set of accounts, including profit and loss accounts and balance sheets.

(b) Institutional units

45.   Institutional units are the core unit of the SNA. Subsequent definitions all embody the definition of this basic unit. Institutional units are transactors in the system and must therefore be capable of engaging in the full range of transactions in their own right and on their own behalf.

46.   Institutional units include persons or groups of persons in the form of households and legal or social entities whose existence is recognized by law or society independently of the persons or other entities that may own or control them.

47.   An institutional unit is capable of owning assets, incurring liabilities and engaging in economic activities and in transactions with other entities. It may own and exchange goods and assets, is legally responsible for the economic transactions that it carries out and may enter into legal contracts. An important attribute of the institutional unit is that a set of economic accounts exists or can be compiled for the unit, and the set includes consolidated financial accounts and/or a balance sheet of assets and liabilities.

48.   The domestic economy is made up of the entire set of institutional units resident in the economy. The institutional sector classification of the SNA defines five mutually exclusive institutional sectors within the economy, which group institutional units by virtue of their economic objectives, principal functions and behaviour.

49.   In the majority of cases, an institutional unit will be a single legal entity. However, some corporations may be composed of legal entities set up for convenience as tax shelters or for other administrative reasons. In such cases, for statistical purposes it is inappropriate and unnecessary to regard each legal entity as a separate institutional unit.

50.   Similarly, if a corporation has a principal activity supported by ancillary activities that are registered as separate legal entities, they, too, would not constitute separate institutional entities.

51.   Because the sector classification distinguishes separate financial and non-financial sectors, it is necessary to define two separate institutional units, as long as the necessary financial accounts are available for each of them, whenever possible, even if the two together have all the other attributes of an institutional unit and consolidated accounts are compiled for them as a single unit.

2. Statistical units in the System of National Accounts

52.   The systematic description of the economy as represented by the System of National Accounts analyses two interrelated types of transactors and transactions for which two levels of statistical units are required. In the income and outlay and capital finance accounts, the concepts of the enterprise and the sector classification, for the analysis of financial transactions, are used. In the production accounts, the concepts of the establishment, the international standard industrial classification and the central product classification, for the analysis of transactions in goods and services, are used.

(a) Enterprise

53.   An institutional unit in its capacity as a producer of goods and services is known as an enterprise.

54.   An enterprise is an economic transactor with autonomy in respect of financial and investment decision-making, as well as authority and responsibility for allocating resources for the production of goods and services. It may be engaged in one or many productive activities.

55.   The enterprise is the level at which financial and balance sheet accounts are maintained and from which international transactions, an international investment position (when applicable) and the consolidated financial position can be derived.

56.   An enterprise may be a corporation (or quasi corporation), a non-profit institution, or an unincorporated enterprise. Corporate enterprises and non-profit institutions are complete institutional units. On the other hand, the term "unincorporated enterprise" refers to an institutional unit - a household or government unit - only in its capacity as a producer of goods and services.

57.   The enterprise is the statistical unit for which financial statistics for the income and outlay accounts and capital finance accounts of the SNA are compiled. They are classified to the sector classification of the SNA.

(b) Establishment

58.   The SNA describes the statistical unit to be defined and delineated for industrial or production statistics as the establishment. The establishment is defined as an enterprise or part of an enterprise that is situated in a single location and in which only a single (non-ancillary) productive activity is carried out or in which the principal productive activity accounts for most of the value added.

59.   ISIC is designed for grouping units engaged in similar activities for the purpose of analysing production and compiling production statistics. Although it is possible to classify enterprises according to their principal activities using ISIC and to group them into industries, some of the resulting industries are likely to be very heterogeneous when enterprises have secondary activities that are very different from their principal activities. It therefore becomes necessary to partition large and complex enterprises into more homogeneous units, for which production data can be compiled. This is particularly important when large enterprises account for a large proportion of the value added of the economy or of particular industries.

60.   Although the definition of an establishment allows for the possibility that there may be one or more secondary activities carried out, they should be small-scale compared with the principal activity. If a

secondary activity within an enterprise is as important, or nearly as important, as the principal activity, then the unit is more like a local unit, described below. It should be subdivided so that the secondary activity is treated as taking place within an establishment separate from that in which the principal activity takes place. The definition of an establishment does not permit an ancillary activity to constitute an establishment on its own.

61.   In the case of most small and medium-sized businesses, the enterprise and the establishment will be identical, though the two different types of data described earlier will be compiled for each. Large and complex enterprises engaged in many activities, belonging to different ISIC industries, will be composed of more than one establishment, provided that smaller, more homogeneous production units for which production data can be compiled, can be identified with the desired geographical precision.

62.   The data to be compiled for an establishment relate to its production activities. They include the following:
(a) The items included in the production account and the generation of income account such as revenues from the sale of goods and services, and all associated costs including employee remuneration, taxes on production and imports, subsidies, depreciation and a meaningful operating surplus;
(b) Statistics of numbers of employees, types of employees and hours worked;
(c) Estimates of the stock of capital and land used;
(d) Estimates of changes in inventories and gross fixed capital formation undertaken.

3. Delineating statistical units

63.   The universe of economic entities is composed of large and complex enterprises engaged in many different activities, horizontally or vertically integrated, that may be undertaken at or from many geographical locations, and small enterprises engaged in one or very few activities undertaken at or from one geographical location.

64.   Enterprises have production units at which or from which they undertake the economic activity of producing goods and services. Production usually takes place at a particular location - for example, at a mine, a factory or a farm. On the other hand, the activity of producing services may take place from a certain location. Transportation services carry the product from the farm or factory gate to the purchaser. They may also carry passengers from one place to another. Even though transportation services are carried out by means of a network that operates over a wide geographical area, it is assumed that the service originates from a certain location. Similarly, telecommunication services are attributed to a particular location from which the service is assumed to be delivered, even though it, too, is carried out through a wired or wireless network that covers a wide geographical area. Certain services may be delivered to the customer at the same location at which it is produced such as accommodation and certain food services. However, others, such as those of engineering consultants, originate at a certain location from which they may be delivered to the location of the customer.

65.   The need to delineate statistical units arises in the case of large and complex economic entities in which the activities in which they are engaged fall into different classes of the standard industrial classification or the production units of which they are composed are located in different geographical areas.

66.   In large and complex entities, the units at which or from which production takes place are grouped for management, administrative, and decision-making purposes into hierarchical structures.

Higher-level organizational units own, control, or manage the lower-level production units at which production decisions are made or production takes place. An economic entity may be structured along geographical, legal, functional or operational lines. They may have one structure or several structures to carry out different functions or to serve different purposes.

67.   In these entities, management of the financial affairs of the business usually occurs at a higher organizational level than does management of production operations. The accounting systems of businesses usually reflect this management structure by mirroring the hierarchy of management responsibility for the operations of the business. The accounts required to support the management and decision-making functions, whether financial or production, are usually maintained for the corresponding level of management responsibility.

68.   Enterprises also have a legal structure. They define and register themselves in terms of legal units for the ownership of assets. These legally constituted units or groups of units form the legal base of the business. An enterprise derives its autonomy from the common ownership and control of its resources irrespective of the number of legal units under which it registers them. They usually submit corporate tax returns to government revenue authorities for the legal units of their legal structure. They may use the same or different units for other administrative purposes such as remitting payroll or value-added taxes to government authorities.

69.   In small enterprises, the operational and legal structures often coincide and may even be embodied in a single unit. For large enterprises, the operational structure may be different from the legal structure, coinciding with it only at the highest level of the business. In such cases, the organizational and production units of the enterprise's operational structure may differ from the units of their legal structure.

70.   The statistical units of large and complex institutional units may be delineated through a process referred to as profiling. Profiling identifies the enterprise, its legal structure, its operating structure, and the production and organizational units that are used to derive the statistical units. Once identified, the enterprise and its constituent establishments constitute the statistical units of the statistical structure. In delineating the statistical structure, functional or other groups in the organizational structure may be ignored and the constituent units regrouped to form the units of the statistical structure. For multi-establishment enterprises, the statistical structure may not coincide with the legal structure in which ownership of assets is registered.

71.   As mentioned earlier for economic analysis, two main types of data are required to describe the economic activities of the units of which the economy is composed: (a) financial statistics organized by institutional or other sectors and (b) production statistics classified by industry and, in some countries, by geographical area. Usually, the data are required for activities carried out within, or from within, domestic boundaries. The two types of data are required separately, as well as integrated into the system of national accounts. Thus, two main statistical units need to be delineated: the enterprise, for the compilation of financial statistics; and the establishment (or kind of activity unit), for the compilation of production statistics.

72.   Economic statistics draw upon the accounting records of businesses. The records that are maintained in support of financial decision-making, management, and control provide the data required for financial statistics. Such records include consolidated profit and loss accounts and balance sheets of assets and liabilities. This is the level at which the enterprise is delineated, as those are the data that need to be compiled for the unit.

73.   The source of information for production statistics and labour income statistics is often management and cost accounts. These accounts record operating revenues earned from the sale of goods and services and the associated costs, wages and salaries, depreciation, and operating profits. Within the organizational structure of the enterprise, the level of autonomy will determine the nature of the data that will be available for the unit. Countries that are more interested in the higher level of autonomy, in terms of decision-making, of the unit, rather than in the geographical location of the activity, may prefer to delineate and use the kind-of-activity unit. This will be the case particularly if they are not interested in compiling comprehensive production statistics for sub-national geographical regions. However, if production statistics at a subnational level of geographic detail are required, then it will be necessary to delineate the smallest unit that is as homogeneous as possible in terms of activity and geography, for which revenues from the sale of goods and services, associated costs and value added can be compiled or estimated.

74.   In those cases where the legal structure and the statistical structure based on production units do not coincide, statistical agencies will need to articulate the statistical structure and compile data with the help of surveys. The legal structure may consist of units created purely for tax purposes that are in no way relevant for the purpose of representing the producing units of the enterprise. However, if it is necessary to draw on tax records for the required data or if survey data need to be supplemented with tax data, statistical agencies will have to decide whether they can find a way to map the legal and statistical structure of the enterprise or whether they prefer to use the legal structure selectively as a proxy for the statistical structure.

75.   The statistical structure delineates and identifies the units about which data are to be compiled. However, the data may have to be collected from higher- or lower-level units which are then described as collection entities. With increasing globalization, some multinational global enterprises are keeping integrated accounting records at the global or the regional level and it is becoming increasingly difficult to separate and extract complete accounts for all the activities taking place within each domestic economy, without obtaining the data from the main or regional head office of the global enterprise. Attributing the value of production and value added to domestic economies is particularly complicated when a global enterprise draws on production carried out in different domestic economies, assembles it in one or another of them, and then manages and maintains accounts for the distribution centres in the different economies under a separate division of the global enterprise. The enterprise may, in the first instance, maintain separate accounting records for all its production activities and all its distribution activities in all the economies in which it operates and, only later, attribute revenues and costs to each domestic economy for purposes of submitting tax returns to the revenue authorities.

4. National differences and application of statistical units

76.   The concept of the establishment combines both an activity dimension and a locality dimension. It is based on the assumption that the aim of the statistical programme is to compile data classified both by activity and by geographical region. However, ISIC can be used to classify numerous variables including those that are needed to analyse production and industrial performance. In examining the accounting and operating structures of enterprises, it is possible that producing units with differing levels of homogeneity with respect to activities and geographical precision will be found and that they may be suitable for the compilation of data on selected variables, for example, numbers employed, or even for the compilation of production statistics because all the information needed with respect to meaningful operating profit is available.

77.   While it may be desirable to give a complete account of possible statistical units, their definition in theoretical terms and in actual statistical applications, their delineation and their use in different forms of statistical data collection, one has to realize that it is impossible to do this at a

worldwide level in a way that would allow their immediate application in any given country. There are many factors that play a role in defining the best statistical unit for a given form of data collection, inter alia, the structure of the legal system in a country, including regulations for the organization of businesses, the particular structure of the industries involved, the type of data collection involved, the purpose and targeted level of data collection etc. The SNA discusses a wider range of statistical units that can serve as models, but may still be adjusted for reasons of national specifics and according to the type of data collection involved. See chapter V of the 1993 SNA for more information.

E. Classification of statistical units

1. General guidelines

78.   In the following paragraphs, a number of general rules of interpretation are given that could be helpful when classifying more complex statistical units. It should be noted that the explanatory notes to some sections and divisions of ISIC also indicate how to treat such cases.

79.   The activity classification of each unit is determined by the ISIC class in which the principal activity, or range of activities, of the unit is included. Secondary and ancillary activities are to be disregarded when classifying a unit. The principal activities of the unit in general can be determined from the goods that it sells or ships or the services that it renders to other units or consumers. The descriptions and explanatory notes of the individual classes in ISIC should be used to determine the activities carried out in terms of ISIC categories, using not only the output structure, but also the input structure and the production process.

80.   Ideally, the principal activity of the unit should be determined by reference to the value added to the goods sold or the services rendered. In practice, it is often not possible to obtain the information on value added for individual products. It is therefore recommended that, in such cases, the principal activity be determined as an approximation by other criteria, such as:
- The proportion of the gross output of the unit that is attributable to the goods or services associated with these kinds of activity
- value of sales of those groups of products
- employment according to the proportion of people engaged in these different kinds of activity.

81.   Instances may arise where considerable proportions of the activities of a unit are included in more than one class of ISIC. These cases may result from the vertical integration of activities, for example, tree felling combined with sawmilling or activities in a clay pit combined with those at a brick works; or the horizontal integration of activities that cannot be segregated into separate statistical units, for example, the manufacture of hides and skins in slaughterhouses; or the combination of any activities that cannot be separated at the level of the statistical unit. In these situations, the unit should be classified according to the rules set out below.

2. Treatment of mixed activities

(a) Treatment of independent multiple activities

82.   If a unit is engaged in several types of independent activities, but the unit itself cannot be segregated into separate statistical units (when, for example, manufacture of bakery products is combined with manufacture of chocolate confectionery), the unit should be classified to the ISIC class with the largest share of value added by using the "top-down" method. In this case, first the appropriate highest

classification (one-digit level) should be determined, then the lower (two- and three-digit) levels and finally the class (four-digit level). If value added cannot be determined for the activities involved, approximations as set out above can be used, provided that their application to the different activities is consistent.

83.   The "top-down" method may identify an activity as the principal activity of the unit, even though this activity does not account for the largest overall share of value added. However, this approach ensures better consistency with aggregated data. Following is an example of applying the top-down method to determine the classification code for a statistical unit.

Example: Identifying the principal activity of a reporting unit using the top-down method

The identification of the principal activity is carried out in five steps:

1. List the activities carried out by the unit, attributing to each appropriate class of ISIC, Rev. 3.1, the value added or another relevant measure (see para. 80) if it is not possible to calculate the value added.
2. Determine the section of ISIC, Rev. 3.1, that has the highest share of the chosen measure.
3. Within this section, determine the division of ISIC, Rev. 3.1, that has the highest share of the chosen measure.
4. Within this division, determine the group of ISIC, Rev. 3.1, that has the highest share of the chosen measure.
5. Within this group, determine the class of ISIC, Rev. 3.1, that has the highest share of the chosen measure. This class identifies the principal activity.

Example

Step 1. A reporting unit may carry out the following activities:

Section	Division	Group	Class	Description of the class	Share of value added (percentage)
D	28	281	2812	Manufacture of tanks, reservoirs and containers of metal	7
	29	291	2915	Manufacture of lifting and handling equipment	8
		292	2921	Manufacture of agricultural and forestry machinery	3
			2922	Manufacture of machine-tools	21
			2924	Manufacture of machinery for mining, quarrying and construction	8
	34	343	3430	Manufacture of parts and accessories for motor vehicles and their engines	5
G	51	511	5110	Wholesale on a fee or contract basis	7
		515	5159	Wholesale of other machinery, equipment and supplies	28
K	74	742	7421	Architectural and engineering activities and related technical consultancy	13

The principal activity is then determined as follows:

Step 2. Identify the section

Section D	Manufacturing	**52**
Section G	Wholesale and retail trade; repair of motor vehicles, motorcycles and personal and household goods	35
Section K	Real estate, renting and business activities	13

Step 3. Identify the division (within section D)

Division 28	Manufacture of fabricated metal products, except machinery and equipment	7
Division 29	Manufacture of machinery and equipment n.e.c.	**40**
Division 34	Manufacture of motor vehicles, trailers and semi-trailers	5

Step 4. Identify the group (within division 29)

| Group 291 | Manufacture of general-purpose machinery | 8 |
| Group 292 | Manufacture of special-purchase machinery | **32·** |

Step 5. Identify the class (within group 292)

Class 2921	Manufacture of agricultural and forestry machinery	3
Class 2922	Manufacture of machine-tools	**21**
Class 2924	Manufacture of machinery for mining, quarrying and construction	8

The principal activity is therefore **2922: Manufacture of machine-tools**, although the class with the biggest share of value added is class 5159: Wholesale of other machinery, equipment and supplies.

If the allocation had been made directly to the class with the largest share of value added, this would have achieved the strange result of putting this enterprise outside manufacturing.

(b) Treatment of vertical integration

84.   Vertical integration of activities occurs where the different stages of production are carried out in succession by the same unit and where the output of one process serves as input to the next, as in the cases, for example, of tree felling combined with sawmilling, a clay pit combined with a brickworks, or production of synthetic fibres associated with a textile mill.

85.   A unit with a vertically integrated chain of activities should generally be classified to the class indicated by the nature of the final products. For instance, in the above example, tree felling combined with sawmilling should be classified as sawmilling in class 2010 (Sawmilling and planing of wood). There are, however, some exceptions made to this general rule for practical reasons. These exceptions are described in the explanatory notes of the affected classes. Some examples of exceptions are illustrated by the following:
* Integrated growing of grapes and manufacture of wine are classified in agriculture (0113), not manufacturing, to account for the specific organization of these activities.

- Finishing of textiles made in the same unit is classified with the manufacture of the textiles in class 1711, 1729 or 1730, reflecting the character of the unit, that is to say, a textile mill etc.
- Retail sale of self-manufactured products is not considered a separate activity and is therefore classified in manufacturing, not in retail trade. If, however, in addition to self-produced goods, other products are also sold, the rules for the treatment of mixed independent activities have to be applied.

(c) Treatment of horizontal integration

86.   Horizontal integration of activities occurs when activities are carried out simultaneously using the same factors of production. In this case, it will not be possible to separate them statistically into different processes, assign them to different units or generally provide separate data for these activities, nor will rules relying on allocation of value added or similar measures be applicable. Alternative indicators, such as gross output, may sometimes be applicable, but there is no general rule for identifying the single activity that best represents the mix included in this horizontal integration. As patterns of horizontal integration have been considered in the preparation of the classification, in many cases, either commonly integrated activities are included in the same class or explicit rules for their treatment have been supplied.

3. E-commerce

87.   Business units receive orders and transact the sale of goods and services produced by a variety of means, for example, telephone, fax, television, electronic data interchange (EDI), Minitel and the Internet. Many countries have chosen to describe the business transaction that transfers the ownership of the goods or service when it is done through the Internet or other electronic means as e-commerce.

88.   There are three stages in the transfer of the ownership of a good or service – the placement of the order, the payment, and the delivery of the good or service. E-commerce transactions may be defined to include situations where only the first, only the first and second, or all three stages are conducted through the Internet or other electronic means.

89.   For many business units, e-commerce is just one of the variety of means by which sales are transacted. The rules for the industrial classification of such units remain unchanged: they are classified to the industry of their principal activity. Increasingly, however, business units that sell goods and supply services exclusively through the Internet are coming into existence. Such units should also be classified to the industry of their principal activity. Business units engaged in e-commerce will therefore be found in any industry of ISIC. It should be noted that the only exception to this rule is the following: in retail trade, business units that undertake their sales exclusively or predominantly through the Internet are classified within industry group 525 (Retail trade not in stores) to class 5251.

4. Repair and maintenance

90.   Units that repair or overhaul capital goods are to be classified in the same class as the units that produce the goods. Three main exceptions exist to this rule:
- Repair and maintenance of motor vehicles and maintenance and repair of motorcycles are classified in class 5020 and in class 5040, respectively.
- Repair of personal and household goods is classified in class 5260.
- Repair and maintenance of computers and office equipment are classified in class 7250.

5. Activities on a fee or contract basis

91.   Except in cases where special categories exist, units carrying out activities on a fee or contract basis are to be classified in the same class as units that produce for their own account and risk. Conversely, units that sell goods or services under their own name and for their own risk but have the actual production carried out by others are to be classified as if they produce the goods or services themselves, provided that they have considerable influence on the conception of the products or, in the case of the manufacturing industry, they own the materials to be transformed.

6. Government activities

92.   ISIC does not make any distinction regarding the institutional sector to which a statistical unit belongs. For instance, there is no category that would describe all activities carried out by the government as such. Activities carried out by government units that are specifically attributable to other areas of ISIC should be classified in the appropriate class of ISIC and not in division 75 (Public administration and defence; compulsory social security). For instance, public hospitals will be classified in class 8511.

7. Classification of enterprises

93.   Since the activities of an enterprise sometimes cover a great variety of ISIC groups or classes, it may be appropriate for certain statistics to classify them at the division level only. In any case, when such a unit is to be classified at a lower level of the classification, the top-down approach, as set out in subsection 2 of the present section (paras. 82-83), should be used.

94.   The classification of a multi-activity enterprise should be determined from the value added by its constituent units. Such a unit should be classified in the category of ISIC that covers the kinds of activity of the constituent units that account for the principal amount of value added. For example, in the case of establishments of an enterprise that make up a vertical chain of production, this principle gives proportional weight to establishments included in each portion of the chain. The use of the principle also makes it feasible to determine the category of an industrial classification to which an enterprise is to be assigned directly from the categories of the classification to which its constituent units are classified.

95.   If data are not available on the value added of the constituent units of enterprises, figures on employment, or wages and salaries paid by these units might be used in order to determine their preponderant class of activities. As far as possible, use should be made of net measures of the activities of the establishment-type units. Figures of the gross output of these units can be misleading. The portion of the gross output of each establishment that is accounted for by the value added there can vary markedly from one unit to another. In some instances, for example, in dealing with industries with a very high investment quota and a relatively low wage quota, the value of assets in each constituent unit may also be taken into account when weighing the different activities to determine the preponderant class.

96.   The classification of entities engaged in ancillary activities, particularly central administrative offices, according to the predominant kind of activity of the establishments served by them may, in some cases, be questionable or difficult. The predominant kind of activity may account for much less than half of the total activity of the establishments served, or these establishments and the central administrative office may be located in different countries. This has led to the provision of a special category for central administrative offices in the case of some national industrial classifications. The special category is included under the equivalent of business activities in ISIC (class 7414).

8. Classification of households

97.   Previous versions of ISIC have included categories for the classification of households when they were employers of domestic personnel. These included households employing maids, gardeners, cooks etc. As employment is generated, data on these units have been collected for various statistics, usually outside of the general business statistics.

98.   Outside of this existing category, the need to describe activities of households for own use has emerged in data collections, such as in labour-force surveys. While market activities should generally be described according to existing rules for identifying the correct ISIC code for an activity, the application of these rules for activities producing goods and services for own use has proved difficult. These activities often combine agricultural, construction, textile manufacturing, repair and other services. In general, it is not possible to assign value-added ratios to these activities and reasonably identify a primary activity. To provide a place for these mixed activities in the classification, two new divisions have been created. These new divisions, 96 (Undifferentiated goods-producing activities of private households for own use) and 97 (Undifferentiated service-producing activities of private households for own use), will normally not be relevant in business statistics, but rather in data collections covering household and subsistence activities.

F.   Structure and coding system of the classification

99.   A comparison of the general structure of ISIC, Rev.2, with that of ISIC, Rev.3, indicates that the former was not essentially changed. However, more detail was introduced, especially at the one- and two-digit levels in the services areas. A request for this change was made by both producers and users of statistics. In the present update to ISIC, Rev.3, there is again no alteration in the structure at any of the higher levels.

100.   The versions of ISIC up to and including Revision 2 used a hierarchical system of categories that were entirely coded using Arabic numerals, based on a decimal system arrangement. This system was considered to be more universally applicable than one employing letters or Roman numerals. It also met the requirements of offices using data-processing equipment. ISIC, Rev.2, had nine one-digit categories which were most of the time further subdivided into a maximum of nine subcategories at each subsequent level.

101.   During the third revision of ISIC, new needs added considerable complexity to the revision process. In addition to maintaining as much comparability as possible by introducing only those changes upon which there was a wide measure of agreement, creating a structure that would achieve greater balance between higher- and lower-level categories than had been the case with ISIC, Rev.2, was also deemed important. In the previous revision, some one-digit categories had been undivided and others were broken down into many subcategories, often up to the four-digit level. As a result, some classes deserved more weight than some categories at higher levels of the classification, in terms of economic importance.

102.   The need for economic statistics to reflect the structure of an economy in a modern way, giving due consideration to the increasing importance of some service industries in terms of their contribution to the gross domestic product (GDP), made the use of a new coding system inevitable. In devising the coding system for ISIC, Rev.3, a separation was introduced in the coding structure in order to make the classification responsive to the tabulation needs of certain users. This was accomplished by

the use of letters at the one-digit level to single out broad tabulation categories, in contrast with the coding itself, which would remain purely numerical at the two-, three- and four-digit levels.

103. The two-digit categories were grouped in clusters of multiples of 5, which theoretically allowed for 20 of such clusters instead of only 10 at the highest level of the classification. They represent the most important sectors of the economy of most countries: agriculture, fishing, mining, manufacturing, energy supply, construction, trade, hotels and restaurants, transport, finance, business activities, public administration, education, health, community service activities, households and extraterritorial bodies. For reasons related to tabulation, these sectors were coded with a Roman capital letter.

104. For quick comparisons, it should be noted that the tabulation categories of ISIC, Rev.3, can easily be converted into the one-digit major divisions of ISIC, Rev.2. This conversion can be carried out as follows: tabulation categories A+B equal old Major Division 1; C equals 2; D equals 3; E equals 4; F equals 5; G+H equal 6; I equals 7; J+K equal 8; L to Q equal 9. The main exception is research and development, which was transferred from Major Division 9 to new section K. These relationships remain unchanged in ISIC, Rev.3.1.

105. The names given to the categories at the different levels in ISIC, Rev. 3, and ISIC, Rev. 3.1, were changed from those in the second revision. This was done for two reasons. First, it seemed better to discontinue the use of a name in combination with a number of digits as in ISIC, Rev.2, in order to prevent confusion of categories from Rev.3 with those from Rev.2. Only the "Division" for the two-digit categories was maintained. The second reason was to harmonize the use of category names with other classifications of the United Nations, for example, the Standard Industrial Trade Classification (SITC)[7] and the Central Product Classification.[8] For practical reasons, the tabulation categories are called "sections", the two-digit categories "divisions", the three-digit categories "groups" and the four-digit categories "classes".

106. While the tabulation categories are assigned capital letters, the Arabic numbers assigned to a given category of ISIC may be read as follows: the first and second digits, taken together, indicate the division in which the category is included; the first three digits identify the group; and all four digits indicate the class. ISIC now comprises 17 sections, which are then further subdivided into a total of 62 divisions, 161 groups and 298 classes. The added detail has considerably increased the number of these categories compared with ISIC, Rev.2. The changes made in the present update to ISIC, Rev.3, have resulted in the creation of only six new classes.

107. In cases where a given level of the classification is not divided into categories of the next more detailed level of classification, "0" is used in the code position for the next more detailed level. For example, the code for the group "Fishing" is 050 since the division "Fishing" (code 05) is not divided into groups. Or, the code for the class "Mining of uranium and thorium ores" is 1200 because the division "Mining of uranium and thorium ores" (code 12) is divided neither into groups nor into classes. The group "Cargo handling" is coded as 6301 since the division "Supporting and auxiliary transport activities" (code 63) is not divided into groups but the group "Supporting and auxiliary transport activities" (code 630) is divided into classes. In computers, the "0" could also indicate that a total of all more detailed categories is being used. Hence, the code 2690 could be used for the total 2691-2699 and 3300 could represent the total 3311-3330. This could of course also be achieved by using the next higher level of the classification, but in some instances it may be appropriate to use the same format, that is to say, number of digits, for all code numbers.

III. Application of the Classification

A. General remarks

108.   The Statistical Commission has recommended that countries classify data according to ISIC, or according to categories convertible to ISIC, in such areas of statistics as production, employment or national accounts. ISIC is being utilized by the United Nations and other international and national bodies in assembling and publishing internationally comparable data for a wide range of statistical series classified according to kind of economic activity. The International Conference of Labour Statisticians has also made explicit references to ISIC in respect of several areas of labour statistics.

109.   The range of application of ISIC extends far beyond the traditional areas such as data collection in industrial statistics. It includes applications for methodological work and policy decisions, such as descriptions of barriers to trade in the system of foreign direct investment, the activities of foreign affiliates for statistics on international trade in services and work related to the functions of government. For many purposes, ISIC is used in conjunction with or as proxy for other classifications, such as the Classifications of Expenditure According to Purpose.[9]

110.   ISIC is intended to meet the needs of those who are looking for data classified according to internationally comparable categories of kind of economic activity. Its purpose is not to supersede national classifications, but to provide a framework for the international comparison of national statistics. Where national classifications differ from the international classification, this comparison may be achieved by regrouping figures obtained under national classifications; but to do this, all the elements required for such a rearrangement need to be obtainable from the national statistics.

111.   In order to attain international comparability, it is suggested that all countries adopt, as far as individual requirements permit, the same general principles and definitions in their industrial classification schemes. The principles and definitions that were developed for this purpose and that are embodied in ISIC are set out above (see chap. II). As a result, it should be feasible to rearrange and combine entire categories of national classifications so that they correspond to one or more categories of ISIC, although not always, inasmuch as certain categories at the most detailed level of ISIC may not be distinguished in the industrial classifications of some countries.

112.   The character and definition of categories of ISIC can also serve as a useful guide to those countries that are developing an activity classification for the first time, or to those that are revising an existing one. A number of countries have utilized ISIC in this way.

113.   The international classification provides categories for economic activities that are important in nearly every country or that, while found only in some countries, are of considerable importance in the world economy. In delineating these individual categories, ISIC reflects the structure of production, that is to say, the way in which economic activities are combined in, and distributed among, producing units in most countries.

114.   The United Nations Statistics Division has put in place mechanisms to distribute relevant information on international classifications, including ISIC, their revisions, their applications and their interpretations and on national specifications and adaptations. With respect to these, ISIC may serve as model and provide guidelines for the development of national classifications. These tools or information about them can be accessed through the web site of the Statistics Division (http://unstats.un.org/unsd/class).

B. Use of ISIC in establishing related national classifications

115. Regarding the relationship between ISIC and related national activity classifications, one may distinguish two broad groups of countries: (a) countries that have developed their own national classifications and perceive ISIC as being essentially based on, or derived from, these; and (b) countries that see their own national classification as one that is based on, or derived from, ISIC. Countries in the second group often lack the infrastructure required to develop and maintain their own activity classification, and may therefore adopt ISIC as their national activity classification with little or no modification.

116. The desire for international comparability does not, however, imply that countries have to adopt ISIC as a whole, without modification. The intention is rather to have countries use ISIC as a guide in adapting their national classifications to the international standard. Adapting ISIC to specifics of the national economy while maintaining international comparability requires observation of a number of rules outlined below.

C. Aggregation and disaggregation of ISIC

117. When adapting ISIC to national circumstances, its categories may be aggregated or further detailed to better reflect the structure of the national economy of the country. If a particular economic sector is economically of great importance or has developed important specializations not separately identified in ISIC, the relevant part of the classification can be further disaggregated. If some other sector of the economy does not exist or is still undeveloped or unimportant in the economy as a whole, the relevant part of the classification can be treated at a more aggregated level. It is not the intention to suggest data collection for categories, which would require all kinds of artificial or arbitrary splits of the existing statistical units.

118. In order to make a national activity classification convertible to ISIC, the categories at the most detailed level of classification in the national scheme should, on the whole, coincide with, or be subdivisions of, the individual classes of ISIC. In other words, any most detailed category of the national classification should not cover selected portions of two or more classes of ISIC. When national categories have to represent combinations of two or more entire classes of ISIC, the classes should be part of the same group. Then the convertibility of the national classification to ISIC would not be affected by the position or the manner of grouping of the categories at the detailed level of the classification in the national scheme.

119. To serve national purposes, categories in the ISIC structure may be disaggregated by subdividing the relevant classes into subclasses. This may be done by appending decimal places to the four-digit code that identifies each class of ISIC. Alternatively, the subdivision of groups into classes in ISIC may be expanded by replacing the existing classes with a greater number of more detailed categories. In order to preserve comparability with the classes of ISIC, the more detailed classes should be delineated so that they may be aggregated to classes.

120. Extending the four-digit codes of ISIC may be unnecessary if, to meet national requirements, the only classes to be subdivided are those that are identical to groups. These classes of ISIC are identified by four-digit codes ending in "0" and may be replaced by as many as nine classes, identified by specific four-digit codes.

121.   ISIC categories may be aggregated, for example, by combining the classes of selected groups into fewer, less detailed classes, or by entirely telescoping classes into groups. It may even, in certain instances, be desirable or necessary to have categories at the most detailed level of the national classification that combine classes of ISIC. This may be because the kinds of activity segregated by selected classes of ISIC are not important enough in a given country. Or, it may be due to a much smaller degree of specialization in the activities of the statistical units than is required in order to use certain classes of ISIC in the national scheme. For example, some countries may not establish categories in their national classifications that are similar to the individual categories of divisions 29 to 32 (Manufacture of machinery), inasmuch as the majority of establishments engaging in activities of class X also carry out the activities of class Y and vice versa, thereby making it impractical to separate these activities in the national classification. They may need to combine some of, or all, the groups or classes into single categories at the most detailed level of their national classification.

122.   It should be kept in mind that combining classes into higher aggregates, either at the group level or elsewhere, will limit comparability of data at the international level to that level or to even higher aggregates. The latter can occur if countries decide to aggregate some of the four-digit classes within, for example, group 291. If two countries aggregate classes within group 291, comparability of their data will not be available at their respective aggregated levels, but only at the higher level of group 291. The combining of classes should therefore be carefully considered in respect of the impact on comparability for data compiled according to these new categories.

D. Capturing information about the activity of units and coding it according to ISIC

123.   The quality as well as the comparability of the statistics produced according to ISIC will depend upon the correctness of the codes assigned to the statistical units. This will again depend on the information available for determining the correct code and upon the tools and procedures used for this determination.

124.   To some extent, the quality of the information will depend upon the type of statistical source. The quality of information collected for administrative registrations will depend on the extent to which this information has a function in the administrative procedures for which the registrations are being made, and what kind of distinctions this function will require, for example, whether tax rules, social security regulations, the rules for investment credits or the services provided by employment agencies will require precise registration of the type of activity undertaken. The statistical offices will therefore frequently need to collect directly from the units the information needed to determine the activity codes of the units, even when the register used as the basis for their surveys is derived from or developed in cooperation with one or more of the administrative agencies. Given the nature of ISIC, the information that is needed to code for the register as well as the surveys will have to describe the main ouputs, that is to say, goods, services or function, of the units' productive activities. For units with a wide range of products, information about them will also be necessary to determine their contributions to the value added or other relevant factors by which to determine the units' main activity. This information must be obtained from the units, and care must be taken to ensure that those individuals who provide the information on behalf of the units understand the type of information needed so that they can find it in the records of the units or from their own knowledge. Thus, testing of question formulations is as important for establishment surveys as it is for household surveys. For household surveys and population censuses, it is recommended that information be obtained both regarding the name and address of the place of work and about the main products made there. Then it may be possible to obtain the correct code either from a matching unit in the register or on the basis of the product information. For the registers as well as for the two types of surveys, finding the correct codes on the basis of product information will be greatly facilitated by a well-organized and comprehensive coding index.

E. Use of different levels of the classification for the presentation of statistics

125.   It may be desirable to utilize less detailed classification categories of kind of economic activity for some types of statistics than for other series, and the number and size of the categories for which reliable statistics are presented may depend on the type of source for the statistics as well as on confidentiality considerations.   For example, it may not be feasible to present data on employment gathered in household inquiries in as great detail as data on employment obtained from establishment inquiries.   Or, it may not be necessary to present data according to kind of economic activity in as great detail in national accounting as in industrial statistics.   By providing for four levels of classification (sections, divisions, groups and classes), ISIC furnishes a framework for comparable classifications of data at different levels of detail. It is important to note, however, that the fact that a category has been defined at the class level in ISIC will not prevent it from being larger in a particular national economy than a category defined at the group level or even at the level of division or section, as will be the case, for example, for division B (Fishing) versus class 8021 (General secondary education) in many countries. Thus, it may be inappropriate to specify tabulation programmes as tabulation for a particular level of aggregation for ISIC.

126.   Similarly, for specialized surveys on a limited number of industries, the detail provided by ISIC, even at its most detailed level, will often not be sufficient for the required analysis. In these cases, ISIC classes can be subdivided further as necessary for specific purposes. It is suggested, however, that the new detailed categories still be aggregable to the existing ISIC classes for comparability reasons.

F. Compilation of homogeneity ratios

127.   Despite the endeavour to define the classes of ISIC or the most detailed level of any other national activity classification in such a way that the two conditions described in paragraph 12 above are satisfied, some of the activities of establishments, or similar units, that are classified to a given class will be characteristic of other classes of the classification. In compiling data classified according to kind of economic activity, it will therefore be valuable to compute measures of homogeneity in respect of kinds of activity for the units falling into the various categories of the scheme of classification.

128.   The two most important ratios for assessing the homogeneity of the various categories are the specialization ratio and the coverage ratio. The specialization ratio of an industry is the output by that industry of goods or services characteristic of that industry in proportion to its total output. The coverage ratio is the output of goods or services characteristic of the industry in proportion to the total output of the same goods or services by the economy as a whole.

129.   When calculating these ratios, a number of problems should be kept in mind. Some products can be characteristic of more than one industry (for example, by-products that occur by necessity); some other products may be non-characteristic of any particular industry (for example, waste); and some may have to be declared characteristic of one or more industries by convention (for example, industrial repair services). In such cases, judgement should be exercised in interpreting the calculated ratios.

130.   It should also be noted that the creation of an industry with high ratios is no guarantee of useful statistics. Nor is a category with low ratios by definition useless. It is possible to create a category with a high specialization or coverage ratio that in economic terms is negligible. On the other hand, a category with a relatively low coverage ratio but a high specialization ratio may very well provide useful information for further analysis. Therefore, the ratios should not be used as the only determining factors

when establishing an industry classification; instead, they should always be used in combination with other criteria.

131. The homogeneity ratios might be computed in respect of the total gross output of the units classified to each class of the classification or – this being more preferable though more burdensome – in respect of the gross output of the individual statistical units. In the latter case, the establishments or similar units that fall into the various categories of the industrial classification would be arrayed according to class intervals of the homogeneity ratio. The specialization ratio especially should be a determining criterion when classifying a unit.

132. Homogeneity ratios can also be calculated in respect of the classification of kind of activity units or establishments to the groups or divisions as well as to the classes of ISIC. It will also be desirable to compute homogeneity ratios in respect of the classification of enterprises to the divisions of the industrial classification. Some enterprises will own establishments the principal kind of activity of which falls outside the scope of the division to which the enterprise is classified. The homogeneity ratios of enterprises might be based on the value added, or, if necessary, the employment, of the constituent units. It would indicate the proportion of the total value added, or employment, of enterprises accounted for by the constituent units classified to the same division as the owning enterprise. Such ratios would be extremely valuable in assessing the degree of comparability of enterprise data from different countries.

IV. Relationship with other classifications

A. General remarks

133. The Statistical Commission at its nineteenth session had requested the Secretariat to prepare a set of classifications that together would form an integrated system for classifying activities, goods and services and that could be used in different kinds of economic statistics. Using the Integrated System of Classifications of Activities and Products (SINAP) as a basis, the work resulted in the revision of ISIC and SITC and the development of CPC. These three classifications are strongly interrelated. ISIC represents the activity side of the system, CPC is the central instrument for classifying goods and services and SITC is the aggregated classification of transportable goods for international trade statistics for analytical purposes. Both CPC and SITC use the headings and sub-headings of the Harmonized Commodity Description and Coding System (HS) as building blocks for their categories.

B. Relationship with product classifications: CPC, HS and SITC, Rev.3

134. The relationship between ISIC on the one hand and the product classifications HS, CPC and SITC on the other is based on the fact that the product classifications in principle combine in one category goods or services that are normally produced in only one industry as defined in ISIC. In HS, this origin criterion was respected as far as possible at the time. In some cases – for instance, when it seemed impossible that a customs officer could make the distinction – the principle was not applied. Still, most headings and sub-headings of HS contain goods that are generally produced in only one ISIC category. The arrangement of headings and sub-headings of HS, however, follows criteria that are quite different from industrial origin and the structure of CPC or SITC.

135. The differences between CPC, HS and SITC result from the fact that they were created for different purposes. HS is the detailed classification for international trade of transportable goods, while SITC is a more aggregated classification for analytical purposes with the same scope as HS, that is to say,

trade of transportable goods. The scope of CPC exceeds that of HS and SITC, in that it is intended to cover the production, trade and consumption of all goods and services. Both CPC and SITC, Rev.3, regroup HS categories, albeit in different ways. SITC follows a traditional order in which the materials used, the stage of processing and the end use are the main considerations. CPC arranges its categories in groups that are similar to ISIC categories. This does not mean, however, that all goods are grouped according to their industrial origin.

136. Although origin had been an important criterion when developing CPC, it was produced as a classification in its own right – one in which classification is based on the physical characteristics and intrinsic nature of goods or on the nature of the services rendered. For example, while meat and hides are both outputs of slaughterhouses (ISIC class 1511, "Production, processing and preserving of meat and meat products"), they appear in different sections of CPC. However, each type of good or service distinguished in CPC is defined so that it is normally produced by only one activity as defined in ISIC. As far as practically possible, an attempt is made to establish a correspondence between the two classifications, each category of CPC being accompanied by a reference to the ISIC class in which the good or service is mainly produced.

137. For SITC, the same relationship with ISIC exists, that is to say, each item (five-digit category) of SITC is generally produced by only one ISIC class. The relationship between SITC and CPC is such that whole items of SITC can be aggregated to one CPC subclass and, conversely, whole CPC subclasses can be aggregated into one group (three-digit category) of SITC[10].

C. Relationship with other classifications of goods and services (BEC, EBOPS)

138. The Classification by Broad Economic Categories (BEC)[11] has been developed by the United Nations. BEC is designed to serve as a means for converting data compiled on SITC –which, as it stands, is not entirely suitable for analysis by end use – to meaningful aggregates for purposes of economic analysis of the use to which goods are put, based on concepts of the SNA (distinction between capital goods, intermediate goods and consumption goods). There is no relationship between ISIC and BEC other than the fact that BEC rearranges the SITC categories in 19 BEC categories. In doing so, it takes no account of the industrial origin of the goods. BEC was revised in 1986, based on the third revision of SITC, and in 2003 to reflect its relationship with the revised version of HS.

139. A correspondence between ISIC and the Extended Balance of Payments Services Classification (EBOPS)[12] has been developed to describe the link between primary activities of enterprises in terms of ISIC with balance-of-payments categories.

D. Other derived and related activity classifications (NACE, ANZSIC, NAEMA, NAICS, ICFA)

140. From the start of the work on harmonization of economic classifications the Statistical Commission emphasized that efforts should be made to harmonize multinational classifications with ISIC, Rev.3. The work of the Expert Group on International Economic and Social Classifications has continued these efforts with the work within the International Family of Economic and Social Classifications. The preamble lays out the foundations of these relationships between reference classifications (such as ISIC for economic activities) and derived and related classifications. The need for convergence of existing activity classifications has been stressed again by the Statistical Commission and will be a key element in the future work on these classifications.

141. The need for convergence does not diminish the need for regional classifications. The work on improved and tailored regional activity classifications, based on the reference classification as the international standard, is an important way to further the application of ISIC. These regional classifications should be derived from ISIC and adjusted to the regional specifics of a group of countries. They will allow for data comparability within the region and serve as more tailored guidelines for the development of national classifications.

1. Derived classifications

142. Through the United Nations Statistical Office/Statistical Office of the European communities (UNSO/SOEC) Joint Working Group and the cooperation of all parties concerned, it was agreed that the revised General Industrial Classification of Economic Activities within the European Communities (NACE) and the related product classification of the European Communities would be identical with, or an extension of, ISIC and CPC, respectively. Also the coding systems used in classifications of the United Nations and the European Communities would be, as far as possible, the same. As a result, data of both organizations became widely compatible. ISIC and NACE are identical up to the two-digit level (divisions) of the classification. At lower levels, NACE has created more detail suitable for European users of the classification. The additional detail created can always be aggregated to ISIC categories at the three- and four-digit levels, within the same structure.

143. The member States of Afristat have developed an activity classification known as Nomenclature d'Activités des Etats Membres d'Afristat (NAEMA)[13], derived from ISIC, Rev.3. Guiding its development was the desire to respect international recommendations, and take into account the needs of member States at the same time. The NAEMA came into force in member States of Afristat in January 2001.

144. NAEMA follows ISIC by using the 17 sections (one-digit level) and 60 divisions (two-digit level) of ISIC, Rev.3, without change. The 149 groups (three-digit level) of this classification are generally identical to those of ISIC. The exceptions relate to aggregations of groups of ISIC when the latter seemed too detailed, relative to the economy of the member States, or to splitting of groups of ISIC for a better breakdown of significant African activities, in particular agriculture and the agricultural processing industry, while observing the procedure of adaptation of the international classifications, as set out in chapter III, sections B and C.

145. Given that the economies of Afristat's member States encompass a significant share of the primary sector (agriculture, breeding, fishing and forestry development) and few developed industrial activities, the work on NAEMA resulted in an increase in the number of classes in the primary sector and a reduction of classes for the activities of manufacturing.

146. The ISIC Categories for Foreign Affiliates (ICFA)[14] is a system of industry groupings drawn from ISIC, provided for use in reporting statistics on foreign affiliates to international organizations. ICFA has been developed to allow the activities of services enterprises to be viewed in the context of the activities of all enterprises.

2. Related classifications

147. The Australian and New Zealand Standard Industrial Classification (ANZSIC), released in 1993, broadly aligns with ISIC at the detailed level. At the class level, ANZSIC has been designed to correspond to individual or aggregate ISIC classes. In some industries, combinations of activities within

Australian and New Zealand economic units cross ISIC boundaries creating a number of m-to-n links. These instances have been kept to the minimum. ISIC concepts and interpretations underpin the ANZSIC without deviation.

148.   The North American Industry Classification System (NAICS) was developed in the mid-1990s. Efforts have been undertaken to minimize the extent to which the lowest levels of NAICS (five-digit, industries) cross the boundaries of the two-digit level of ISIC, Rev.3. This allows statistical data collected according to NAICS to be reaggregated into the two-digit divisions of ISIC, Rev.3, and reflects a striving to ensure comparability of data, even if NAICS has been developed on a different conceptual basis than ISIC.

E. Relationship of other international classifications with ISIC

149.   There are other classifications developed by the United Nations or its subsidiary organs that have some relationship with ISIC or that make use of parts of ISIC in defining their own scope or categories. They have been developed for the description of statistics on occupations, employment, expenditures, education, tourism and environment. These are the Classification of the Functions of Government (COFOG), the International Standard Classification of Education (ISCED),[15] the International Standard Classification of Occupations (ISCO)[16] and the activity classification of the Tourism Satellite Account (TSA)[17].

150.   COFOG, which was developed by the former Statistical Office of the United Nations Secretariat mainly for use in the System of National Accounts, was first published in 1980 and revised in 2000. COFOG is in practice very similar to ISIC. In principle, its unit of classification is the individual transaction, but for many types of outlays, the unit will be the same government unit as for ISIC. Moreover, the criteria of classification - function in the case of COFOG and activity for ISIC - are conceptually rather similar. However, COFOG is more appropriate than ISIC for classifying government expenditures because the COFOG list of functions is more detailed than the ISIC list of activities, having been drawn up specifically to take account of the range and diversity of government activities. Although there are similarities between the criteria of the two classifications, problems may arise when comparing data collected according to ISIC and COFOG. For instance, COFOG covers not only direct outlays on government-owned schools, but also the subsidizing of privately owned schools and outlays on subsidiary services to education such as school transport, food and lodging for students etc. A correspondence table between COFOG and ISIC categories is shown in part five, section A, of this publication.

151.   ISCED was developed by the United Nations Educational, Scientific and Cultural Organization (UNESCO) as an instrument for assembling, compiling and presenting statistics of education both within individual countries and internationally and was last updated in 1997. It is a multi-purpose classification of educational programmes to be used for statistics on student enrolment, and human or financial resources invested in education as well as statistics on the educational attainment of the population as obtained, for example, from population censuses or labour-force surveys. The statistical unit as classified in ISCED at the lowest level is the programme or programme group.

152.   Educational institutions are classified according to ISCED on the basis of the type of programmes that they provide. In principle, these institutions may be considered equivalent to the basic units to be classified by ISIC. The definitions of the ISIC categories for education services have been changed since the last revision of ISIC so as to bring them in line with the changes applied in the last ISCED revision.

153.   The International Standard Classification of Occupations (ISCO) has been developed by the International Labour Organization (ILO). It provides a basis for comparing occupational statistics for different countries as well as communicating other occupational information, for example, for the recruitment or admission of migrant workers. It also serves as a model for countries when they develop their national occupational classifications or revise their existing ones.

154.   The primary units to be classified to ISCO are jobs. Jobs are classified to ISCO on the basis of the type of work performed, that is to say, the task and duties to be carried out. As ISIC and ISCO have entirely different functions and conceptual foundations – in other words, they measure very different aspects of the economy – there is no need to "harmonize" their structures. However, ISCO makes use of appropriate references to ISIC when defining similarities and differences between certain groups, when these are based on the type of distinctions that are reflected in ISIC, that is to say, between the type of products, namely, goods and services, that are being produced or sold. In ISCO-88, such references are given for distinctions made between the unit groups in minor groups 122 ("Production and operations department managers") and 131 ("General managers").

155.   A new international standard, the Tourism Satellite Account (TSA), has recently been developed and was approved by the Statistical Commission at its thirty-first session in 2000.[18] It sets the measurement of tourism and its impact on the economy within the macroeconomic framework of the SNA. The list of tourism-related activities that appeared in annex II of part two of ISIC, Rev.3, has been superseded by the TSA which identifies tourism in terms of characteristic products purchased by visitors and the activities that produce them, and lists them in terms of CPC and ISIC. Tourism characteristic activities are defined as those productive activities that produce one or more tourism characteristic products as a typical output of the production process characterizing the activity. The concepts, definitions and classifications to be used as well as the recommended methodological framework are described in *Tourism Satellite Account: Recommended Methodological Framework*. Tourism characteristic products and tourism characteristic activities are listed in annex II of that publication.

V. Other topics

A. Changes in ISIC, Rev.3.1, as compared with ISIC, Rev.3

156.   The current update to ISIC, Rev.3, has been limited in respect of its impact on the structure of the classification. Some changes were necessary to allow proper aggregation of complete ISIC classes into the alternate aggregations shown in part four of this publication. Only two ISIC groups had to be split to accomplish this. Since these groups (515 and 722) have not been subdivided before, countries unable to implement this new detail of the classification can still produce data at the three-digit level, that is to say, the group level, without compromising comparability with other, newer time series.

157.   ISIC group 050 (Fishing, aquaculture and service activities incidental to fishing) has been subdivided into two classes: 0501 (Fishing) and 0502 (Aquaculture) to account for the differences in the nature, and the importance, of these two activities.

158.   ISIC group 515 (Wholesale of machinery, equipment and supplies) has been subdivided into three classes: 5151 (Wholesale of computers, computer peripheral equipment and software), 5152 (Wholesale of electronic and telecommunications parts and equipment) and 5159 (Wholesale of other machinery, equipment and supplies).

159. ISIC group 722 (Software publishing, consultancy and supply) has been subdivided into two classes: 7221 (Software publishing) and 7229 (Other software consultancy and supply). In addition, these classes now include the creation and publication of software for all kinds of platforms, including video games.

160. ISIC section M (Education) has been adjusted to take account of the changes in the International Standard Classification of Education (ISCED), which was revised in 1997. Most notably, the treatment of adult education at various levels has been changed.

161. Two new divisions have been included in ISIC, Rev.3.1 (division 96: Undifferentiated goods-producing activities of private households for own use; and division 97: Undifferentiated service-producing activities of private households for own use) in order to cover production activities carried out by private households for their own use. Hence, these divisions would normally not be relevant in business statistics, but useful in data collections covering household and subsistence activities.

162. A number of smaller corrections have been made to the classifications. Details of these corrections are reflected in the correspondence tables between ISIC, Rev.3, and ISIC, Rev.3.1, contained in part five of this publication. A more detailed description of these corrections is available in the Classifications Registry on the United Nations Statistics Division web site (http://unstats.un.org/unsd/class).

B. Indexes to the classification

163. Alphabetical and numerical indexes are very useful tools for further detailing classification categories and greatly simplify their application. The indexes are designed to be of assistance in adapting ISIC to the classification requirements of individual countries, in comparing national classifications to ISIC and in classifying data according to ISIC. They should also provide a guide to the correct classification of statistical units.

164. New interpretations of the classification, usually related to new activities, can be easily reflected in the index, while usually no change in the classification or its related texts is necessary. Indexes for ISIC were published in printed form for ISIC, Rev.2, in 1971[19]. Indexes for this new version of ISIC will be available in machine-readable form only, published in the Classifications Registry on the United Nations Statistics Division web site (http://unstats.un.org/unsd/class).

C. Correspondence tables

165. Correspondence tables are an important tool for comparing statistical data that have been collected and presented using different classifications. They become necessary when the classification changes over time or when different underlying frameworks do not allow classifications to be closely related. Correspondence tables between different versions of the same classification are used to describe the detailed changes that have taken place in the revision process.

166. Since ISIC has been used for the collection and presentation of statistics in many areas, there has been a strong need for correspondence tables between ISIC and other classifications. This publication includes correspondence tables between ISIC, Rev.3.1, and ISIC, Rev.2, to allow for comparison of historical data, as well as correspondence tables between ISIC, Rev.3.1, and ISIC, Rev.3, to detail the changes that have been made in the current revision.

167.   When drafting ISIC, Rev.3, and simultaneously CPC, a strong link was established between the two classifications. By rearranging the CPC categories according to their industrial origin, and using the link between CPC, SITC and HS, a detailed correspondence table between HS, SITC, CPC and ISIC was established, but has not been included in this publication.

168.   There is a strong need to link ISIC and the Classification of the Functions of Government (COFOG). While the latter classifies transactions and not transactors, there is usually an activity characteristic for the transactions classified in COFOG that allows linking the transactions with the appropriate statistical units. It should be noted that ISIC does not make any distinctions between government-owned and privately owned businesses. A correspondence between the two classifications is provided in part five of this publication.

D. Special-purpose groupings of ISIC/alternate aggregations

169.   Economic analysis and presentation of statistics on specific subjects often require aggregation of data, collected according to ISIC, in ways that are different from the aggregation provided by the ISIC structure. For these special purposes, standard aggregations have been created to meet these demands, such as those presented in part four of this publication (for the information sector, the information and communication technologies (ICT) sector and the informal sector) and those defined in other statistical frameworks (for "Tourism activities", "Environmental activities" etc.). These alternate aggregations may use either complete ISIC classes, such as the alternate aggregation for the information sector, or only parts of ISIC classes, if the underlying concept for the aggregation is not comparable with the principle used in ISIC (see part four for more detailed information).

170.   Annex II on tourism-related industries found in part two of ISIC, Rev. 3, has not been reproduced in ISIC, Rev. 3.1, as the simple approach of showing a list of tourism-related industries (Standard International Classification of Tourism Activities (SICTA)) as an annex to ISIC has been superseded by a much more comprehensive satellite account framework, as described in paragraph 155 above.

E. Support for ISIC users

171.   The United Nations Statistics Division is responsible for the development and maintenance of ISIC. The developers of national activity classifications and other institutions using ISIC may find it in their interest to establish contact with the Statistics Division. Users of ISIC may thus receive notification about plans for updates or revisions, information concerning interpretations and rulings and, in general, technical support in applying the classification. Users are encouraged to bring to the attention of the Statistics Division any difficulties they encounter in the implementation of ISIC, to request clarification and to share their experience and remarks with regard to its adequacy and provide ideas or proposals for enhancing its usefulness.

172.   Updated information on ISIC, indexes, proposals for revisions and the revision process are available in the Classifications Registry on the United Nations international economic and social classifications web site (http://unstats.un.org/unsd/class).

173.   Communications may be sent to the Director, United Nations Statistics Division, Attention: Statistical Classifications Section, by mail (address: 2 United Nations Plaza, Room DC2-1670, New York, NY 10017, USA); by fax (1-212-963-1374); or through the Classifications Hotline by e-mail (chl@un.org).

Notes:

1 Statistical Papers, Series M, No. 4, Lake Success, New York, 31 October 1949.

2 *International Standard Industrial Classification of All Economic Activities*, Statistical Papers, Series M, No. 4, Rev. 1 (United Nations publication, Sales No. E.58.XVII.7).

3 *International Standard Industrial Classification of All Economic Activities*, Statistical Papers, Series M, No. 4, Rev. 2 (United Nations publication, Sales No. E.68.XVII.8).

4 *International Standard Industrial Classification of All Economic Activities*, Statistical Papers, Series M, No. 4, Rev. 3 (United Nations publication, Sales No. E.90.XVII.11).

5 See *official records of the Economic and Social Council, 1999, Supplement No. 4 (E/1999/24)*, para. 108 (b).

6 Commission of the European Communities, International Monetary Fund, Organisation for Economic Co-operation and Development, United Nations and World Bank, *System of National Accounts, 1993* (United Nations publication, Sales No. E.94.XVII.4).

7 *Standard International Trade Classification, Revision 3*, Statistical Papers, Series M, No. 34, Rev. 3, and corrigenda (United Nations publication, Sales No. E.86.XVII.12 and Corr. 1 and 2).

8 *Central Product Classification (CPC), Version 1.1*, Statistical Papers, Series M, No. 77, Ver.1.1 (United Nations publication, Sales No. E.03.XVII.3).

9 *Classifications of Expenditure According to Purpose: Classification of the Functions of Government (COFOG), Classification of Individual Consumption According to Purpose (COICOP), Classification of the Purposes of Non-Profit Institutions Serving Households (COPNI), Classification of the Outlays of Producers According to Purpose (COPP)*, Statistical Papers, Series M, No. 84 (United Nations publication, Sales No. E.00.XVII.6).

10 See *Central Product Classification (CPC), Version 1.0*, Statistical papers, Series M, No. 77, Ver.1.0 (United Nations publication, sales No. E.98.XVII.5), part one, paras. 35, 36, 44.

11 *Classification by Broad Economic Categories: Defined in Terms of the Standard International Trade Classification, Rev. 3 and the Harmonized Commodity Description and Coding System (2002)*, Statistical Papers, Series M, No. 53, Rev.4 (United Nations publication, Sales No. E.03.XVII.8).

12 International Monetary Fund, *Balance of Payments Manual*, 5th ed. (Washington, D.C., IMF, 1993).

13 *Nomenclature d'Activités des Etats Membres d'Afristat (NAEMA)*, Série Méthodes, No. 3 (Bamako, Afristat, December 2000).

14 See United Nations, European Commission, International Monetary Fund, Organisation for Economic Co-operation and Development, United Nations Conference on Trade and Development and World Trade Organization, *Manual on Statistics of International Trade in Services*, Statistical Papers, Series M, No. 86 (United Nations publication, Sales No. E.02.XVII.11).

15 *International Standard Classification of Education (ISCED 1997)* (Paris, UNESCO, November 1097).

16 *International Standard Classification of Occupations (ISCO-1988)* (Geneva, ILO, 1988).

17 Commission of the European Communities, Organisation for Economic Co-operation and Development, United Nations and World Tourism Organization, *Tourism Satellite Account: Recommended Methodological Framework*, Statistical Papers, Series F, No. 80 (United Nations publication, Sales No. E.01.XVII.9).

18 See *Official Records of the Economic and Social Council, 2000, Supplement No. 4 (E/2002/24)*, para. 18.

19 *Indexes to the International Standard Industrial Classification of All Economic Activities*, Statistical Papers, Series M, No. 4, Rev.2, Add.1 (United Nations publications, Sales No. E.71.XVII.8).

Part two

Broad and detailed structure

I. Broad structure

The individual categories of ISIC have been aggregated into the following 17 sections:

Section	Divisions	Description
A	01, 02	Agriculture, hunting and forestry
B	05	Fishing
C	10-14	Mining and quarrying
D	15-37	Manufacturing
E	40, 41	Electricity, gas and water supply
F	45	Construction
G	50-52	Wholesale and retail trade; repair of motor vehicles, motorcycles and personal and household goods
H	55	Hotels and restaurants
I	60-64	Transport, storage and communications
J	65-67	Financial intermediation
K	70-74	Real estate, renting and business activities
L	75	Public administration and defence; compulsory social security
M	80	Education
N	85	Health and social work
O	90-93	Other community, social and personal service activities
P	95-97	Activities of private households as employers and undifferentiated production activities of private households
Q	99	Extraterritorial organizations and bodies

II. Detailed structure

Section/Division	Group	Class	Description
Section A			**Agriculture, hunting and forestry**
Division 01			**Agriculture, hunting and related service activities**
	011		Growing of crops; market gardening; horticulture
		0111	Growing of cereals and other crops n.e.c.
		0112	Growing of vegetables, horticultural specialties and nursery products
		0113	Growing of fruit, nuts, beverage and spice crops
	012		Farming of animals
		0121	Farming of cattle, sheep, goats, horses, asses, mules and hinnies; dairy farming
		0122	Other animal farming; production of animal products n.e.c.
	013	0130	Growing of crops combined with farming of animals (mixed farming)
	014	0140	Agricultural and animal husbandry service activities, except veterinary activities
	015	0150	Hunting, trapping and game propagation including related service activities
Division 02			**Forestry, logging and related service activities**
	020	0200	Forestry, logging and related service activities
Section B			**Fishing**
Division 05			**Fishing, aquaculture and service activities incidental to fishing**
	050		Fishing, aquaculture and service activities incidental to fishing
		0501	Fishing
		0502	Aquaculture
Section C			**Mining and quarrying**
Division 10			**Mining of coal and lignite; extraction of peat**
	101	1010	Mining and agglomeration of hard coal
	102	1020	Mining and agglomeration of lignite
	103	1030	Extraction and agglomeration of peat
Division 11			**Extraction of crude petroleum and natural gas; service activities incidental to oil and gas extraction, excluding surveying**
	111	1110	Extraction of crude petroleum and natural gas
	112	1120	Service activities incidental to oil and gas extraction excluding surveying
Division 12			**Mining of uranium and thorium ores**
	120	1200	Mining of uranium and thorium ores
Division 13			**Mining of metal ores**
	131	1310	Mining of iron ores
	132	1320	Mining of non-ferrous metal ores, except uranium and thorium ores

Division 14			**Other mining and quarrying**
	141	1410	Quarrying of stone, sand and clay
	142		Mining and quarrying n.e.c.
		1421	Mining of chemical and fertilizer minerals
		1422	Extraction of salt
		1429	Other mining and quarrying n.e.c.
Section D			**Manufacturing**
Division 15			**Manufacture of food products and beverages**
	151		Production, processing and preservation of meat, fish, fruit, vegetables, oils and fats
		1511	Production, processing and preserving of meat and meat products
		1512	Processing and preserving of fish and fish products
		1513	Processing and preserving of fruit and vegetables
		1514	Manufacture of vegetable and animal oils and fats
	152	1520	Manufacture of dairy products
	153		Manufacture of grain mill products, starches and starch products, and prepared animal feeds
		1531	Manufacture of grain mill products
		1532	Manufacture of starches and starch products
		1533	Manufacture of prepared animal feeds
	154		Manufacture of other food products
		1541	Manufacture of bakery products
		1542	Manufacture of sugar
		1543	Manufacture of cocoa, chocolate and sugar confectionery
		1544	Manufacture of macaroni, noodles, couscous and similar farinaceous products
		1549	Manufacture of other food products n.e.c.
	155		Manufacture of beverages
		1551	Distilling, rectifying and blending of spirits; ethyl alcohol production from fermented materials
		1552	Manufacture of wines
		1553	Manufacture of malt liquors and malt
		1554	Manufacture of soft drinks; production of mineral waters
Division 16			**Manufacture of tobacco products**
	160	1600	Manufacture of tobacco products
Division 17			**Manufacture of textiles**
	171		Spinning, weaving and finishing of textiles
		1711	Preparation and spinning of textile fibres; weaving of textiles
		1712	Finishing of textiles
	172		Manufacture of other textiles
		1721	Manufacture of made-up textile articles, except apparel
		1722	Manufacture of carpets and rugs
		1723	Manufacture of cordage, rope, twine and netting
		1729	Manufacture of other textiles n.e.c.
	173	1730	Manufacture of knitted and crocheted fabrics and articles

Division 18   **Manufacture of wearing apparel; dressing and dyeing of fur**

181	1810	Manufacture of wearing apparel, except fur apparel
182	1820	Dressing and dyeing of fur; manufacture of articles of fur

Division 19   **Tanning and dressing of leather; manufacture of luggage, handbags, saddlery, harness and footwear**

191		Tanning and dressing of leather; manufacture of luggage, handbags, saddlery and harness
	1911	Tanning and dressing of leather
	1912	Manufacture of luggage, handbags and the like, saddlery and harness
192	1920	Manufacture of footwear

Division 20   **Manufacture of wood and of products of wood and cork, except furniture; manufacture of articles of straw and plaiting materials**

201	2010	Sawmilling and planing of wood
202		Manufacture of products of wood, cork, straw and plaiting materials
	2021	Manufacture of veneer sheets; manufacture of plywood, laminboard, particle board and other panels and boards
	2022	Manufacture of builders' carpentry and joinery
	2023	Manufacture of wooden containers
	2029	Manufacture of other products of wood; manufacture of articles of cork, straw and plaiting materials

Division 21   **Manufacture of paper and paper products**

210		Manufacture of paper and paper products
	2101	Manufacture of pulp, paper and paperboard
	2102	Manufacture of corrugated paper and paperboard and of containers of paper and paperboard
	2109	Manufacture of other articles of paper and paperboard

Division 22   **Publishing, printing and reproduction of recorded media**

221		Publishing
	2211	Publishing of books, brochures and other publications
	2212	Publishing of newspapers, journals and periodicals
	2213	Publishing of music
	2219	Other publishing
222		Printing and service activities related to printing
	2221	Printing
	2222	Service activities related to printing
223	2230	Reproduction of recorded media

Division 23   **Manufacture of coke, refined petroleum products and nuclear fuel**

231	2310	Manufacture of coke oven products
232	2320	Manufacture of refined petroleum products
233	2330	Processing of nuclear fuel

Division 24   **Manufacture of chemicals and chemical products**

241		Manufacture of basic chemicals

		2411	Manufacture of basic chemicals, except fertilizers and nitrogen compounds
		2412	Manufacture of fertilizers and nitrogen compounds
		2413	Manufacture of plastics in primary forms and of synthetic rubber
	242		Manufacture of other chemical products
		2421	Manufacture of pesticides and other agrochemical products
		2422	Manufacture of paints, varnishes and similar coatings, printing ink and mastics
		2423	Manufacture of pharmaceuticals, medicinal chemicals and botanical products
		2424	Manufacture of soap and detergents, cleaning and polishing preparations, perfumes and toilet preparations
		2429	Manufacture of other chemical products n.e.c.
	243	2430	Manufacture of man-made fibres

Division 25   **Manufacture of rubber and plastics products**

	251		Manufacture of rubber products
		2511	Manufacture of rubber tyres and tubes; retreading and rebuilding of rubber tyres
		2519	Manufacture of other rubber products
	252	2520	Manufacture of plastics products

Division 26   **Manufacture of other non-metallic mineral products**

	261	2610	Manufacture of glass and glass products
	269		Manufacture of non-metallic mineral products n.e.c.
		2691	Manufacture of non-structural non-refractory ceramic ware
		2692	Manufacture of refractory ceramic products
		2693	Manufacture of structural non-refractory clay and ceramic products
		2694	Manufacture of cement, lime and plaster
		2695	Manufacture of articles of concrete, cement and plaster
		2696	Cutting, shaping and finishing of stone
		2699	Manufacture of other non-metallic mineral products n.e.c.

Division 27   **Manufacture of basic metals**

	271	2710	Manufacture of basic iron and steel
	272	2720	Manufacture of basic precious and non-ferrous metals
	273		Casting of metals
		2731	Casting of iron and steel
		2732	Casting of non-ferrous metals

Division 28   **Manufacture of fabricated metal products, except machinery and equipment**

	281		Manufacture of structural metal products, tanks, reservoirs and steam generators
		2811	Manufacture of structural metal products
		2812	Manufacture of tanks, reservoirs and containers of metal
		2813	Manufacture of steam generators, except central heating hot water boilers
	289		Manufacture of other fabricated metal products; metalworking service activities

		2891	Forging, pressing, stamping and roll-forming of metal; powder metallurgy
		2892	Treatment and coating of metals; general mechanical engineering on a fee or contract basis
		2893	Manufacture of cutlery, hand tools and general hardware
		2899	Manufacture of other fabricated metal products n.e.c.

Division 29   **Manufacture of machinery and equipment n.e.c.**

	291		Manufacture of general-purpose machinery
		2911	Manufacture of engines and turbines, except aircraft, vehicle and cycle engines
		2912	Manufacture of pumps, compressors, taps and valves
		2913	Manufacture of bearings, gears, gearing and driving elements
		2914	Manufacture of ovens, furnaces and furnace burners
		2915	Manufacture of lifting and handling equipment
		2919	Manufacture of other general-purpose machinery
	292		Manufacture of special-purpose machinery
		2921	Manufacture of agricultural and forestry machinery
		2922	Manufacture of machine tools
		2923	Manufacture of machinery for metallurgy
		2924	Manufacture of machinery for mining, quarrying and construction
		2925	Manufacture of machinery for food, beverage and tobacco processing
		2926	Manufacture of machinery for textile, apparel and leather production
		2927	Manufacture of weapons and ammunition
		2929	Manufacture of other special-purpose machinery
	293	2930	Manufacture of domestic appliances n.e.c.

Division 30   **Manufacture of office, accounting and computing machinery**

	300	3000	Manufacture of office, accounting and computing machinery

Division 31   **Manufacture of electrical machinery and apparatus n.e.c.**

	311	3110	Manufacture of electric motors, generators and transformers
	312	3120	Manufacture of electricity distribution and control apparatus
	313	3130	Manufacture of insulated wire and cable
	314	3140	Manufacture of accumulators, primary cells and primary batteries
	315	3150	Manufacture of electric lamps and lighting equipment
	319	3190	Manufacture of other electrical equipment n.e.c.

Division 32   **Manufacture of radio, television and communication equipment and apparatus**

	321	3210	Manufacture of electronic valves and tubes and other electronic components
	322	3220	Manufacture of television and radio transmitters and apparatus for line telephony and line telegraphy
	323	3230	Manufacture of television and radio receivers, sound or video recording or reproducing apparatus, and associated goods

Division 33   **Manufacture of medical, precision and optical instruments, watches and clocks**

	331		Manufacture of medical appliances and instruments and appliances for measuring, checking, testing, navigating and other purposes, except optical instruments
		3311	Manufacture of medical and surgical equipment and orthopaedic appliances
		3312	Manufacture of instruments and appliances for measuring, checking, testing, navigating and other purposes, except industrial process control equipment
		3313	Manufacture of industrial process control equipment
	332	3320	Manufacture of optical instruments and photographic equipment
	333	3330	Manufacture of watches and clocks
Division 34			**Manufacture of motor vehicles, trailers and semi-trailers**
	341	3410	Manufacture of motor vehicles
	342	3420	Manufacture of bodies (coachwork) for motor vehicles; manufacture of trailers and semi-trailers
	343	3430	Manufacture of parts and accessories for motor vehicles and their engines
Division 35			**Manufacture of other transport equipment**
	351		Building and repairing of ships and boats
		3511	Building and repairing of ships
		3512	Building and repairing of pleasure and sporting boats
	352	3520	Manufacture of railway and tramway locomotives and rolling stock
	353	3530	Manufacture of aircraft and spacecraft
	359		Manufacture of transport equipment n.e.c.
		3591	Manufacture of motorcycles
		3592	Manufacture of bicycles and invalid carriages
		3599	Manufacture of other transport equipment n.e.c.
Division 36			**Manufacture of furniture; manufacturing n.e.c.**
	361	3610	Manufacture of furniture
	369		Manufacturing n.e.c.
		3691	Manufacture of jewellery and related articles
		3692	Manufacture of musical instruments
		3693	Manufacture of sports goods
		3694	Manufacture of games and toys
		3699	Other manufacturing n.e.c.
Division 37			**Recycling**
	371	3710	Recycling of metal waste and scrap
	372	3720	Recycling of non-metal waste and scrap
Section E			**Electricity, gas and water supply**
Division 40			**Electricity, gas, steam and hot water supply**
	401	4010	Production, transmission and distribution of electricity
	402	4020	Manufacture of gas; distribution of gaseous fuels through mains
	403	4030	Steam and hot water supply
Division 41			**Collection, purification and distribution of water**
	410	4100	Collection, purification and distribution of water

Section F			**Construction**
Division 45			**Construction**
	451	4510	Site preparation
	452	4520	Building of complete constructions or parts thereof; civil engineering
	453	4530	Building installation
	454	4540	Building completion
	455	4550	Renting of construction or demolition equipment with operator
Section G			**Wholesale and retail trade; repair of motor vehicles, motorcycles and personal and household goods**
Division 50			**Sale, maintenance and repair of motor vehicles and motorcycles; retail sale of automotive fuel**
	501	5010	Sale of motor vehicles
	502	5020	Maintenance and repair of motor vehicles
	503	5030	Sale of motor vehicle parts and accessories
	504	5040	Sale, maintenance and repair of motorcycles and related parts and accessories
	505	5050	Retail sale of automotive fuel
Division 51			**Wholesale trade and commission trade, except of motor vehicles and motorcycles**
	511	5110	Wholesale on a fee or contract basis
	512		Wholesale of agricultural raw materials, live animals, food, beverages and tobacco
		5121	Wholesale of agricultural raw materials and live animals
		5122	Wholesale of food, beverages and tobacco
	513		Wholesale of household goods
		5131	Wholesale of textiles, clothing and footwear
		5139	Wholesale of other household goods
	514		Wholesale of non-agricultural intermediate products, waste and scrap
		5141	Wholesale of solid, liquid and gaseous fuels and related products
		5142	Wholesale of metals and metal ores
		5143	Wholesale of construction materials, hardware, plumbing and heating equipment and supplies
		5149	Wholesale of other intermediate products, waste and scrap
	515		Wholesale of machinery, equipment and supplies
		5151	Wholesale of computers, computer peripheral equipment and software
		5152	Wholesale of electronic and telecommunications parts and equipment
		5159	Wholesale of other machinery, equipment and supplies
	519	5190	Other wholesale
Division 52			**Retail trade, except of motor vehicles and motorcycles; repair of personal and household goods**
	521		Non-specialized retail trade in stores
		5211	Retail sale in non-specialized stores with food, beverages or tobacco predominating
		5219	Other retail sale in non-specialized stores
	522	5220	Retail sale of food, beverages and tobacco in specialized stores

	523		Other retail trade of new goods in specialized stores
		5231	Retail sale of pharmaceutical and medical goods, cosmetic and toilet articles
		5232	Retail sale of textiles, clothing, footwear and leather goods
		5233	Retail sale of household appliances, articles and equipment
		5234	Retail sale of hardware, paints and glass
		5239	Other retail sale in specialized stores
	524	5240	Retail sale of second-hand goods in stores
	525		Retail trade not in stores
		5251	Retail sale via mail order houses
		5252	Retail sale via stalls and markets
		5259	Other non-store retail sale
	526	5260	Repair of personal and household goods

Section H   **Hotels and restaurants**

Division 55   **Hotels and restaurants**

	551	5510	Hotels; camping sites and other provision of short-stay accommodation
	552	5520	Restaurants, bars and canteens

Section I   **Transport, storage and communications**

Division 60   **Land transport; transport via pipelines**

	601	6010	Transport via railways
	602		Other land transport
		6021	Other scheduled passenger land transport
		6022	Other non-scheduled passenger land transport
		6023	Freight transport by road
	603	6030	Transport via pipelines

Division 61   **Water transport**

	611	6110	Sea and coastal water transport
	612	6120	Inland water transport

Division 62   **Air transport**

	621	6210	Scheduled air transport
	622	6220	Non-scheduled air transport

Division 63   **Supporting and auxiliary transport activities; activities of travel agencies**

	630		Supporting and auxiliary transport activities; activities of travel agencies
		6301	Cargo handling
		6302	Storage and warehousing
		6303	Other supporting transport activities
		6304	Activities of travel agencies and tour operators; tourist assistance activities n.e.c.
		6309	Activities of other transport agencies

Division 64   **Post and telecommunications**

	641		Post and courier activities

		6411	National post activities
		6412	Courier activities other than national post activities
	642	6420	Telecommunications

Section J — **Financial intermediation**

Division 65 — **Financial intermediation, except insurance and pension funding**

651		Monetary intermediation
	6511	Central banking
	6519	Other monetary intermediation
659		Other financial intermediation
	6591	Financial leasing
	6592	Other credit granting
	6599	Other financial intermediation n.e.c.

Division 66 — **Insurance and pension funding, except compulsory social security**

660		Insurance and pension funding, except compulsory social security
	6601	Life insurance
	6602	Pension funding
	6603	Non-life insurance

Division 67 — **Activities auxiliary to financial intermediation**

671		Activities auxiliary to financial intermediation, except insurance and pension funding
	6711	Administration of financial markets
	6712	Security dealing activities
	6719	Activities auxiliary to financial intermediation n.e.c.
672	6720	Activities auxiliary to insurance and pension funding

Section K — **Real estate, renting and business activities**

Division 70 — **Real estate activities**

701	7010	Real estate activities with own or leased property
702	7020	Real estate activities on a fee or contract basis

Division 71 — **Renting of machinery and equipment without operator and of personal and household goods**

711		Renting of transport equipment
	7111	Renting of land transport equipment
	7112	Renting of water transport equipment
	7113	Renting of air transport equipment
712		Renting of other machinery and equipment
	7121	Renting of agricultural machinery and equipment
	7122	Renting of construction and civil engineering machinery and equipment
	7123	Renting of office machinery and equipment (including computers)
	7129	Renting of other machinery and equipment n.e.c.
713	7130	Renting of personal and household goods n.e.c.

Division 72 — **Computer and related activities**

	721	7210	Hardware consultancy
	722		Software publishing, consultancy and supply
		7221	Software publishing
		7229	Other software consultancy and supply
	723	7230	Data processing
	724	7240	Database activities and online distribution of electronic content
	725	7250	Maintenance and repair of office, accounting and computing machinery
	729	7290	Other computer-related activities

Division 73 — **Research and development**

	731	7310	Research and experimental development on natural sciences and engineering (NSE)
	732	7320	Research and experimental development on social sciences and humanities (SSH)

Division 74 — **Other business activities**

	741		Legal, accounting, bookkeeping and auditing activities; tax consultancy; market research and public opinion polling; business and management consultancy
		7411	Legal activities
		7412	Accounting, bookkeeping and auditing activities; tax consultancy
		7413	Market research and public opinion polling
		7414	Business and management consultancy activities
	742		Architectural, engineering and other technical activities
		7421	Architectural and engineering activities and related technical consultancy
		7422	Technical testing and analysis
	743	7430	Advertising
	749		Business activities n.e.c.
		7491	Labour recruitment and provision of personnel
		7492	Investigation and security activities
		7493	Building-cleaning and industrial-cleaning activities
		7494	Photographic activities
		7495	Packaging activities
		7499	Other business activities n.e.c.

Section L — **Public administration and defence; compulsory social security**

Division 75 — **Public administration and defence; compulsory social security**

	751		Administration of the State and the economic and social policy of the community
		7511	General (overall) public service activities
		7512	Regulation of the activities of agencies that provide health care, education, cultural services and other social services, excluding social security
		7513	Regulation of and contribution to more efficient operation of business
		7514	Supporting service activities for the government as a whole
	752		Provision of services to the community as a whole
		7521	Foreign affairs

		7522	Defence activities
		7523	Public order and safety activities
	753	7530	Compulsory social security activities

Section M — Education

Division 80 — Education

	801	8010	Primary education
	802		Secondary education
		8021	General secondary education
		8022	Technical and vocational secondary education
	803	8030	Higher education
	809	8090	Other education

Section N — Health and social work

Division 85 — Health and social work

	851		Human health activities
		8511	Hospital activities
		8512	Medical and dental practice activities
		8519	Other human health activities
	852	8520	Veterinary activities
	853		Social work activities
		8531	Social work activities with accommodation
		8532	Social work activities without accommodation

Section O — Other community, social and personal service activities

Division 90 — Sewage and refuse disposal, sanitation and similar activities

	900	9000	Sewage and refuse disposal, sanitation and similar activities

Division 91 — Activities of membership organizations n.e.c.

	911		Activities of business, employers and professional organizations
		9111	Activities of business and employers organizations
		9112	Activities of professional organizations
	912	9120	Activities of trade unions
	919		Activities of other membership organizations
		9191	Activities of religious organizations
		9192	Activities of political organizations
		9199	Activities of other membership organizations n.e.c.

Division 92 — Recreational, cultural and sporting activities

	921		Motion picture, radio, television and other entertainment activities
		9211	Motion picture and video production and distribution
		9212	Motion picture projection
		9213	Radio and television activities
		9214	Dramatic arts, music and other arts activities
		9219	Other entertainment activities n.e.c.
	922	9220	News agency activities
	923		Library, archives, museums and other cultural activities

		9231	Library and archives activities
		9232	Museums activities and preservation of historic sites and buildings
		9233	Botanical and zoological gardens and nature reserves activities
	924		Sporting and other recreational activities
		9241	Sporting activities
		9249	Other recreational activities

Division 93   **Other service activities**

	930		Other service activities
		9301	Washing and (dry-)cleaning of textile and fur products
		9302	Hairdressing and other beauty treatment
		9303	Funeral and related activities
		9309	Other service activities n.e.c.

Section P   **Activities of private households as employers and undifferentiated production activities of private households**

Division 95   **Activities of private households as employers of domestic staff**

	950	9500	Activities of private households as employers of domestic staff

Division 96   **Undifferentiated goods-producing activities of private households for own use**

	960	9600	Undifferentiated goods-producing activities of private households for own use

Division 97   **Undifferentiated service-producing activities of private households for own use**

	970	9700	Undifferentiated service-producing activities of private households for own use

Section Q   **Extraterritorial organizations and bodies**

Division 99   **Extraterritorial organizations and bodies**

	990	9900	Extraterritorial organizations and bodies

Part three

Detailed structure and explanatory notes

A   Agriculture, hunting and forestry

Section A covers the exploitation of vegetal and animal natural resources. The section comprises the activities of growing crops, raising animals, harvesting timber, and harvesting other plants and animals from a farm or their natural habitats.

01   Agriculture, hunting and related service activities

Division 01 distinguishes two basic activities:
- Production of crop products (011: Growing of crops)
- Production of animal products (012: Farming of animals).

Within 011 a distinction is made between:
- Production of field crops whose growth generally follows a yearly cycle (0111, 0112) such as cereals, vegetables and flowers
- Production of crops with a long cycle such as those grown in plantations (e.g. coffee, cocoa etc.), vineyards and orchards (0113).

Within group 012 (Farming of animals), the activities are grouped according to the type of animal and not according to the type of product produced (e.g. meat, milk, hide etc.) and without distinguishing between total confinement (non-grazing) and open range pasture farming.

Group 013 (Mixed farming) breaks with the usual principles for identifying main activity. It accepts that many agricultural holdings have reasonably balanced crop and animal production, and that it would be arbitrary to classify them in one category or the other.

Certain operations, such as soil preparation, planting, harvesting, and management, that are normally part of farm operation, may be carried out by agricultural support units on a fee or contract basis as agricultural or animal husbandry (0140) service activities.

Agricultural activity excludes any subsequent processing of the agricultural products (classified under division 15 (Manufacture of food products and beverages) and division 16 (Manufacture of tobacco products)), beyond that needed to prepare them for the primary markets. However, as an exception to the general rule for classification of integrated activities, a unit growing grapes and producing wine at the same location is classified to 01, even though the output normally is the product of division 15.

The division excludes field construction (e.g. agricultural land terracing, drainage, preparing rice paddies etc.) classified in division 45 (Construction) and buyers and cooperative associations engaged in the marketing of farm products classified in section G.

011   Growing of crops; market gardening; horticulture

This group includes the growing of crops, vegetables and fruits in the open and under cover.

0111   Growing of cereals and other crops n.e.c.

This class includes:
- growing of temporary and permanent crops
- cereal grains: rice, hard and soft wheat, rye, barley, oats, maize, corn (except sweetcorn) etc.
- growing of potatoes, yams, sweet potatoes or cassava
- growing of sugar beet, sugar cane or grain sorghum
- growing of tobacco, including its preliminary processing: harvesting and drying of tobacco leaves
- growing of oilseeds or oleaginous fruit and nuts: peanuts, soya, colza etc.
- production of sugar beet seeds and forage plant seeds (including grasses)
- growing of hop cones, roots and tubers with a high starch or inulin content

- growing of cotton or other vegetal textile materials
- retting of plants bearing vegetable fibres (jute, flax, coir)
- growing of rubber trees, harvesting of latex
- growing of leguminous vegetables such as field peas and beans
- growing of plants used chiefly in pharmacy or for insecticidal, fungicidal or similar purposes
- growing of crops n.e.c.

This class excludes:
- *growing of melons, see 0112*
- *growing of sweet corn, see 0112*
- *growing of other vegetables, see 0112*
- *growing of flowers, see 0112*
- *production of flower and vegetable seeds, see 0112*
- *growing of horticultural specialties, see 0112*
- *growing of olives, see 0113*
- *growing of beverage crops, see 0113*
- *growing of spice crops, see 0113*
- *growing of edible nuts, see 0113*
- *gathering of forest products and other wild growing material (cork, resins, balsam etc.), see 0200*

0112   Growing of vegetables, horticultural specialties and nursery products

This class includes:
- growing of vegetables: tomatoes, melons, pumpkins, onions, cabbages, lettuce, cucumbers, carrots, beans, sweetcorn, courgettes, aubergines (eggplants), leeks
- growing of seasoning herbs and vegetables: capers, "peppers", fennel, parsley, chervil, tarragon, cress, sweet marjoram
- growing of mushrooms, gathering of forest mushrooms or truffles
- growing of flowers or flower buds
- production of seeds for flowers, fruit or vegetables
- growing of plants for planting or ornamental purposes, including turf for transplanting
- gathering of sap and production of maple syrup and sugar

This class excludes:
- *growing of potatoes, see 0111*
- *growing of sugar beets, see 0111*
- *growing of oilseeds and oleaginous fruit, see 0111*
- *growing of roots and tubers with a high starch or inulin content, see 0111*
- *growing of cotton or other vegetable textile materials, see 0111*
- *growing of spice crops, see 0113*
- *growing of coffee, cocoa beans, tea or maté, see 0113*
- *growing of olives, see 0113*
- *operation of forest tree nurseries, see 0200*
- *growing of Christmas trees, see 0200*

0113   Growing of fruit, nuts, beverage and spice crops

This class includes:
- growing of fruit: apples, pears, citrus fruit, apricots, strawberries, berries, cherries, peaches, bananas, avocados, guava, dates etc.
- growing of wine grapes and table grapes
- production of wine from self-produced grapes (included by exception)
- growing of edible nuts, including coconuts
- growing of beverage crops such as coffee, cocoa, tea, maté
- growing of spice crops such as:
  • seeds: anise, coriander, cumin

- leaves: bay, basil, thyme
- flowers: cinnamon
- fruit: cloves
- other spices: ginger, nutmeg
- growing of olives

This class also includes:
- gathering of berries or nuts

This class excludes:
- *growing of peanuts, see 0111*
- *growing of hop cones, see 0111*
- *growing of fruit bearing vegetables, e.g. tomatoes, melons, cucumbers etc., see 0112*
- *growing of fresh "peppers", parsley and tarragon, see 0112*
- *production of olive oil, see 1514*
- *manufacture of cocoa, see 1543*
- *processing of tea leaves and coffee, see 1549*
- *production of wines other than from self-produced grapes, see 1552*

012   Farming of animals

0121   Farming of cattle, sheep, goats, horses, asses, mules and hinnies; dairy farming

This class includes:
- farming of cattle
- farming and breeding of horses, asses, mules or hinnies
- farming of sheep and goats
- production of raw cow milk
- production of raw sheep or goat milk
- production of raw wool
- production of bovine semen

This class excludes:
- *sheep shearing on a fee or contract basis, see 0140*
- *farm animal boarding, breeding and care, see 0140*
- *production of pulled wool, see 1511*
- *processing of milk outside the farm, see 1520*
- *operation of racing stables and riding academies, see 9241*

0122   Other animal farming; production of animal products n.e.c.

This class includes:
- farming of swine
- farming of poultry:
  - turkeys, ducks, chickens, geese and guinea fowl or guinea hens
- production of eggs
- operation of poultry hatcheries
- raising of semi-domesticated or wild live animals:
  - birds, insects, rabbits and other fur animals
- production of fur skins, reptile or bird skins from ranching operation
- operation of dog and cat farms, worm farms, land mollusc farms, frog farms etc.
- raising of silk worms, production of silk worm cocoons
- bee-keeping and production of honey and beeswax
- raising of diverse animals

This class excludes:
- *farm animal boarding and care, see 0140*
- *production of hides and skins originating from hunting and trapping, see 0150*

- *operation of fish farms, see 0502*
- *production of hides and skins from slaughterhouses, see 1511*
- *production of feathers or down, see 1511*
- *training of dogs for security reasons, see 7492*
- *training of pet animals, see 9309*

013   Growing of crops combined with farming of animals (mixed farming)

0130   Growing of crops combined with farming of animals (mixed farming)

This class includes:
- crop growing in combination with farming of livestock at mixed activity units with a specialization ratio in neither one of 66 per cent or more of standard gross margins

This class excludes:
- *mixed cropping or mixed livestock units, see their main activity*

014   Agricultural and animal husbandry service activities, except veterinary activities

0140   Agricultural and animal husbandry service activities, except veterinary activities

This class includes:
- agricultural activities on a fee or contract basis (except veterinary activities):
  - farm operation
  - preparation of fields
  - establishing a crop
  - treatment of crops
  - crop spraying, including by air
  - trimming of fruit trees and vines
  - transplanting of rice, thinning of beets
  - harvesting and preparation of crops for primary markets, i.e. cleaning, trimming, grading, disinfecting, wax covering, polishing, wrapping, decorticating, retting, cooling or bulk packaging including packing in oxygen-free gases
  - cotton ginning
  - activities to promote propagation, growth and output of animals
  - herd testing services, droving services, agistment services, poultry caponizing, coop cleaning etc.
  - activities related to artificial insemination
  - sheep shearing
  - farm animal boarding and care
  - pest control (including rabbits) in connection with agriculture
- operation of irrigation systems
- landscape gardening for constructing, maintaining and redesigning landscapes such as:
  - parks and gardens for
    - private and public housing
    - public and semi-public buildings (schools, hospitals, administrative buildings, church buildings etc.)
    - municipal grounds (parks, green areas, cemeteries etc.)
    - highway greenery (roads, train lines and tramlines, waterways, ports)
    - industrial and commercial buildings
  - greenery for buildings (roof gardens, facade greenery, indoor gardens)
  - sports grounds, play grounds and other recreational parks (sports grounds, play grounds, lawns for sunbathing, golf courses)
  - stationary and flowing water (basins, alternating wet areas, ponds, swimming pools, ditches, watercourses, plant sewage systems)
  - plantings and landscaping for protection against noise, wind, erosion, visibility and dazzling

- landscaping measures for protecting the environment and nature as well as landscape maintenance (renaturalization, recultivation, melioration, retention areas, anti-flooding basins etc.)
- arboriculture and tree surgery, including tree pruning and hedge trimming, replanting of big trees

This class also includes:
- provision of agricultural machinery with operators and crew

This class excludes:
- *provision of feed lot services, see 0121, 0122*
- *service activities to promote commercial hunting and trapping, see 0150*
- *preparation of vegetable fibres for textile use, see 1711*
- *marketing activities of commission merchants and cooperative associations, see division 51*
- *activities of agronomists and agricultural economists, see 7414*
- *landscape architecture, see 7421*
- *organization of agricultural shows and fairs, see 7499*
- *veterinary activities, see 8520*
- *pet boarding, see 9309*

015   Hunting, trapping and game propagation including related service activities

0150   Hunting, trapping and game propagation including related service activities

This class includes:
- hunting and trapping on a commercial basis
- taking of animals (dead or alive) for food, fur, skin, or for use in research, in zoos or as pets
- production of fur skins, reptile or bird skins from hunting or trapping activities
- game propagation
- service activities to promote commercial hunting and trapping

This class also includes:
- catching of sea mammals such as walrus and seal (except whales)

This class excludes:
- *production of fur skins, reptile or bird skins from ranching operations, see 0122*
- *raising of game animals on ranching operations, see 0122*
- *catching of whales, see 0501*
- *production of hides and skins originating from slaughterhouses, see 1511*
- *hunting for sport or recreation and related service activities, see 9241*

02   Forestry, logging and related service activities

Forestry covers the production of standing timber as well as the extraction and gathering of wild growing forest materials except for mushrooms, truffles, berries and nuts. Besides the production of timber, forestry results in products that undergo little processing, such as wood for fuel or industrial use (e.g. pit-props, pulpwood etc.).

Further processing of wood beginning with sawmilling and planing of wood, which is generally done away from the logging area, is classified to division 20 (Manufacture of wood and wood products).

020   Forestry, logging and related service activities

0200   Forestry, logging and related service activities

This class includes:
- growing of standing timber: planting, replanting, transplanting, thinning and conserving of forests and timber tracts

- growing of coppice and pulpwood
- operation of forest tree nurseries
- growing of Christmas trees
- logging: felling of timber and production of wood in the rough such as pit-props, split poles, pickets or fuel wood
- forestry service activities: forestry inventories, timber evaluation, fire fighting and protection, forest management including afforestation and reforestation
- logging service activities: transport of logs within the forest
- production of charcoal, when done in the forest

This class also includes:
- gathering of wild growing forest materials, except mushrooms, truffles, berries or nuts: balata and other rubber-like gums, cork, lac, resins, balsams, vegetable hair, eelgrass, acorns, horse chestnuts, mosses, lichens

This class excludes:
- *growing and gathering of mushrooms or truffles, see 0112*
- *gathering of berries or nuts, see 0113*
- *production of wood chips, see 2010*
- *production of charcoal through distillation of wood, see 2411*

B   Fishing

See description of division 05.

05   Fishing, aquaculture and service activities incidental to fishing

Fishing is defined as the use of fishery resources from marine or freshwater environments, with the goal of capturing or gathering fish, crustaceans, molluscs and other marine products (e.g. pearls, sponges etc).

Division 05 also includes fish farming and aquaculture activities that produce similar products. It includes activities that are normally integrated in the process of production for own account (e.g. seeding oysters for pearl production).

Division 05 does not include building and repairing of ships and boats (3511, 3512) and sport or recreational fishing activities (9249). Processing of fish, crustaceans or molluscs is excluded, whether at land-based plants or on factory ships (fish industry: 1512). However, processing taking place on board of ships that also fish is classified in division 05.

050   Fishing, aquaculture and service activities incidental to fishing

0501   Fishing

This class includes:
- fishing on a commercial basis in ocean, coastal or inland waters
- taking of marine and freshwater crustaceans and molluscs
- whale catching
- hunting of aquatic animals: turtles, sea squirts, tunicates, sea urchins etc.

This class also includes:
- activities of vessels engaged both in fishing, and in processing and preserving of fish
- gathering of marine materials: natural pearls, sponges, coral and algae
- service activities incidental to fishing

This class excludes:
- *capturing of sea mammals, except whales, e.g. walruses, seals, see 0150*
- *processing of fish, crustaceans and molluscs not connected to fishing, i.e. on vessels*

61

engaged only in processing and preserving of fish, or in factories ashore, see 1512
- *fishing inspection, protection and patrol services, see 7523*
- *fishing practised for sport or recreation and related services, see 9241*
- *operation of sport fishing preserves, see 9241*

0502   Aquaculture

This class includes:
- production of oyster spat, mussel, lobsterlings, shrimp post-larvae, fish fry and fingerlings
- growing of laver and other edible seaweeds
- fish farming in sea water and freshwater including farming of ornamental fish
- cultivation of oysters
- operation of fish hatcheries

This class also includes:
- service activities incidental to the operation of fish hatcheries and fish farms

This class excludes:
- *frog farming, see 0122*
- *operation of sport fishing preserves, see 9241*

C   Mining and quarrying

Mining and quarrying include the extraction of minerals occurring naturally as solids (coal and ores), liquids (petroleum) or gases (natural gas). Extraction can be achieved by underground or surface mining or well operation.

This section includes supplementary activities aimed at preparing the crude materials for marketing, for example, crushing, grinding, cleaning, drying, sorting, concentrating ores, liquefaction of natural gas and agglomeration of solid fuels. These operations are often accomplished by the units that extracted the resource and/or others located nearby.

Mining activities are classified into divisions, groups and classes on the basis of the principal mineral produced. Divisions 10, 11 and 12 are concerned with mining and quarrying of energy producing materials (coal, lignite and peat, hydrocarbons, uranium ore); divisions 13 and 14 concern non-energy producing materials (metal ores, various minerals and quarry products).

Some of the technical operations of this section, particularly concerning the extraction of hydrocarbons, may also be carried out for third parties by specialized units as an industrial service.

This section also includes:
- agglomeration of coals and ores

This section excludes:
- *processing of the extracted materials, see section D*
- *usage of the extracted materials without a further transformation for construction purposes, see section F*
- *bottling of natural spring and mineral waters at springs and wells, see 1554*
- *crushing, grinding or otherwise treating certain earths, rocks and minerals not carried on in conjunction with mining and quarrying, see 2699*
- *collection, purification and distribution of water, see 4100*
- *site preparation for mining, see 4510*
- *mineral prospecting, see 7421*

10   Mining of coal and lignite; extraction of peat

The extraction of solid mineral fuels covers underground or open-cast mining and includes operations (e.g. grading, cleaning etc.) leading to a marketable product including briquetting (e.g. briquettes and ovoids). It does not include coking (see 2310).

101   Mining and agglomeration of hard coal

1010   Mining and agglomeration of hard coal

This class includes:
- mining of hard coal: underground or surface mining
- cleaning, sizing, grading, pulverizing etc. of coal to classify, improve quality or facilitate transport
- agglomeration of hard coal, including manufacture of briquettes or other solid fuels consisting chiefly of hard coal

This class also includes:
- recovery of hard coal from culm banks

This class excludes:
- *lignite mining and production of briquettes or agglomerations of lignite, see 1020*
- *peat digging and agglomeration of peat, see 1030*
- *coke ovens producing solid fuels, see 2310*
- *work performed to develop or prepare properties for coal mining, see 4510*

102   Mining and agglomeration of lignite

1020   Mining and agglomeration of lignite

This class includes:
- mining of lignite (brown coal): underground or surface mining
- washing, dehydrating, pulverizing of lignite to improve quality, facilitate transport or storage
- agglomeration of lignite, including manufacture of briquettes or other solid fuels consisting chiefly of lignite

This class excludes:
- *hard coal mining and production of briquettes or agglomerations of hard coal, see 1010*
- *peat digging and agglomeration of peat, see 1030*
- *work performed to develop or prepare properties for coal mining, see 4510*

103   Extraction and agglomeration of peat

1030   Extraction and agglomeration of peat

This class includes:
- peat digging
- peat agglomeration

This class excludes:
- *manufacture of articles of peat, see 2699*

11   Extraction of crude petroleum and natural gas; service activities incidental to oil and gas extraction, excluding surveying

This division includes the production of crude petroleum, the mining and extraction of oil from oil shale and oil sands, and the production of natural gas and recovery of hydrocarbon liquids. This division includes the activities of operating and/or developing oil and gas field properties. Such activities may include drilling, completing, and equipping wells; operating separators, emulsion breakers, desilting equipment, and field gathering lines for crude petroleum; and all other activities in the preparation of oil and gas up to the point of shipment from the producing property. Support services, on a fee or contract basis, required for the drilling or operation of oil and gas wells, are also included.

This division excludes:
- *refining of petroleum products, see 2320*
- *test drilling and boring, see 4510*
- *geophysical surveying and mapping, see 7421*
- *oil and gas well exploration, see 7421*

111 Extraction of crude petroleum and natural gas

1110 Extraction of crude petroleum and natural gas

This class includes:
- extraction of crude petroleum oils
- production of crude gaseous hydrocarbon (natural gas)
- extraction of condensates
- draining and separation of liquid hydrocarbon fractions
- liquefaction and regasification of natural gas for transportation, at the mine site
- gas desulphurization
- mining operations: drilling, completing and equipping wells (except on a fee or contract basis)

This class also includes:
- extraction of bituminous or oil shale and tar sand
- production of crude petroleum from bituminous shale and sand
- processes to obtain crude oils: decantation, desalting, dehydration, stabilization etc.

This class excludes:
- *service activities incidental to oil and gas extraction, see 1120*
- *manufacture of refined petroleum products, see 2320*
- *recovery of liquefied petroleum gases in the refining of petroleum, see 2320*
- *manufacture of industrial gases, see 2411*
- *operation of pipelines, see 6030*
- *oil and gas exploration, see 7421*

112 Service activities incidental to oil and gas extraction excluding surveying

1120 Service activities incidental to oil and gas extraction excluding surveying

This class includes:
- oil and gas extraction service activities provided on a fee or contract basis:
  • directional drilling and redrilling; "spudding in"; derrick erection in situ, repairing and dismantling; cementing oil and gas well casings; pumping of wells; plugging and abandoning wells etc.

This class also includes:
- test drilling in connection with petroleum or gas extraction

This class excludes:
- *service activities performed by operators of oil or gas fields, see 1110*
- *geophysical, geologic and seismographic surveys, see 7421*

12 Mining of uranium and thorium ores

120 Mining of uranium and thorium ores

1200 Mining of uranium and thorium ores

This class includes:
- mining of ores chiefly valued for uranium and thorium content: pitchblende etc.
- concentration of such ores
- manufacture of yellowcake

This class excludes:
- *enrichment of uranium and thorium ores, see 2330*
- *production of fissile or fertile material, see 2330*
- *production of uranium metal from pitchblende or other ores, see 2330*

13   Mining of metal ores

This division includes:
- underground and open-cast extraction of metal ores and native metals
- preparation of ores:
  • crushing and grinding of ores, washing of ores
  • concentrating of ores by magnetic or gravimetric separation
  • flotation, screening, grading, drying, calcination and roasting of ores

This division excludes:
- *mining of uranium and thorium ores, see 1200*
- *roasting of iron pyrites, see 2411*
- *production of aluminium oxide, see 2720*

131   Mining of iron ores

1310   Mining of iron ores

This class includes:
- mining of ores valued chiefly for iron content
- beneficiation and agglomeration of iron ores

This class excludes:
- *mining and preparation of iron pyrite and pyrrhotite, see 1421*

132   Mining of non-ferrous metal ores, except uranium and thorium ores

1320   Mining of non-ferrous metal ores, except uranium and thorium ores

This class includes:
- mining and preparation of ores valued chiefly for non-ferrous metal content:
  • aluminium (bauxite), copper, lead, zinc, tin, manganese, chrome, nickel, cobalt, molybdenum, tantalum, vanadium etc.
  • precious metals: gold, silver, platinum

This class excludes:
- *mining and preparation of uranium and thorium ores, see 1200*
- *production of aluminium oxide and mattes of nickel or of copper, see 2720*

14   Other mining and quarrying

This division covers extraction from a quarry, but also dredging of alluvial deposits, rock crushing and the use of salt marshes. The products are used most notably in construction (e.g. sands, stones etc.), manufacture of materials (e.g. clay, gypsum, calcium etc.), manufacture of chemicals etc.

This division does not include processing (except crushing, grinding, cutting, cleaning, drying, sorting and mixing) of the minerals extracted. Vertically integrated units that are processing self-extracted mineral materials are classified under manufacturing (e.g. cement plants or brick making plants). Salt production includes refining salt, to render it suitable for human consumption.

141   Quarrying of stone, sand and clay

1410   Quarrying of stone, sand and clay

This class includes:
- quarrying, rough trimming and sawing of monumental and building stone such as marble, granite, sandstone etc.
- quarrying, crushing and breaking of limestone
- mining of gypsum and anhydrite
- mining of chalk and uncalcined dolomite
- extraction and dredging of industrial sand, sand for construction and gravel
- breaking and crushing of stone, gravel and sand
- mining of clays, refractory clays and kaolin

This class excludes:
- *mining of bituminous sand, see 1110*
- *mining of chemical and fertilizer minerals, see 1421*
- *production of calcined dolomite, see 2694*
- *cutting, shaping and finishing of stone outside quarries, see 2696*

142   Mining and quarrying n.e.c.

1421   Mining of chemical and fertilizer minerals

This class includes:
- mining of natural phosphates and natural potassium salts
- mining of native sulphur
- extraction and preparation of pyrites and pyrrhotite, except roasting
- mining of natural barium sulphate and carbonate (barytes and witherite), natural borates, natural magnesium sulphates (kieserite)
- mining of earth colours, fluorspar and other minerals valued chiefly as a source of chemicals

This class also includes:
- guano mining

This class excludes:
- *production of salt, see 1422*
- *roasting of iron pyrites, see 2411*
- *manufacture of synthetic fertilizers and nitrogen compounds, see 2412*

1422   Extraction of salt

This class includes:
- extraction of salt from underground including by dissolving and pumping
- salt production by evaporation of sea water or other saline waters
- crushing, purification and refining of salt

This class excludes:
- *processing of purchased salt, see 2429*
- *potable water production by evaporation of saline water, see 4100*

1429   Other mining and quarrying n.e.c.

This class includes:
- mining and quarrying of various minerals and materials:
  - abrasive materials, asbestos, siliceous fossil meals, natural graphite, steatite (talc), feldspar etc.
  - gemstones, quartz, mica etc.
  - natural asphalt and bitumen

D   Manufacturing

Manufacturing comprises units engaged in the physical or chemical transformation of materials, substances, or components into new products. The materials, substances, or components transformed are raw materials that are products of agriculture, forestry, fishing, mining or quarrying as well as products of other manufacturing activities.

The units in the manufacturing section are often described as plants, factories or mills and characteristically use power-driven machines and materials-handling equipment. However, units that transform materials or substances into new products by hand or in the worker's home and those engaged in selling to the general public products made on the same premises from which they are sold, such as bakeries and custom tailors, are also included in this section.

Manufacturing units may process materials or may contract with other units to process their materials for them. Both types of units are included in manufacturing.

The new product of a manufacturing unit may be finished in the sense that it is ready for utilization or consumption, or it may be semi-finished in the sense that it is to become an input for further manufacturing. For example, the product of the alumina refinery is the input used in the primary production of aluminium; primary aluminium is the input to an aluminium wire drawing plant; and aluminium wire is the input for a fabricated wire product manufacturing unit.

Assembly of the component parts of manufactured products is considered manufacturing. This includes the assembly of manufactured products from either self-produced or purchased components. Assembly of self-produced prefabricated components of constructions at the construction site is classified as manufacturing when the manufacturing and assembly are integrated activities. When the assembly is performed by separate units, the activity is appropriately classified in division 45 (Construction). Therefore, assembly on the site of not self-produced prefabricated, integral parts into bridges, water tanks, storage and warehouse facilities, railroad and elevated rights of way, lift and escalator, plumbing, sprinkler, central heating, ventilating and air conditioning, lighting, electrical and telecommunications wiring systems of buildings, and all kinds of structures, is classified in Construction.

Assembly and installation of machinery and equipment in mining, manufacturing, commercial or other units, when carried out as a specialized activity, are classified in the same class of manufacturing as manufacture of the item installed.

Assembly and installation of machinery and equipment that are performed as a service incidental to the sale of the goods by a unit primarily engaged in manufacturing, wholesale trade or retail trade, are classified with its main activity.

Activities of units primarily engaged in maintenance and repair of industrial, commercial and similar machinery and equipment are, in general, classified in the same class of manufacturing as those specializing in manufacturing the goods. However, units engaged in repair of office and computing machinery are classified in class 7250. Units the main activity of which is repair of household appliances, equipment and furnishings, motor vehicles and other consumer goods are, as a general rule, classified in the appropriate class of division 50 (Sale, maintenance and repair of motor vehicles and motorcycles; retail sale of automotive fuel) or 52 (Retail trade, except of motor vehicles and motorcycles; repair of personal and household goods) in accordance with the kind of goods that are repaired.

Substantial alteration, renovation or reconstruction of goods is generally considered to be manufacturing.

Manufacture of specialized components and parts of, and accessories and attachments to, machinery and equipment is, as a general rule, classified in the same class as the manufacture of the machinery and equipment for which the parts and accessories are intended. Manufacture of unspecialized components and parts of machinery and equipment, e.g. engines, pistons, electric motors, electrical assemblies, valves, gears, roller bearings, is classified in the appropriate class of manufacturing, without regard to the machinery and equipment in which these items may be included. However, making specialized components and accessories by moulding or extruding plastics materials is included in class 2520.

The recycling of waste is also included in Manufacturing.

Remark: The boundaries of manufacturing and the other sectors of the classification system can be somewhat blurry. As a general rule, the units in the manufacturing sector are engaged in the transformation of materials into new products. Their output is a new product. However, the definition of what constitutes a new product can be somewhat subjective. As clarification, the following activities are considered manufacturing in ISIC:
- Milk pasteurizing and bottling (see 1520);
- Fresh fish processing (oyster shucking, fish filleting), not done on a fishing boat (see 1512);
- Printing and related activities (see 2221, 2222);
- Ready-mixed concrete production (see 2695);
- Leather converting (see 1911);
- Wood preserving (see 2010);
- Electroplating, plating, metal heat treating, and polishing (see 2892);
- Rebuilding or remanufacturing machinery (e.g., automobile engines, see 3410);
- Ship repair and renovation (see 3511);
- Tyre retreading (see 2511).

Conversely, there are activities that though sometimes considered manufacturing, are classified in another section of ISIC (in other words, they are not classified as manufacturing). They include:
- Logging, classified in section A (Agriculture, hunting and forestry);
- Beneficiating of ores and other minerals, classified in section C (Mining);
- Construction of structures and fabricating operations performed at the site of construction, classified in section F (Construction);
- Activities of breaking of bulk and redistribution in smaller lots, including packaging, repackaging, or bottling products, such as liquors or chemicals; the customized assembly of computers; sorting of scrap; mixing paints to customer order; and cutting metals to customer order, produce a modified version of the same product, not a new product, and are classified to section G (Wholesale and retail trade).

15   Manufacture of food products and beverages

The food industry processes the products of agriculture, animal husbandry and fishing into food and drink for humans or animals, and includes the production of various intermediate products that are not directly food products. The activity often generates associated products of greater or lesser value (for example, hides from slaughtering, or oilcake from oil production).

This division is organized by activities dealing with different kinds of products: meat, fish, fruit and vegetables, fats and oils, milk products, grain mill products, animal feeds, other food products and beverages. Production can be carried out for own account, as well as for third parties, as in custom slaughtering.

Some activities are considered manufacturing (for example, those performed in bakeries, pastry shops, and prepared meat shops etc. which sell their own production) even though there is retail sale of the products in the producers' own shop. However, where the processing is minimal and does not lead to a real transformation (as is the case, for example, for butchers, fishmongers etc.), the unit is classified to Wholesale and retail trade (section G).

Production of animal feeds from slaughter waste or by-products is classified in 1533, while processing food and beverage waste into secondary raw material is classified to 3720, and disposal of food and beverage waste in 9000.

151   **Production, processing and preservation of meat, fish, fruit, vegetables, oils and fats**

1511   **Production, processing and preserving of meat and meat products**

This class includes:
- operation of slaughterhouses engaged in killing, dressing or packing meat
- production of fresh, chilled or frozen meat, in carcasses
- production of fresh, chilled or frozen meat, in cuts
- slaughtering of poultry
- preparation of poultry meat
- production of fresh or frozen poultry meat in individual portions
- production of dried, salted or smoked meat
- production of meat products:
  - sausages, salami, puddings, "andouillettes", saveloys, bolognas, pâtés, rillettes, boiled ham, meat extracts and juices
- production of prepared fresh meat dishes

This class also includes:
- slaughtering and processing of whales on land or on specialized vessels
- production of hides and skins originating from slaughterhouses, including fellmongery
- rendering of lard and other edible fats of animal origin
- processing of animal offal
- production of pulled wool
- slaughtering of rabbits and the like
- preparation of rabbit meat and the like
- production of feathers and down

This class excludes:
- *manufacture of soup containing meat, see 1549*
- *manufacture of prepared frozen meat and poultry dishes, see 1549*
- *packaging of meat for own account by the wholesale trade, see 5122*
- *packaging of meat on a fee or contract basis, see 7495*

1512   **Processing and preserving of fish and fish products**

This class includes:
- preparation and preservation of fish, crustaceans and molluscs: freezing, deep-freezing, drying, smoking, salting, immersing in brine, canning etc.
- manufacture of fish, crustacean and mollusc products: cooked fish, fish fillets, roes, caviar, caviar substitutes etc.
- manufacture of prepared fish dishes
- manufacture of fishmeal for human consumption or animal feed
- manufacture of meals and solubles from fish and other aquatic animals unfit for human consumption

This class also includes:
- activities of vessels engaged only in the processing and preserving of fish

This class excludes:
- *activities of vessels engaged both in fishing, and in processing and preserving of fish, see 0501*
- *processing of whales on land or specialized vessels, see 1511*
- *production of oils and fats from marine material, see 1514*
- *manufacture of fish soups, see 1549*

1513   **Processing and preserving of fruit and vegetables**

This class includes:
- manufacture of food consisting chiefly of fruit or vegetables
- preserving of fruit, nuts or vegetables: freezing, drying, immersing in oil or in vinegar, canning etc.

- manufacture of fruit or vegetable food products
- manufacture of fruit or vegetable juices
- manufacture of jams, marmalades and table jellies
- processing and preserving of potatoes:
  - manufacture of prepared frozen potatoes
  - manufacture of dehydrated mashed potatoes
  - manufacture of potato snacks
  - manufacture of potato crisps
  - manufacture of potato flour and meal
- manufacture of prepared dishes of vegetables
- roasting of nuts
- manufacture of nut foods and pastes

This class also includes:
- industrial peeling of potatoes
- production of concentrates

This class excludes:
- *manufacture of flour or meal of dried leguminous vegetables, see 1531*
- *preservation of fruit and nuts in sugar, see 1543*

1514   Manufacture of vegetable and animal oils and fats

This class includes the manufacture of crude and refined oils and fats from vegetable or animal materials, except rendering or refining of lard and other edible animal fats.

This class includes:
- manufacture of crude vegetable oils: olive oil, soya-bean oil, palm oil, sunflower-seed oil, cotton-seed oil, rape, colza or mustard oil, linseed oil etc.
- manufacture of non-defatted flour or meal of oilseeds, oil nuts or oil kernels
- manufacture of refined vegetable oils: olive oil, soya-bean oil etc.
- processing of vegetable oils: blowing, boiling, dehydration, hydrogenation etc.
- manufacture of margarine
- manufacture of melanges and similar spreads
- manufacture of compound cooking fats

This class also includes:
- manufacture of non-edible animal oils and fats
- extraction of fish and marine mammal oils

Note: Cotton linters, oilcakes and other residual products of oil production are by-products of this class.

This class excludes:
- *rendering and refining of lard and other edible animal fats, see 1511*
- *wet corn milling, see 1532*
- *production of essential oils, see 2429*
- *treatment of oil and fats by chemical processes, see 2429*

152   Manufacture of dairy products

1520   Manufacture of dairy products

This class includes:
- manufacture of fresh liquid milk, pasteurized, sterilized, homogenized and/or ultra heat treated
- manufacture of milk-based soft drinks
- manufacture of cream from fresh liquid milk, pasteurized, sterilized, homogenized
- manufacture of dried or concentrated milk whether or not sweetened
- manufacture of milk or cream in solid form

- manufacture of butter
- manufacture of yoghurt
- manufacture of cheese and curd
- manufacture of whey
- manufacture of casein or lactose
  • manufacture of ice cream and other edible ice such as sorbet

This class excludes:
- *production of raw milk, see 0121*
- *manufacture of non-dairy milk and cheese substitutes, see 1549*
- *activities of ice cream parlours, see 5520*

153   Manufacture of grain mill products, starches and starch products, and prepared animal feeds

1531   Manufacture of grain mill products

This class includes:
- grain milling: production of flour, groats, meal or pellets of wheat, rye, oats, maize (corn) or other cereal grains
- rice milling: production of husked, milled, polished, glazed, parboiled or converted rice; production of rice flour
- vegetable milling: production of flour or meal of dried leguminous vegetables, of roots or tubers, or of edible nuts
- manufacture of cereal breakfast foods
- manufacture of flour mixes and prepared blended flour and dough for bread, cakes, biscuits or pancakes

This class excludes:
- *manufacture of potato flour and meal, see 1513*
- *wet corn milling, see 1532*

1532   Manufacture of starches and starch products

This class includes:
- manufacture of starches from rice, potatoes, maize etc.
- wet corn milling
- manufacture of glucose, glucose syrup, maltose, inulin etc.
- manufacture of gluten
- manufacture of tapioca and tapioca substitutes prepared from starch
- manufacture of corn oil

This class excludes:
- *manufacture of lactose (milk sugar), see 1520*
- *production of cane or beet sugar, see 1542*

1533   Manufacture of prepared animal feeds

This class includes:
- manufacture of prepared feeds for pets, including dogs, cats, birds, fish etc.
- manufacture of prepared feeds for farm animals, including animal feed concentrated and feed supplements
- preparation of unmixed (single) feeds for farm animals

This class also includes:
- treatment of slaughter waste to produce animal feeds

This class excludes:
- *production of fishmeal for animal feed, see 1512*
- *production of oilseed cake, see 1514*
- *activities resulting in by-products usable as animal feed without special treatment, e.g. oilseeds (see 1514), grain milling residues (see 1531) etc.*

154   Manufacture of other food products

1541   Manufacture of bakery products

This class includes:
- manufacture of fresh, frozen or dry bakery products
- manufacture of bread and rolls
- manufacture of fresh pastry, cakes, pies, tarts etc.
- manufacture of rusks, biscuits and other "dry" bakery products
- manufacture of preserved pastry goods and cakes
- manufacture of snack products (cookies, crackers, pretzels etc.), whether sweet or salted
- manufacture of tortillas
- manufacture of frozen bakery products: pancakes, waffles, rolls etc.

This class excludes:
- *manufacture of farinaceous products (pastas), see 1544*
- *manufacture of potato snacks, see 1513*

1542   Manufacture of sugar

This class includes:
- manufacture or refining of sugar (sucrose) and sugar substitutes from the juice of cane, beet, maple and palm
- manufacture of sugar syrups
- manufacture of molasses

This class excludes:
- *integrated gathering of sap and production of maple syrup and sugar, see 0112*
- *manufacture of glucose, glucose syrup, maltose, see 1532*

1543   Manufacture of cocoa, chocolate and sugar confectionery

This class includes:
- manufacture of cocoa, cocoa butter, cocoa fat, cocoa oil
- manufacture of chocolate and chocolate confectionery
- manufacture of sugar confectionery: caramels, cachous, nougats, fondant, white chocolate
- manufacture of chewing gum
- preserving in sugar of fruit, nuts, fruit peels and other parts of plants
- manufacture of confectionery lozenges and pastilles

This class excludes:
- *manufacture of sucrose sugar, see 1542*

1544   Manufacture of macaroni, noodles, couscous and similar farinaceous products

This class includes:
- manufacture of pastas such as macaroni and noodles, whether or not cooked or stuffed
- manufacture of couscous
- manufacture of canned or frozen pasta products

This class excludes:
- *manufacture of soup containing pasta, see 1549*

1549   Manufacture of other food products n.e.c.

This class includes:
- decaffeinating and roasting of coffee
- production of coffee products:
  - ground coffee
  - soluble coffee
  - extracts and concentrates of coffee
- manufacture of coffee substitutes
- blending of tea and maté
- packing of tea including packing in tea bags
- manufacture of soups and broths
- manufacture of spices, sauces and condiments:
  - mayonnaise
  - mustard flour and meal
  - prepared mustard etc.
- manufacture of vinegar
- manufacture of foods for particular nutritional uses:
  - infant formulas
  - follow-up milk and other follow-up foods
  - baby foods
  - other foods containing homogenized ingredients (including meat, fish, fruit etc.)
- manufacture of artificial honey and caramel
- manufacture of fresh or frozen pizza
- manufacture of frozen meat, poultry dishes
- manufacture of canned stews and vacuum-prepared meals

This class also includes:
- manufacture of herb infusions (mint, vervain, camomile etc.)
- manufacture of yeast
- manufacture of extracts and juices of meat, fish, crustaceans or molluscs
- manufacture of non-dairy milk and cheese substitutes

This class excludes:
- *growing of spice crops, see 0113*
- *manufacture of table salt, see 1422*
- *manufacture of frozen fish dishes, including fish and chips, see 1512*
- *manufacture of inulin, see 1532*
- *manufacture of herb infusions if they are considered medical products, see 2423*

155   Manufacture of beverages

1551   Distilling, rectifying and blending of spirits; ethyl alcohol production from fermented materials

This class includes:
- manufacture of distilled, potable, alcoholic beverages: whisky, brandy, gin, liqueurs, "mixed drinks" etc.
- blending of distilled spirits
- production of ethyl alcohol from fermented materials
- production of neutral spirits

This class excludes:
- *manufacture of non-distilled alcoholic beverages, see 1552, 1553*
- *manufacture of denatured ethyl alcohol, see 2411*
- *merely bottling and labelling, see 5122 (if performed as part of wholesale) and 7495 (if performed on a fee or contract basis)*

1552   Manufacture of wines

This class includes:
- manufacture of wine from grapes not grown by the same unit
- manufacture of sparkling wine
- manufacture of wine from concentrated grape must
- manufacture of fermented but not distilled alcoholic beverages: sake, cider, perry, mead, other fruit wines and mixed beverages containing alcohol
- manufacture of vermouth and the like

This class also includes:
- blending of wine
- manufacture of low or non-alcoholic wine

This class excludes:
- *production of wine from self-produced grapes, see 0113*
- *merely bottling and labelling, see 5122 (if performed as part of wholesale) and 7495 (if performed on a fee or contract basis)*

1553   Manufacture of malt liquors and malt

This class includes:
- manufacture of malt liquors, such as beer, ale, porter and stout
- manufacture of malt

This class also includes:
- manufacture of low alcohol or non-alcoholic beer

1554   Manufacture of soft drinks; production of mineral waters

This class includes:
- manufacture of non-alcoholic beverages, except non-alcoholic beer and wine
- production of natural mineral waters
- manufacture of soft drinks:
    • non-alcoholic flavoured and/or sweetened waters: lemonade, orangeade, cola, fruit drinks, tonic waters etc.

This class excludes:
- *production of fruit and vegetable juice, see 1513*
- *manufacture of non-alcoholic wine, see 1552*
- *manufacture of non-alcoholic beer, see 1553*
- *merely bottling and labelling, see 5122 (if performed as part of wholesale) and 7495 (if performed on a fee or contract basis)*

16   Manufacture of tobacco products

This division includes the processing of an agricultural product, tobacco, into a form suitable for final consumption.

160   Manufacture of tobacco products

1600   Manufacture of tobacco products

This class includes:
- manufacture of tobacco products and products of tobacco substitutes: cigarettes, cigarette tobacco, cigars, pipe tobacco, chewing tobacco, snuff
- manufacture of "homogenized" or "reconstituted" tobacco

This class excludes:
- *growing or preliminary processing of tobacco, see 0111*

17 Manufacture of textiles

This division includes preparation and spinning of textile fibres as well as textile weaving, finishing of textiles and wearing apparel, manufacture of made-up textile articles, except apparel (e.g. household linen, blankets, rugs, cordage etc.) and manufacture of knitted and crocheted fabrics and articles thereof (e.g. socks and pullovers). Growing of natural fibres falls under division 01, while manufacture of synthetic fibres is a chemical process that has to be classified in class 2430. Manufacture of wearing apparel falls under division 18.

171 Spinning, weaving and finishing of textiles

1711 Preparation and spinning of textile fibres; weaving of textiles

This class includes:
- preparatory operations on textile fibres:
  - reeling and washing of silk
  - degreasing and carbonizing of wool and dyeing of wool fleece
  - carding and combing of all kinds of animal, vegetable and man-made fibres
- spinning and manufacture of yarn or thread for weaving or sewing, for the trade or for further processing
  - texturizing, twisting, folding, cabling and dipping of synthetic or artificial filament yarns
- manufacture of broad woven cotton-type, woollen-type, worsted-type or silk-type fabrics, including from mixtures or artificial or synthetic yarns
- manufacture of other broad woven fabrics, using flax, ramie, hemp, jute, bast fibres and special yarns
- manufacture of made-up textile articles, made from self-produced woven fabric

This class also includes:
- manufacture of paper yarn
- manufacture of woven pile or chenille fabrics, terry towelling, gauze etc.
- manufacture of woven fabrics of glass fibres
- manufacture of imitation fur by weaving

This class excludes:
- *preparatory operations carried out in combination with agriculture or farming, see 01, 02*
- *retting of plants bearing vegetable textile fibres (jute, flax, coir etc.), see 0111*
- *cotton ginning, see 0140*
- *manufacture of textile floor coverings, see 1722*
- *manufacture of non-woven fabrics and felts, see 1729*
- *manufacture of narrow fabrics, see 1729*
- *manufacture of knitted and crocheted fabrics, see 1730*
- *manufacture of synthetic or artificial fibres and tows, manufacture of single yarns (including high-tenacity yarn and yarn for carpets) of synthetic or artificial fibres, see 2430*
- *manufacture of glass fibres, see 2610*
- *spinning of asbestos yarn, see 2699*

1712 Finishing of textiles

This class includes:
- bleaching, dyeing and printing (including thermoprinting) of not self-produced textile fibres, yarns, fabrics and textile articles, including wearing apparel
- dressing, drying, steaming, shrinking, mending, Sanforizing, mercerizing of not self-produced textiles and textile articles, including wearing apparel

This class also includes:
- bleaching of jeans
- pleating and similar work on textiles

This class excludes:
- *manufacture of textile fabric impregnated, coated, covered or laminated with rubber, where rubber is the chief constituent, see 2519*
- *"while-you-wait" printing on textile articles, see 5260*

172   Manufacture of other textiles

1721   Manufacture of made-up textile articles, except apparel

This class includes:
- manufacture, from fabrics not made in the same unit, of made-up articles of any textile material, including of knitted or crocheted fabrics:
  - blankets, including travelling rugs
  - bed, table, toilet or kitchen linen
  - quilts, eiderdowns, cushions, pouffes, pillows, sleeping bags etc.
- manufacture of made-up furnishing articles:
  - curtains, valances, blinds, bedspreads, furniture or machine covers etc.
  - tarpaulins, tents, camping goods, sails, sunblinds, loose covers for cars, machines or furniture etc.
  - flags, banners, pennants etc.
  - dustcloths, dishcloths and similar articles, life jackets, parachutes etc.

This class also includes:
- manufacture of the textile part of electric blankets
- manufacture of hand-woven tapestries

This class excludes:
- *manufacture of textile articles from self-produced materials, see 1711, 1729 and 1730*
- *manufacture of textile articles for technical use, see 1729*

1722   Manufacture of carpets and rugs

This class includes:
- manufacture of textile floor coverings:
  - carpets, rugs and mats, tiles

This class also includes:
- manufacture of needle-loom felt floor coverings

This class excludes:
- *manufacture of mats and matting of plaiting materials, see 2029*
- *manufacture of floor coverings of cork, rubber or plastic materials, even when textile-backed, see 2029, 2519, 2520*
- *manufacture of linoleum and hard non-plastic surface floor coverings, see 3699*

1723   Manufacture of cordage, rope, twine and netting

This class includes:
- manufacture of twine, cordage, rope and cables of textile fibres or strip or the like, whether or not impregnated, coated, covered or sheathed with rubber or plastics
- manufacture of knotted netting of twine, cordage or rope
- manufacture of products of rope or netting: fishing nets, ships' fenders, unloading cushions, loading slings, rope or cable fitted with metal rings etc.

This class excludes:
- *manufacture of hairnets, see 1810*

1729 **Manufacture of other textiles n.e.c.**

This class includes all activities related to textiles or textile products, not specified elsewhere in division 17 or 18 or anywhere else in this classification, involving a large number of processes and a great variety of goods produced.

This class includes:
- manufacture of narrow woven fabrics, including fabrics consisting of warp without weft assembled by means of an adhesive
- manufacture of labels, badges etc.
- manufacture of ornamental trimmings: braids, tassels, pompons etc.
- manufacture of felt
- manufacture of tulles and other net fabrics, and of lace and embroidery, in the piece, in strips or in motifs
- manufacture of fabrics impregnated, coated, covered or laminated with plastics
- manufacture of textile wadding and articles of wadding: sanitary towels, tampons etc.
- manufacture of metallized yarn or gimped yarn, rubber thread and cord covered with textile material, textile yarn or strip covered, impregnated, coated or sheathed with rubber or plastics
- manufacture of made-up textile articles, made from self-produced fabrics in this class
- manufacture of tyre cord fabric of high-tenacity man-made yarn
- manufacture of other treated or coated fabrics: tracing cloth, canvas prepared for use by painters, buckram and similar stiffened textile fabrics, fabrics coated with gum or amylaceous substances
- manufacture of diverse textile articles: textile wicks, incandescent gas mantles and tubular gas
- mantle fabric, hosepiping, transmission or conveyor belts or belting (whether or not reinforced with metal or other material), bolting cloth, straining cloth

This class excludes:
- *manufacture of needle-loom felt floor coverings, see 1722*
- *manufacture of transmission or conveyor belts of textile fabric, yarn or cord impregnated, coated, covered or laminated with rubber, where rubber is the chief constituent, see 2519*
- *manufacture of plates or sheets of cellular rubber or plastic combined with textiles for reinforcing purposes only, see 2519, 2520*
- *manufacture of cloth of woven metal wire, see 2899*

173 **Manufacture of knitted and crocheted fabrics and articles**

1730 **Manufacture of knitted and crocheted fabrics and articles**

This class includes:
- manufacture and processing in the same unit of knitted or crocheted fabrics:
  - pile and terry fabrics
  - net and window furnishing type fabrics knitted on raschel or similar machines
  - other knitted or crocheted fabrics
- manufacture of hosiery, including socks, tights and pantyhose
- manufacture of knitted or crocheted wearing apparel and other made-up articles directly into shape: pullovers, cardigans, jerseys, waistcoats and similar articles

This class also includes:
- manufacture of imitation fur by knitting

This class excludes:
- *manufacture of net and window furnishing type fabrics of lace knitted on raschel or similar machines, see 1729*
- *manufacture of knitted clothing from fabric not knitted in the same unit, see 1810*

18 Manufacture of wearing apparel; dressing and dyeing of fur

The clothing industry covers all tailoring (ready-to-wear or made-to-measure), in all materials (e.g. leather, fabric, knitted and crocheted fabrics etc.), of all items of clothing (e.g. outerwear, underwear for men, women or children; work, city or casual clothing etc.) and accessories from materials not made in the same unit. There is no distinction made between clothing for adults and clothing for children, or between modern and traditional clothing. Division 18 also includes the fur industry (fur skins and wearing apparel).

181 Manufacture of wearing apparel, except fur apparel

1810 Manufacture of wearing apparel, except fur apparel

This class includes manufacture of wearing apparel made of material not made in the same unit. The material used may be of any kind and may be coated, impregnated or rubberized.

This class includes:
- manufacture of wearing apparel made of leather or composition leather
- manufacture of work wear
- manufacture of other outerwear made of woven, knitted or crocheted fabric, non-wovens etc. for men, women and children:
  - coats, suits, ensembles, jackets, trousers, skirts etc.
- manufacture of underwear and nightwear made of woven, knitted or crocheted fabric, lace etc. for men, women and children:
  - shirts, T-shirts, underpants, briefs, pyjamas, nightdresses, dressing gowns, blouses, slips, brassieres, corsets etc.
- manufacture of babies' garments, tracksuits, ski suits, swimwear etc.
- manufacture of hats and caps
- manufacture of other clothing accessories: gloves, belts, shawls, ties, cravats, hairnets etc.

This class also includes:
- custom tailoring
- manufacture of headgear of fur skins
- manufacture of footwear of textile material without applied soles
- manufacture of parts of the products listed

This class excludes:
- *manufacture of clothing of fabrics knitted in the same unit, see 1730*
- *manufacture of wearing apparel of fur skins (except headgear), see 1820*
- *manufacture of footwear, see 1920*
- *manufacture of wearing apparel of rubber or plastics not assembled by stitching but merely sealed together, see 2519, 2520*
- *manufacture of safety headgear (except sports headgear), see 2520, 2899*
- *manufacture of asbestos apparel and headgear, see 2699*
- *manufacture of leather sports gloves and sports headgear, see 3693*
- *repair of wearing apparel, see 5260*

182 Dressing and dyeing of fur; manufacture of articles of fur

1820 Dressing and dyeing of fur; manufacture of articles of fur

This class includes:
- dressing and dyeing of fur skins and hides with the hair on: scraping, currying, tanning, bleaching, shearing and plucking and dyeing of fur skins
- manufacture of articles made of fur skins:
  - fur wearing apparel and clothing accessories
  - assemblies of fur skins such as "dropped" fur skins, plates, mats, strips etc.
  - diverse articles of fur skins: rugs, unstuffed pouffes, industrial polishing cloths

This class also includes:
- manufacture of artificial fur and articles thereof

This class excludes:
- *production of raw fur skins, see 0122, 0150*
- *production of raw hides and skins, see 1511*
- *manufacture of imitation furs (long-hair cloth obtained by weaving or knitting), see 1711, 1712, 1730*
- *manufacture of fur hats, see 1810*
- *manufacture of apparel trimmed with fur, see 1810*
- *manufacture of boots or shoes containing fur parts, see 1920*

19 Tanning and dressing of leather; manufacture of luggage, handbags, saddlery, harness and footwear

This division includes the transformation of hides into leather by tanning or curing and fabricating the leather into products for final consumption. It also includes the manufacture of similar products from other materials (imitation leathers or leather substitutes), such as rubber footwear, textile luggage etc. The products made from leather substitutes are included here, since they are made in ways similar to those in which leather products are made (e.g. luggage) and are often produced in the same unit.

191 Tanning and dressing of leather; manufacture of luggage, handbags, saddlery and harness

1911 Tanning and dressing of leather

This class includes:
- production of tanned leather
- manufacture of chamois dressed, parchment dressed, patent or metallized leathers
- manufacture of composition leather

This class excludes:
- *production of hides and skins as part of ranching, see 0122*
- *production of hides and skins as part of slaughtering, see 1511*
- *manufacture of leather apparel, see 1810*
- *tanning or dressing of fur skins or hides with the hair on, see 1820*
- *manufacture of imitation leather not based on natural leather, see 1711, 2519, 2520*

1912 Manufacture of luggage, handbags and the like, saddlery and harness

This class includes:
- manufacture of luggage, handbags and the like, of leather, composition leather or any other material, such as plastic sheeting, textile materials, vulcanized fibre or paperboard, where the same technology is used as for leather
- manufacture of saddlery and harness
- manufacture of non-metallic watch straps
- manufacture of diverse articles of leather or composition leather: driving belts, packings etc.

This class excludes:
- *manufacture of leather wearing apparel, see 1810*
- *manufacture of leather gloves and hats, see 1810*
- *manufacture of footwear, see 1920*
- *manufacture of metallic watch straps, see 3330*
- *manufacture of saddles for bicycles, see 3592*

192   **Manufacture of footwear**

1920   **Manufacture of footwear**

This class includes:
- manufacture of footwear for all purposes, of any material, by any process, including moulding
- manufacture of gaiters, leggings and similar articles
- manufacture of parts of footwear: manufacture of uppers and parts of uppers, outer and inner soles, heels etc.

This class excludes:
- *manufacture of footwear of textile material without applied soles, see 1810*
- *manufacture of footwear of asbestos, see 2699*
- *manufacture of orthopaedic shoes, see 3311*

20   **Manufacture of wood and of products of wood and cork, except furniture; manufacture of articles of straw and plaiting materials**

This division includes manufacture of wood products, such as lumber, plywood, veneers, wood containers, wood flooring, wood trusses, and prefabricated wood buildings. The production processes include sawing, planing, shaping, laminating, and assembling of wood products starting from logs that are cut into bolts, or lumber that may then be cut further, or shaped by lathes or other shaping tools. The lumber or other transformed wood shapes may also be subsequently planed or smoothed, and assembled into finished products, such as wood containers.

With the exception of sawmills and wood preservation units, the units are grouped into industries mainly based on the specific products manufactured.

This division does not include either the manufacture of furniture (3610), or the installation of not self-manufactured wooden fittings and the like (4540).

201   **Sawmilling and planing of wood**

2010   **Sawmilling and planing of wood**

This class includes:
- sawing, planing and machining of wood
- slicing, peeling or chipping logs
- manufacture of wooden railway sleepers
- manufacture of unassembled wooden flooring
- manufacture of wood wool, wood flour, chips, particles

This class also includes:
- drying of wood
- impregnation or chemical treatment of wood with preservatives or other materials

This class excludes:
- *logging and production of wood in the rough, see 0200*
- *manufacture of veneer sheets thin enough for use in plywood, boards and panels, see 2021*
- *manufacture of shingles and shakes, beadings and mouldings, see 2022*

202   **Manufacture of products of wood, cork, straw and plaiting materials**

2021   **Manufacture of veneer sheets; manufacture of plywood, laminboard, particle board and other panels and boards**

This class includes:
- manufacture of veneer sheets thin enough to be used for veneering, making plywood or other purposes:

80

- smoothed, dyed, coated, impregnated, reinforced (with paper or fabric backing)
  - made in the form of motifs
- manufacture of plywood, veneer panels and similar laminated wood boards and sheets
- manufacture of particle board and fibreboard
- manufacture of densified wood

2022   Manufacture of builders' carpentry and joinery

This class includes:
- manufacture of wooden goods intended to be used primarily in the construction industry:
  - beams, rafters, roof struts
  - glue-laminated and prefabricated wooden trusses
  - doors, windows, shutters and their frames, whether or not containing metal fittings, such as hinges, locks etc.
  - stairs, railings
  - wooden beadings and mouldings, shingles and shakes
  - parquet floor blocks, strips etc., assembled into panels
- manufacture of prefabricated buildings, or elements thereof, predominantly of wood

This class excludes:
- *manufacture of unassembled wooden flooring, see 2010*
- *manufacture of kitchen cabinets, bookcases, wardrobes etc., see 3610*

2023   Manufacture of wooden containers

This class includes:
- manufacture of packing cases, boxes, crates, drums and similar packings of wood
- manufacture of pallets, box pallets and other load boards of wood
- manufacture of barrels, vats, tubs and other coopers' products of wood
- manufacture of wooden cable-drums

This class excludes:
- *manufacture of luggage, see 1912*
- *manufacture of cases of plaiting material, see 2029*

2029   Manufacture of other products of wood; manufacture of articles of cork, straw and plaiting materials

This class includes:
- manufacture of various wood products:
  - wooden handles and bodies for tools, brooms, brushes
  - wooden boot or shoe lasts and trees, clothes hangers
  - household utensils and kitchenware of wood
  - wooden statuettes and ornaments, wood marquetry, inlaid wood
  - wooden cases for jewellery, cutlery and similar articles
  - wooden spools, cops, bobbins, sewing thread reels and similar articles of turned wood
  - other articles of wood
- natural cork processing, manufacture of agglomerated cork
- manufacture of articles of natural or agglomerated cork, including floor coverings
- manufacture of plaits and products of plaiting materials: mats, matting, screens, cases etc.
- manufacture of basket-ware and wickerwork

This class excludes:
- *manufacture of mats or matting of textile materials, see 1722*
- *manufacture of luggage, see 1912*
- *manufacture of wooden footwear, see 1920*
- *manufacture of wooden spools and bobbins that are part of textile machinery, see 2926*
- *manufacture of clock cases, see 3330*

- *manufacture of furniture, see 3610*
- *manufacture of wooden toys, see 3694*
- *manufacture of brushes and brooms, see 3699*
- *manufacture of walking sticks and umbrella handles, see 3699*
- *manufacture of matches, see 3699*
- *manufacture of caskets, see 3699*

21   Manufacture of paper and paper products

This division includes the manufacture of pulp, paper, or converted paper products. The manufacturing of these products is grouped together because they constitute a series of vertically connected processes. More than one activity is often carried out in a single unit. There are essentially three activities. The manufacturing of pulp involves separating the cellulose fibers from other impurities in wood or used paper. The manufacturing of paper involves matting these fibers into a sheet. Converted paper products are made from paper and other materials by various cutting and shaping techniques, including coating and laminating activities. The paper articles may be printed (e.g. wallpaper, gift wrap etc.), as long as the printing of information is not the main purpose.

The production of pulp, paper and paperboard in bulk is included in class 2101, while the remaining classes include the production of further-processed paper and paper products.

210   Manufacture of paper and paper products

2101   Manufacture of pulp, paper and paperboard

This class includes:
- manufacture of bleached, semi-bleached or unbleached paper pulp by mechanical, chemical (dissolving or non-dissolving) or semi-chemical processes
- manufacture of cotton-linters pulp
- removal of ink and manufacture of pulp from waste paper
- manufacture of paper and paperboard intended for further industrial processing

This class also includes:
- further processing of paper and paperboard:
  • coating, covering and impregnation of paper and paperboard
  • manufacture of crêped or crinkled paper
- manufacture of handmade paper
- manufacture of newsprint and other printing or writing paper
- manufacture of cellulose wadding and webs of cellulose fibres

This class excludes:
- *manufacture of corrugated paper and paperboard, see 2102*
- *manufacture of further-processed articles of paper, paperboard or pulp, see 2109*
- *manufacture of abrasive paper, see 2699*
- *manufacture of coated or impregnated paper, where the coating or impregnant is the main ingredient, see class in which the manufacture of the coating or impregnant is classified*

2102   Manufacture of corrugated paper and paperboard and of containers of paper and paperboard

This class includes:
- manufacture of corrugated paper and paperboard
- manufacture of containers of corrugated paper or paperboard
- manufacture of folding paperboard containers
- manufacture of containers of solid board
- manufacture of other containers of paper and paperboard
- manufacture of sacks and bags of paper

- manufacture of office box files and similar articles

This class excludes:
- *manufacture of envelopes, see 2109*
- *manufacture of moulded or pressed articles of paper pulp (e.g. boxes for packing eggs, moulded pulp paper plates), see 2109*

2109   Manufacture of other articles of paper and paperboard

This class includes:
- manufacture of household and personal hygiene paper and cellulose wadding products:
  - cleansing tissues
  - handkerchiefs, towels, serviettes
  - toilet paper
  - sanitary towels and tampons, napkins and napkin liners for babies
  - cups, dishes and trays
- manufacture of printing and writing paper ready for use
- manufacture of computer printout paper ready for use
- manufacture of self-copy paper ready for use
- manufacture of duplicator stencils and carbon paper ready for use
- manufacture of gummed or adhesive paper ready for use
- manufacture of envelopes and letter-cards
- manufacture of boxes, pouches, wallets and writing compendiums containing an assortment of paper stationery
- manufacture of wallpaper and similar wall coverings, including vinyl-coated and textile wallpaper
- manufacture of labels, whether printed or not
- manufacture of filter paper and paperboard
- manufacture of paper and paperboard bobbins, spools, cops etc.
- manufacture of egg trays and other moulded pulp packaging products etc.

This class excludes:
- *manufacture of paper or paperboard in bulk, see 2101*
- *manufacture of playing cards, see 3694*
- *manufacture of games and toys of paper or paperboard, see 3694*

22   Publishing, printing and reproduction of recorded media

This division includes printing and publishing whether or nor connected with printing. Publishing involves financial, technical, artistic, legal and marketing activities, among others, but not predominantly. The primary breakdown of this division is by units engaged in publishing, whether or not connected with printing (group 221) versus units engaged in printing only (group 222). The breakdown of publishing activities into classes is based on the type of printed matter or recorded media published.

This division includes units engaged in the publishing of newspapers, magazines, other periodicals, and books. In general, these units, which are known as publishers, issue copies of works for which they usually possess copyright. Works may be in one or more formats including traditional print form and electronic form. Publishers may publish works originally created by others for which they have obtained the rights and/or works that they have created in-house.

The printing activities print products, such as newspapers, books, periodicals, business forms, greeting cards, and other materials, and perform support activities, such as bookbinding, plate-making services, and data imaging. The support activities included here are an integral part of the printing industry, and a product (a printing plate, a bound book, or a computer disk or file) that is an integral part of the printing industry is almost always provided by these operations.

Processes used in printing include a variety of methods for transferring an image from a plate, screen, or computer file to some medium, such as paper, plastics, metal, textile articles, or wood. The most prominent of these methods entails the transfer of the image from a plate or screen to the medium (lithographic, gravure, screen, and flexographic printing). A rapidly growing new technology uses a computer file to directly "drive" the printing mechanism to create the image and new electrostatic and other types of equipment (digital or non-impact printing).

Though printing and publishing can be carried out by the same unit (a newspaper, for example), it is less and less the case that these distinct activities are carried out in the same physical location. When publishing and printing are done in the same unit, the unit is classified in group 221 (Publishing) even if the receipts for printing exceed those for publishing.

Units engaged in both online publishing and other publishing are included here, as represented, for example, by a newspaper publisher who also publishes an online version of the newspaper.

This division excludes units engaged exclusively in online publishing, see 7240.

This division excludes publishing of software, see 7221, and the publishing of motion pictures and videotapes, see 9211.

221   Publishing

2211   Publishing of books, brochures and other publications

This class includes:
- publishing of books, brochures, leaflets and similar publications, including publishing of dictionaries and encyclopedias
- publishing of atlases, maps and charts
- publishing of audiobooks
- publishing of encyclopedias etc. on CD-ROM

This class excludes:
- *exclusive publishing of these products online, see 7240*

2212   Publishing of newspapers, journals and periodicals

This class includes:
- publishing of newspapers, including advertising newspapers
- publishing of periodicals, trade journals, comic books etc.

This class excludes:
- *exclusive publishing of these products online, see 7240*

2213   Publishing of music

This class includes:
- publishing of gramophone records, compact discs and tapes with music or other sound recordings
- publishing of printed music

This class also includes:
- publishing of other sound recordings

This class excludes:
- *publishing of software, see 7221*
- *exclusive publishing of these products online, see 7240*
- *publishing of motion pictures, videotapes and movies on digital video disc (DVD) or similar media, see 9211*
- *production of master copies for records or audio material, see 9211*

2219   Other publishing

This class includes:
- publishing of:
  - photos, engravings and postcards
  - greeting cards
  - timetables
  - forms
  - posters, reproduction of works of art
  - other printed matter

222   Printing and service activities related to printing

2221   Printing

This class includes:
- printing of newspapers, magazines and other periodicals, books and brochures, music and music manuscripts, maps, atlases, posters, advertising catalogues, prospectuses and other printed advertising, postage stamps, taxation stamps, documents of title, cheques and other security papers, registers, albums, diaries, calendars, business forms and other commercial printed matter, personal stationery and other printed matter by letterpress, offset, photogravure, flexographic, screen printing and other printing presses, duplication machines, computer printers, embossers, photocopiers and thermocopiers

This class excludes:
- *printing of labels, see 2109*
- *publishing of printed matter, see 2211, 2212, 2219*

2222   Service activities related to printing

This class includes:
- binding of printed sheets, e.g. into books, brochures, magazines, catalogues etc., by folding, assembling, stitching, glueing, collating, basting, adhesive binding, trimming, gold stamping
- composition, typesetting, phototypesetting, pre-press data input including scanning and optical character recognition, electronic make-up
- plate-making services including imagesetting and plate-setting (for the printing processes letterpress and offset)
- engraving or etching of cylinders for gravure
- plate processes direct to plate (also photopolymer plates)
- preparation of plates and dies for relief stamping or printing
- proofs
- artistic work including litho stones and prepared woodblocks
- production of reprographic products
- design of printing products e.g. sketches, layouts, dummies etc.
- other graphic activities such as die-sinking or die-stamping, braille copying, punching and drilling, embossing, varnishing and laminating, collating and insetting, creasing

223   Reproduction of recorded media

2230   Reproduction of recorded media

This class includes:
- reproduction from master copies of gramophone records, compact discs and tapes with music or other sound recordings
- reproduction from master copies of records, compact discs and tapes with motion pictures and other video recordings
- reproduction from master copies of software and data on discs and tapes

This class excludes:
- *reproduction of printed matter, see 2221*
- *publishing of software, see 7221*
- *publishing of motion pictures, videotapes and movies on DVD or similar media, see 9211*
- *production of master copies for records or audio material, see 9211*
- *reproduction of motion picture films for theatrical distribution, see 9211*

23   Manufacture of coke, refined petroleum products and nuclear fuel

This division is based on the transformation of crude petroleum and coal into usable products and also includes the nuclear industries. It constitutes the manufacturing part of the energy sector which begins in section C (extraction) and is also present in section E (electricity, gas and water supply). The dominant process is petroleum refining which involves the separation of crude petroleum into component products through such techniques as cracking and distillation. This division also covers the manufacture for own account of characteristic products (e.g. coke, butane, propane, petrol, kerosene, fuel oil, nuclear fuel etc.) as well as processing services (e.g. custom refining, treatment of nuclear waste).

This division includes the manufacture of gases such as ethane, propane and butane as products of petroleum refineries. Not included is the manufacture of such gases in other units (2411), manufacture of industrial gases (2411), extraction of natural gas (methane, ethane, butane or propane) (1110), and manufacture of fuel gas, other than petroleum gases (e.g. coal gas, water gas, producer gas, gasworks gas) (4020).

Units that manufacture petrochemicals from refined petroleum are classified in division 24.

231   Manufacture of coke oven products

2310   Manufacture of coke oven products

This class includes:
- operation of coke ovens
- production of coke and semi-coke
- production of coke oven gas
- production of crude coal and lignite tars
- agglomeration of coke

This class excludes:
- *agglomeration of hard coal, see 1010*
- *agglomeration of lignite, see 1020*
- *manufacture of pitch, pitch coke and coal tar, see 2411*

232   Manufacture of refined petroleum products

2320   Manufacture of refined petroleum products

This class includes the manufacture of liquid or gaseous fuels or other products from crude petroleum, bituminous minerals or their fractionation products.

This class includes:
- production of motor fuel: gasoline, kerosene etc.
- production of fuel: light, medium and heavy fuel oil, refinery gases such as ethane, propane, butane etc.
- manufacture of oil-based lubricating oils or greases, including from waste oil
- manufacture of products for the petrochemical industry and for the manufacture of road coverings
- manufacture of various products: white spirit, vaseline, paraffin wax, petroleum jelly etc.

233   Processing of nuclear fuel

2330   Processing of nuclear fuel

This class includes:
- extraction of uranium metal from pitchblende or other ores
- production of natural and enriched uranium, plutonium; compounds, alloys, dispersions and mixtures thereof
- production of fuel elements for nuclear reactors
- reprocessing of nuclear fuels
- production of radioactive elements for industrial or medical use
- treatment of radioactive nuclear waste

This class excludes:
- *mining and concentration of uranium and thorium ores, see 1200*
- *manufacture of yellowcake, see 1200*
- *disposal of transition radioactive waste (i.e. decaying within the period of temporary storage) from hospitals etc., see 9000*

24   Manufacture of chemicals and chemical products

This division is based on the transformation of organic and inorganic raw materials by a chemical process and the formation of products. It distinguishes the production of basic chemicals that constitute the first industry group from the production of intermediate and end products produced by further processing of basic chemicals that make up the remaining industry classes.

241   Manufacture of basic chemicals

2411   Manufacture of basic chemicals, except fertilizers and nitrogen compounds

This class includes:
- manufacture of liquefied or compressed inorganic industrial or medical gases:
  - elemental gases
  - liquid or compressed air
  - refrigerant gases
  - mixed industrial gases
  - inert gases such as carbon dioxide
  - isolating gases
- manufacture of dyes and pigments from any source in basic form or as concentrate
- manufacture of chemical elements except metals and radioactive elements produced by the nuclear fuels industry
- manufacture of inorganic acids except nitric acid
- manufacture of alkalis, lyes and other inorganic bases except ammonia
- manufacture of other inorganic compounds
- manufacture of basic organic chemicals:
  - acyclic hydrocarbons, saturated and unsaturated
  - cyclic hydrocarbons, saturated and unsaturated
  - acyclic and cyclic alcohols, including synthetic ethyl alcohol
  - mono- and polycarboxylic acids, including acetic acid
  - other oxygen-function compounds, including aldehydes, ketones, quinones and dual or poly oxygen-function compounds
  - synthetic glycerol
  - nitrogen-function organic compounds, including amines
  - other organic compounds, including wood distillation products (e.g. charcoal) etc.
- production of pitch and pitch coke
- manufacture of synthetic aromatic products

- distillation of coal tar
- roasting of iron pyrites

This class also includes:
- manufacture of products of a kind used as fluorescent brightening agents or as luminophores

This class excludes:
- *extraction of methane, ethane, butane or propane, see 1110*
- *manufacture of ethyl alcohol from fermented materials, see 1551*
- *manufacture of fuel gases such as ethane, butane or propane in a petroleum refinery, see 2320*
- *manufacture of nitrogenous fertilizers and nitrogen compounds, see 2412*
- *manufacture of ammonia, see 2412*
- *manufacture of ammonium chloride, see 2412*
- *manufacture of nitrites and nitrates of potassium, see 2412*
- *manufacture of ammonium carbonates, see 2412*
- *manufacture of plastics in primary forms, see 2413*
- *manufacture of synthetic rubber in primary forms, see 2413*
- *manufacture of prepared dyes and pigments, see 2422*
- *manufacture of salicylic and O-acetylsalicylic acids, see 2423*
- *manufacture of crude glycerol, see 2424*
- *manufacture of natural essential oils, see 2429*

2412   Manufacture of fertilizers and nitrogen compounds

This class includes:
- manufacture of fertilizers:
  - straight or complex nitrogenous, phosphatic or potassic fertilizers
  - urea, crude natural phosphates and crude natural potassium salts
  - compost
- manufacture of associated nitrogen products:
  - nitric and sulphonitric acids, ammonia, ammonium chloride, ammonium carbonate, nitrites and nitrates of potassium

This class excludes:
- *mining of guano, see 1421*
- *manufacture of agrochemical products, such as pesticides, see 2421*

2413   Manufacture of plastics in primary forms and of synthetic rubber

This class includes:
- manufacture of plastics in primary forms:
  - polymers, including those of ethylene, propylene, styrene, vinyl chloride, vinyl acetate and acrylics
  - polyamides
  - phenolic and epoxide resins and polyurethanes
  - alkyd and polyester resins and polyethers
  - silicones
  - ion-exchangers based on polymers
- manufacture of synthetic rubber in primary forms:
  - synthetic rubber
  - Factice
- manufacture of mixtures of synthetic rubber and natural rubber or rubber-like gums (e.g. balata)

This class also includes:
- manufacture of cellulose and its chemical derivatives

This class excludes:
- *manufacture of artificial and synthetic fibres, filaments and yarn, see 2430*
- *recycling of plastics, see 3720*

242   Manufacture of other chemical products

2421   Manufacture of pesticides and other agrochemical products

This class includes:
- manufacture of insecticides, rodenticides, fungicides, herbicides
- manufacture of anti-sprouting products, plant growth regulators
- manufacture of disinfectants (for agricultural and other use)
- manufacture of other agrochemical products n.e.c.

This class excludes:
- *manufacture of fertilizers and nitrogen compounds, see 2412*

2422   Manufacture of paints, varnishes and similar coatings, printing ink and mastics

This class includes:
- manufacture of paints and varnishes, enamels or lacquers
- manufacture of prepared pigments and dyes, opacifiers and colours
- manufacture of vitrifiable enamels and glazes and engobes and similar preparations
- manufacture of mastics
- manufacture of caulking compounds and similar non-refractory filling or surfacing preparations
- manufacture of organic composite solvents and thinners
- manufacture of prepared paint or varnish removers
- manufacture of printing ink

This class excludes:
- *manufacture of dyestuffs, pigments and turpentine, see 2411*
- *manufacture of writing and drawing ink, see 2429*

2423   Manufacture of pharmaceuticals, medicinal chemicals and botanical products

This class includes:
- manufacture of medicinal active substances to be used for their pharmacological properties in the manufacture of medicaments: antibiotics, basic vitamins, salicylic and O-acetylsalicylic acids etc.
- processing of blood
- manufacture of medicaments:
  - antisera and other blood fractions
  - vaccines
  - diverse medicaments, including homeopathic preparations
- manufacture of chemical contraceptive products for external use and hormonal contraceptive medicaments
- manufacture of dental fillings and bone reconstruction cements
- manufacture of medical diagnostic preparations, including pregnancy tests

This class also includes:
- manufacture of chemically pure sugars
- processing of glands and manufacture of extracts of glands etc.
- manufacture of medical impregnated wadding, gauze, bandages, dressings, surgical gut string etc.
- preparation of botanical products (grinding, grading, milling) for pharmaceutical use

This class excludes:
- *packaging of pharmaceuticals for own account, see 5139, 5231*
- *packaging of pharmaceuticals on a fee or contract basis, see 7495*

2424 **Manufacture of soap and detergents, cleaning and polishing preparations, perfumes and toilet preparations**

This class includes:
- manufacture of organic surface-active agents
- manufacture of soap
- manufacture of paper, wadding, felt etc. coated or covered with soap or detergent
- manufacture of crude glycerol
- manufacture of surface-active preparations:
  • washing powders in solid or liquid form and detergents
  • dish-washing preparations
  • textile softeners
- manufacture of cleaning and polishing products:
  • preparations for perfuming or deodorizing rooms
  • artificial waxes and prepared waxes
  • polishes and creams for leather
  • polishes and creams for wood
  • polishes for coachwork, glass and metal
  • scouring pastes and powders, including paper, wadding etc. coated or covered with these
- manufacture of perfumes and toilet preparations:
  • perfumes and toilet water
  • beauty and make-up preparations
  • sunburn prevention and suntan preparations
  • manicure and pedicure preparations
  • shampoos, hair lacquers, waving and straightening preparations
  • dentifrices and preparations for oral hygiene, including denture fixative preparations
  • shaving preparations, including pre-shave and aftershave preparations
  • deodorants and bath salts
  • depilatories

This class excludes:
- *manufacture of separate, chemically defined compounds, see 2411*
- *manufacture of glycerol, synthesized from petroleum products, see 2411*
- *extraction and refining of natural essential oils, see 2429*

2429 **Manufacture of other chemical products n.e.c.**

This class includes:
- manufacture of propellant powders
- manufacture of explosives and pyrotechnic products, including percussion caps, detonators, signalling flares etc.
- manufacture of gelatine and its derivatives, glues and prepared adhesives, including rubber-based glues and adhesives
- manufacture of extracts of natural aromatic products
- manufacture of resinoids
- manufacture of aromatic distilled waters
- manufacture of mixtures of odoriferous products for the manufacture of perfumes or food
- manufacture of photographic plates, films, sensitized paper and other sensitized unexposed materials
- manufacture of chemical preparations for photographic uses
- manufacture of unrecorded media for sound or video recording
- manufacture of unrecorded computer disks and tapes
- manufacture of various chemical products:
  • peptones, peptone derivatives, other protein substances and their derivatives n.e.c.
  • essential oils
  • chemically modified oils and fats

- materials used in the finishing of textiles and leather
- powders and pastes used in soldering, brazing or welding
- substances used to pickle metal
- prepared additives for cements
- activated carbon, lubricating oil additives, prepared rubber accelerators, catalysts and other chemical products for industrial use
- anti-knock preparations, antifreeze preparations
- composite diagnostic or laboratory reagents

This class also includes:
- manufacture of writing and drawing ink
- manufacture of processed salt

This class excludes:
- *manufacture of chemically defined products in bulk, see 2411*
- *manufacture of synthetic aromatic products, see 2411*
- *manufacture of printing ink, see 2422*
- *manufacture of perfumes and toilet preparations, see 2424*
- *manufacture of asphalt-based adhesives, see 2699*

243 Manufacture of man-made fibres

2430 Manufacture of man-made fibres

This class includes:
- manufacture of synthetic or artificial filament tow
- manufacture of synthetic or artificial staple fibres, not carded, combed or otherwise processed for spinning
- manufacture of synthetic or artificial filament yarn, including high-tenacity yarn
- manufacture of synthetic or artificial monofilament or strip

This class excludes:
- *spinning of synthetic or artificial fibres, see 1711*
- *manufacture of yarns made of man-made staple, see 1711*
- *manufacture of processed yarns from filaments, tow, staple, yarn not made in the same unit, see 1711*

25 Manufacture of rubber and plastics products

The rubber and plastic industries are characterized by the raw materials used. However, this does not mean that all products made of these materials necessarily fall under this activity. Most notably, manufacture of apparel and footwear is classified in division 18 and 19, even when plastic or rubber is the main constituent.

251 Manufacture of rubber products

2511 Manufacture of rubber tyres and tubes; retreading and rebuilding of rubber tyres

This class includes:
- manufacture of rubber tyres for vehicles, equipment, mobile machinery, aircraft, toy, furniture and other uses:
  - pneumatic tyres
  - solid or cushion tyres
- manufacture of inner tubes for tyres
- manufacture of interchangeable tyre treads, tyre flaps, "camelback" strips for retreading tyres etc.
- tyre rebuilding and retreading

This class excludes:
- *manufacture of tube repair materials, see 2519*
- *tyre and tube repair, fitting or replacement, see 5020*

2519   Manufacture of other rubber products

This class includes:
- manufacture of other products of natural or synthetic rubber, unvulcanized, vulcanized or hardened:
  - rubber plates, sheets, strip, rods, profile shapes
  - tubes, pipes and hoses
  - rubber conveyor or transmission belts or belting
  - rubber hygienic articles: sheath contraceptives, teats, hot water bottles etc.
  - rubber articles of apparel (if only sealed together, not sewn)
  - rubber floor coverings
  - rubber thread and rope
  - rubberized yarn and fabrics
  - rubber rings, fittings and seals
  - rubber roller coverings
  - inflatable rubber mattresses
  - inflatable balloons

This class also includes:
- manufacture of rubber repair materials
- manufacture of textile fabric impregnated, coated, covered or laminated with rubber, where rubber is the chief constituent

This class excludes:
- *manufacture of tyre cord fabrics, see 1729*
- *manufacture of apparel of elastic fabrics, see 1810*
- *manufacture of rubber footwear, see 1920*
- *manufacture of glues and adhesives based on rubber, see 2429*
- *manufacture of "camelback" strips, see 2511*
- *manufacture of inflatable rafts and boats, see 3511, 3512*
- *manufacture of mattresses of uncovered cellular rubber, see 3610*
- *manufacture of rubber sports requisites, except apparel, see 3693*
- *manufacture of rubber games and toys, see 3694*
- *reclaiming of rubber, see 3720*

252   Manufacture of plastics products

2520   Manufacture of plastics products

This class includes:
- manufacture of semi-manufactures of plastic products:
  - plastic plates, sheets, blocks, film, foil, strip etc. (whether self-adhesive or not)
- manufacture of finished plastic products:
  - plastic tubes, pipes and hoses; hose and pipe fittings
- manufacture of plastic articles for the packing of goods:
  - plastic bags, sacks, containers, boxes, cases, carboys, bottles etc.
- manufacture of builders' plastics ware:
  - plastic doors, windows, frames, shutters, blinds, skirting boards
  - tanks, reservoirs
  - plastic floor, wall or ceiling coverings in rolls or in the form of tiles etc.
  - plastic sanitary ware:
    - plastic baths, shower-baths, washbasins, lavatory pans, flushing cisterns etc.
- manufacture of plastic tableware, kitchenware and toilet articles

- manufacture of diverse plastic products:
  - plastic headgear, insulating fittings, parts of lighting fittings, office or school supplies, articles of apparel (if only sealed together, not sewn), fittings for furniture, statuettes, transmission and conveyer belts etc.

This class excludes:
- *manufacture of plastic luggage, see 1912*
- *manufacture of plastic footwear, see 1920*
- *manufacture of plastics in primary forms, see 2413*
- *manufacture of articles of synthetic or natural rubber, see 251*
- *manufacture of plastic medical and dental appliances, see 3311*
- *manufacture of plastic optical elements, see 3320*
- *manufacture of plastic furniture, see 3610*
- *manufacture of mattresses of uncovered cellular plastic, see 3610*
- *manufacture of plastic sports requisites, see 3693*
- *manufacture of plastic games and toys, see 3694*
- *manufacture of linoleum and hard non-plastic surface floor coverings, see 3699*

26 Manufacture of other non-metallic mineral products

This division groups different areas that are all related to a single substance of mineral origin. This division includes glass and glass products (e.g. flat glass, hollow glass, fibres, technical glassware etc.); and ceramic products, tiles and baked clay products, and cement and plaster, from raw materials to finished articles. Shaped and finished stone and other mineral products complete the division.

261 Manufacture of glass and glass products

2610 Manufacture of glass and glass products

This class includes glass in all its forms, made by any process, and articles of glass.

This class includes:
- manufacture of flat glass, including wired, coloured or tinted flat glass
- manufacture of toughened or laminated flat glass
- manufacture of glass in rods or tubes
- manufacture of glass paving blocks
- manufacture of glass mirrors
- manufacture of multiple-walled insulating units of glass
- manufacture of bottles and other containers of glass or crystal
- manufacture of drinking glasses and other domestic glass or crystal articles
- manufacture of glass fibres, including glass wool and non-woven products thereof
- manufacture of laboratory, hygienic or pharmaceutical glassware
- manufacture of clock or watch glasses, optical glass and optical elements not optically worked
- manufacture of glassware used in imitation jewellery
- manufacture of glass insulators and glass insulating fittings
- manufacture of glass envelopes for lamps

This class excludes:
- *manufacture of woven fabrics of glass yarn, see 1711*
- *manufacture of optical fibre cables for coded data transmission, see 3130*
- *manufacture of syringes and other medical laboratory equipment, see 3311*
- *manufacture of optical elements optically worked, see 3320*
- *manufacture of optical fibres and optical fibre cables for live transmission of images, see 3320*
- *manufacture of glass toys, see 3694*

269   Manufacture of non-metallic mineral products n.e.c.

2691   Manufacture of non-structural non-refractory ceramic ware

This class includes:
- manufacture of ceramic tableware and other domestic or toilet articles
- manufacture of statuettes and other ornamental ceramic articles
- manufacture of electrical insulators and insulating fittings of ceramics
- manufacture of ceramic laboratory, chemical and industrial products
- manufacture of ceramic pots, jars and similar articles of a kind used for conveyance or packing of goods
- manufacture of ceramic furniture
- manufacture of ceramic products n.e.c.

This class excludes:
- *manufacture of refractory ceramic goods, see 2692*
- *manufacture of ceramic building materials, see 2693*
- *manufacture of artificial teeth, see 3311*
- *manufacture of ceramic toys, see 3694*
- *manufacture of imitation jewellery, see 3699*

2692   Manufacture of refractory ceramic products

This class includes:
- manufacture of refractory mortars, concretes etc.
- manufacture of refractory ceramic goods:
  - heat-insulating ceramic goods of siliceous fossil meals
  - refractory bricks, blocks and tiles etc.
  - retorts, crucibles, muffles, nozzles, tubes, pipes etc.

This class also includes:
- manufacture of refractory articles containing magnesite, dolomite or cromite

This class excludes:
- *manufacture of non-refractory ceramic goods, see 2691, 2693*

2693   Manufacture of structural non-refractory clay and ceramic products

This class includes:
- manufacture of non-refractory ceramic hearth or wall tiles, mosaic cubes etc.
- manufacture of non-refractory ceramic flags and paving
- manufacture of structural non-refractory clay building materials:
  - manufacture of ceramic bricks, roofing tiles, chimney pots, pipes, conduits etc.
- manufacture of flooring blocks in baked clay

This class excludes:
- *manufacture of non-structural non-refractory ceramic products, see 2691*
- *manufacture of refractory ceramic products, see 2692*

2694   Manufacture of cement, lime and plaster

This class includes:
- manufacture of clinkers and hydraulic cements, including portland, aluminous cement, slag cement and superphosphate cements
- manufacture of quicklime, slaked lime and hydraulic lime
- manufacture of plasters of calcined gypsum or calcined sulphate
- manufacture of calcined dolomite

This class excludes:
- *manufacture of cements used in dentistry, see 2423*
- *manufacture of refractory mortars, concrete etc., see 2692*
- *manufacture of articles of cement, see 2695*
- *manufacture of articles of plaster, see 2695*
- *manufacture of ready-mixed and dry-mix concrete and mortars, see 2695*

2695   Manufacture of articles of concrete, cement and plaster

This class includes:
- manufacture of precast concrete, cement or artificial stone articles for use in construction:
  - tiles, flagstones, bricks, boards, sheets, panels, pipes, posts etc.
- manufacture of prefabricated structural components for building or civil engineering of cement, concrete or artificial stone
- manufacture of plaster articles for use in construction:
  - boards, sheets, panels etc.
- manufacture of building materials of vegetable substances (wood wool, straw, reeds, rushes) agglomerated with cement, plaster or other mineral binder
- manufacture of articles of asbestos-cement or cellulose fibre-cement or the like:
  - corrugated sheets, other sheets, panels, tiles, tubes, pipes, reservoirs, troughs, basins, sinks, jars, furniture, window frames etc.
- manufacture of other articles of concrete, plaster, cement or artificial stone:
  - statuary, furniture, bas- and haut-reliefs, vases, flowerpots etc.
- manufacture of powdered mortars
- manufacture of ready-mix and dry-mix concrete and mortars

This class excludes:
- *manufacture of refractory cements and mortars, see 2692*

2696   Cutting, shaping and finishing of stone

This class includes:
- cutting, shaping and finishing of stone for use in construction, in cemeteries, on roads, as roofing etc.
- manufacture of stone furniture

This class excludes:
- *activities carried out by operators of quarries, e.g. production of rough cut stone, see 1410*
- *production of millstones, abrasive stones and similar products, see 2699*

2699   Manufacture of other non-metallic mineral products n.e.c.

This class includes:
- manufacture of millstones, sharpening or polishing stones and natural or artificial abrasive products, including abrasive products on a soft base (e.g. sandpaper)
- manufacture of non-metallic mineral yarn and fabric, clothing, headgear, footwear, cord, string, paper, felt etc. (e.g. from asbestos)
- manufacture of friction material and unmounted articles thereof with a base of mineral substances or of cellulose
- manufacture of mineral insulating materials:
  - slag wool, rock wool and similar mineral wools; exfoliated vermiculite, expanded clays and similar heat-insulating, sound-insulating or sound-absorbing materials
- manufacture of articles of diverse mineral substances:
  - worked mica and articles of mica, of peat, of graphite (other than electrical articles) etc.
- manufacture of articles of asphalt or similar material, e.g. asphalt-based adhesives, coal tar pitch etc.

This class excludes:
- *manufacture of glass wool and non-woven glass wool products, see 2610*

27 Manufacture of basic metals

This division includes the activities of smelting and/or refining ferrous and non-ferrous metals from ore, pig or scrap, using electrometallurgic and other process metallurgic techniques. Units in this division also manufacture metal alloys and super-alloys by introducing other chemical elements to pure metals. The output of smelting and refining, usually in ingot form, is used in rolling, drawing and extruding operations to make sheet, strip, bar, rod or wire, and in molten form to make castings and other basic metal products.

271 Manufacture of basic iron and steel

2710 Manufacture of basic iron and steel

This class includes:
- operation of blast furnaces, steel converters, rolling and finishing mills
- production of pig iron and spiegeleisen in pigs, blocks or other primary forms
- production of ferro-alloys
- production of semi-finished products of iron or non-alloy steel
- production of ingots, other primary forms and semi-finished products of stainless steel or other alloy steel
- production of angles, shapes and sections of stainless steel or other alloy steel
- production of bars and rods of stainless steel or other alloy steel
- production of flat-rolled products of iron or non-alloy steel
- production of angles, shapes and sections of iron or non-alloy steel
- production of bars and rods of iron or non-alloy steel
- production of sheet piling
- production of railway track materials (unassembled rails)
- manufacture of cast-iron tubes and cast-iron or steel centrifugally cast tubes
- manufacture of cast-iron fittings: non-malleable and malleable cast-iron fittings and cast-steel fittings for which connection is obtained by screwing for threaded fittings, by contact for socket fittings or by bolting for flange fittings
- manufacture of seamless tubes, by hot rolling, hot extrusion or hot drawing, or by cold drawing or cold rolling
- manufacture of welded tubes by cold or hot forming and welding, by forming and cold drawing, or by hot forming and reducing
- manufacture of steel tube fittings:
  • flat flanges and flanges with forged collars of steel
  • butt welding fittings of steel
  • threaded fittings and other fittings of steel
- manufacture of steel bars or sections by cold drawing, grinding or peeling
- manufacture of open sections by progressive forming on a roll mill or folding on a press of flat-rolled products of steel
- manufacture of steel wire by cold drawing or stretching
- production of granular iron and iron powder; production of iron of exceptional purity by electrolysis or other chemical processes

This class excludes:
- *forging or casting operations in connection with the manufacture of metal products, see divisions 28-36*

272 Manufacture of basic precious and non-ferrous metals

2720 Manufacture of basic precious and non-ferrous metals

This class includes:
- production of basic precious metals:
  • production and refining of unwrought or wrought precious metals: gold, silver, platinum etc. from ore and scrap

- production of precious metal alloys
- production of precious metal semi-products
- production of silver rolled onto base metals
- production of gold rolled onto base metals or silver
- production of platinum and platinum group metals rolled onto gold, silver or base metals
- production of aluminium from alumina
- production of aluminium from electrolytic refining of aluminium waste and scrap
- production of aluminium alloys
- semi-manufacturing of aluminium
- production of lead, zinc and tin from ores
- production of lead, zinc and tin from electrolytic refining of lead, zinc and tin waste and scrap
- production of lead, zinc and tin alloys
- semi-manufacturing of lead, zinc and tin
- production of copper from ores
- production of copper from electrolytic refining of copper waste and scrap
- production of copper alloys
- manufacture of fuse wire or strip
- semi-manufacturing of copper
- production of chrome, manganese, nickel etc. from ores or oxides
- production of chrome, manganese, nickel etc. from electrolytic and aluminothermic refining of chrome, manganese, nickel etc., waste and scrap
- production of alloys of chrome, manganese, nickel etc.
- semi-manufacturing of chrome, manganese, nickel etc.
- production of mattes of nickel

This class also includes:
- manufacture of wire of these metals by drawing
- production of aluminium oxide (alumina)
- production of aluminium wrapping foil

This class excludes:
- *manufacture of precious metal watch cases, see 3330*
- *manufacture of precious metal jewellery, see 3691*
- *forging or casting operations in connection with the manufacture of metal products, see divisions 28-36*

273   Casting of metals

This group includes:
- manufacture of semi-finished products and various castings produced for third parties according to their specifications

This group excludes:
- *manufacture of finished cast products such as pipes and related items, see 2710; boilers and radiators, see 2812; cast household items, see 2899, etc.*

2731   Casting of iron and steel

This class includes activities of iron and steel foundries.

This class includes:
- casting of semi-finished iron products
- casting of grey iron castings
- casting of spheroidal graphite iron castings
- casting of malleable cast-iron products
- casting of semi-finished steel products
- casting of steel castings

This class excludes:
- *casting carried out in connection with the manufacture of metal products, see divisions 27 - 36*

2732   Casting of non-ferrous metals

This class includes:
- casting of semi-finished products of aluminium, magnesium, titanium, zinc etc.
- casting of light metal castings
- casting of heavy metal castings
- casting of precious metal castings
- die-casting of non-ferrous metal castings

This class excludes:
- *casting carried out in connection with the manufacture of metal products, see divisions 27 - 36*

28   Manufacture of fabricated metal products, except machinery and equipment

While division 28 deals with the manufacture of "pure" metal products (such as parts, containers and structures), usually with a static, immovable function, divisions 29-36 concern combinations or assemblies of such metal products (sometimes with other materials) into more complex units that, unless they are purely electrical, electronic or optical, work with moving parts.

281   Manufacture of structural metal products, tanks, reservoirs and steam generators

2811   Manufacture of structural metal products

This class includes:
- manufacture of metal frameworks or skeletons for construction and parts thereof (towers, masts, trusses, bridges etc.)
- manufacture of industrial frameworks in metal (frameworks for blast furnaces, lifting and handling equipment etc.)
- manufacture of prefabricated buildings mainly of metal:
  • site huts, modular exhibition elements etc.
- manufacture of metal doors, windows and their frames, shutters and gates

This class excludes:
- *manufacture of parts for marine or power boilers, see 2813*
- *manufacture of assembled railway track fixtures, see 2899*
- *manufacture of sections of ships, see 3511*

2812   Manufacture of tanks, reservoirs and containers of metal

This class includes:
- manufacture of reservoirs, tanks and similar containers of metal, of types normally installed as fixtures for storage or manufacturing use
- manufacture of metal containers for compressed or liquefied gas
- manufacture of central heating boilers and radiators

This class excludes:
- *manufacture of metal casks, drums, cans, pails, boxes etc. of a kind normally used for carrying and packing of goods (irrespective of size), see 2899*
- *manufacture of transport containers, see 3420*

2813   Manufacture of steam generators, except central heating hot water boilers

This class includes:
- manufacture of steam or other vapour generators
- manufacture of auxiliary plant for use with steam generators:
  • condensers, economizers, superheaters, steam collectors and accumulators

- manufacture of nuclear reactors, except isotope separators
- manufacture of parts for marine or power boilers

This class excludes:
- *manufacture of central heating hot-water boilers and radiators, see 2812*
- *manufacture of boiler-turbine sets, see 2911*
- *manufacture of isotope separators, see 2929*

289   Manufacture of other fabricated metal products; metalworking service activities

2891   Forging, pressing, stamping and roll-forming of metal; powder metallurgy

This class includes:
- forging, pressing, stamping and roll forming of metal
- powder metallurgy: production of metal objects directly from metal powders by heat treatment (sintering) or under pressure

This class excludes:
- *production of metal powder, see 2710, 2720*

2892   Treatment and coating of metals; general mechanical engineering on a fee or contract basis

This class includes:
- plating, anodizing etc. of metal
- heat treatment of metal
- deburring, sandblasting, tumbling, cleaning of metals
- colouring, engraving, printing of metal
- non-metallic coating of metal:
  • plastifying, enamelling, lacquering etc.
- hardening, buffing of metal
- boring, turning, milling, eroding, planing, lapping, broaching, levelling, sawing, grinding, sharpening, polishing, welding, splicing etc. of metalwork pieces
- cutting of and writing on metals by means of laser beams

This class excludes:
- *rolling precious metals onto base metals or other metals, see 2720*
- *"while-you-wait" engraving services, see 5260*

2893   Manufacture of cutlery, hand tools and general hardware

This class includes:
- manufacture of domestic cutlery such as knives, forks, spoons etc.
- manufacture of other articles of cutlery:
  • cleavers and choppers
  • razors and razor blades
  • scissors and hair clippers
- manufacture of knives and cutting blades for machines or for mechanical appliances
- manufacture of hand tools such as pliers, screwdrivers etc.
- manufacture of non-power-driven agricultural hand tools
- manufacture of saws and sawblades, including circular sawblades and chainsaw blades
- manufacture of interchangeable tools for hand tools, whether or not power-operated, or for machine tools: drills, punches, dies, milling cutters
- manufacture of blacksmiths' tools: forges, anvils etc.
- manufacture of vices, clamps
- manufacture of padlocks, locks, keys, hinges and the like, hardware for buildings, furniture, vehicles etc.
- manufacture of cutlasses, swords, bayonets etc.

This class excludes:
- *manufacture of hollowware (pots, kettles etc.), dinnerware (bowls, platters etc.) or flatware (plates, saucers etc.), see 2899*
- *manufacture of power-driven hand tools, see 2922*
- *manufacture of cutlery of precious metal, see 3691*

2899   Manufacture of other fabricated metal products n.e.c.

This class includes:
- manufacture of pails, cans, drums, buckets, boxes
- manufacture of tins and cans for food products, collapsible tubes and boxes
- manufacture of metallic closures
- manufacture of metal cable, plaited bands and similar articles
- manufacture of uninsulated metal cable or insulated cable not capable of being used as a conductor of electricity
- manufacture of articles made of wire: barbed wire, wire fencing, grill, netting, cloth etc.
- manufacture of nails and pins
- manufacture of rivets, washers and similar non-threaded products
- manufacture of screw machine products
- manufacture of bolts, screws, nuts and similar threaded products
- manufacture of springs (except watch springs):
  - leaf springs, helical springs, torsion bar springs
  - leaves for springs
- manufacture of chain, except power transmission chain
- manufacture of metal household articles:
  - flatware: plates, saucers etc.
  - hollowware: pots, kettles etc.
  - dinnerware: bowls, platters etc.
  - saucepans, frying pans and other non-electrical utensils for use at the table or in the kitchen
  - small hand-operated kitchen appliances and accessories
  - metal scouring pads
- manufacture of baths, sinks, washbasins and similar articles
- manufacture of metal goods for office use, except furniture
- manufacture of safes, strongboxes, armoured doors etc.
- manufacture of various metal articles:
  - ship propellers and blades therefor
  - anchors
  - bells
  - assembled railway track fixtures
  - metal safety headgear
  - clasps, buckles, hooks
  - sign plates

This class excludes:
- *manufacture of tanks and reservoirs, see 2812*
- *manufacture of swords, bayonets, see 2893*
- *manufacture of power transmission chain, see 2913*
- *manufacture of wire and cable for electricity transmission, see 3130*
- *manufacture of clock or watch springs, see 3330*
- *manufacture of metal furniture, see 3610*
- *manufacture of sports goods, see 3693*
- *manufacture of games and toys, see 3694*

29   Manufacture of machinery and equipment n.e.c.

This division covers the manufacture of machinery and equipment that act independently on materials either mechanically or thermally or perform operations on materials (such as handling, spraying, weighing or packing), including their mechanical components that produce and apply force, and any specially manufactured primary parts. This category includes fixed and mobile or hand-held devices, regardless of whether they are designed for industrial, building and civil engineering, agricultural, military or home use. The manufacture of weapons and special equipment for passenger or freight transport within demarcated premises also belongs within this division.

The manufacture of metal products for general use (division 28), associated control devices, computer equipment, measurement and testing equipment, electricity distribution and control apparatus (divisions 30-33) and general-purpose motor vehicles (divisions 34 and 35) is excluded.

Division 29 distinguishes between the manufacture of general-purpose machinery and components and those with special applications and includes the manufacture of:
- motors and engines (except electric motors), turbines, pumps, compressors, valves and transmissions
- ovens, burners, lifting and handling equipment, cooling and ventilation equipment, other general-purpose machinery (e.g. packaging equipment, weighing machines and water purification equipment)
- agricultural machinery, machine tools, machinery for other specific industrial purposes (e.g. for metal production, building and civil engineering, mining or the manufacture of foodstuffs, textiles, paper, printed matter, plastic and rubber products)
- weapons and munitions
- domestic appliances (electrical and non-electrical)

291   Manufacture of general-purpose machinery

2911   Manufacture of engines and turbines, except aircraft, vehicle and cycle engines

This class includes:
- manufacture of internal combustion piston engines and parts thereof, except motor vehicle, aircraft and cycle propulsion engines:
  - marine engines
  - railway engines
- manufacture of turbines and parts thereof:
  - steam turbines and other vapour turbines
  - hydraulic turbines, waterwheels and regulators thereof
  - wind turbines
  - gas turbines, except turbojets or turbopropellers for aircraft propulsion
- manufacture of boiler-turbine sets

This class excludes:
- *manufacture of electric generator sets, see 3110*
- *manufacture of electrical equipment and components of internal combustion engines, see 3190*
- *manufacture of motor vehicle, aircraft or cycle propulsion engines, see 3410, 3530, 3591*
- *manufacture of turbojets and turbopropellers, see 3530*

2912   Manufacture of pumps, compressors, taps and valves

This class includes:
- manufacture of air or vacuum pumps, air or other gas compressors
- manufacture of pumps for liquids whether or not fitted with a measuring device

- manufacture of pumps designed for fitting to internal combustion engines: oil, water and fuel pumps for motor vehicles etc.

This class also includes:
- manufacture of fluid power equipment and pneumatic engines and motors
- manufacture of industrial taps and valves, including regulating valves and intake taps
- manufacture of sanitary taps and valves
- manufacture of heating taps and valves
- manufacture of hand pumps

This class excludes:
- *manufacture of valves of unhardened vulcanized rubber, glass or of ceramic materials, see 2519, 2610 or 2691*
- *manufacture of hydraulic transmission equipment, see 2913*
- *manufacture of household-type fans, see 2930*
- *manufacture of inlet and exhaust valves of internal combustion engines, see 3430, 3530*

2913 **Manufacture of bearings, gears, gearing and driving elements**

This class includes:
- manufacture of ball and roller bearings and parts thereof
- manufacture of mechanical power transmission equipment:
  • transmission shafts and cranks: camshafts, crankshafts, cranks etc.
  • bearing housings and plain shaft bearings
- manufacture of gears, gearing and gear boxes and other speed changers
- manufacture of clutches and shaft couplings
- manufacture of flywheels and pulleys
- manufacture of articulated link chain
- manufacture of power transmission chain
- manufacture of hydraulic transmission equipment

This class excludes:
- *manufacture of other chain, see 2899*
- *manufacture of electromagnetic clutches, see 3190*
- *manufacture of sub-assemblies of power transmission equipment identifiable as parts of vehicles or aircraft, see divisions 34 and 35*

2914 **Manufacture of ovens, furnaces and furnace burners**

This class includes:
- manufacture of electrical and other industrial and laboratory furnaces and ovens, including incinerators
- manufacture of burners

This class also includes:
- manufacture of mechanical stokers, grates, ash dischargers etc.

This class excludes:
- *manufacture of agricultural dryers, see 2925*
- *manufacture of bakery ovens, see 2925*
- *manufacture of dryers for wood, paper pulp, paper or paperboard, see 2929*
- *manufacture of household ovens, see 2930*
- *manufacture of medical, surgical or laboratory sterilizers, see 3311*

2915 **Manufacture of lifting and handling equipment**

This class includes:
- manufacture of hand-operated or power-driven lifting, handling, loading or unloading machinery:
  • pulley tackle and hoists, winches, capstans and jacks

- derricks, cranes, mobile lifting frames, straddle carriers etc.
- works trucks, whether or not fitted with lifting or handling equipment, whether or not self-propelled, of the type used in factories
- mechanical manipulators and industrial robots specifically designed for lifting, handling, loading or unloading
- manufacture of conveyors, teleferics etc.
- manufacture of lifts, escalators and moving walkways
- manufacture of parts specialized for lifting and handling equipment

This class also includes:
- maintenance of lifts and escalators

This class excludes:
- *manufacture of continuous-action elevators and conveyors for underground use, see 2924*
- *manufacture of mechanical shovels, excavators and shovel loaders, see 2924*
- *manufacture of industrial robots for multiple uses, see 2929*
- *manufacture of floating cranes, railway cranes, crane-lorries, see 3511, 3520*
- *installation of lifts and elevators, see 4530*

2919   Manufacture of other general-purpose machinery

This class includes:
- manufacture of refrigerating or freezing industrial equipment, including assemblies of major components
- manufacture of air-conditioning machines, including for motor vehicles
- manufacture of non-domestic fans
- manufacture of weighing machinery (other than sensitive laboratory balances):
  - household and shop scales, platform scales, scales for continuous weighing, weighbridges, weights etc.
- manufacture of filtering or purifying machinery and apparatus for liquids
- manufacture of equipment for projecting, dispersing or spraying liquids or powders:
  - spray guns, fire extinguishers, sandblasting machines, steam cleaning machines etc.
- manufacture of packing and wrapping machinery:
  - filling, closing, sealing, capsuling or labelling machines etc.
- manufacture of machinery for cleaning or drying bottles and for aerating beverages
- manufacture of distilling or rectifying plant for petroleum refineries, chemical industries, beverage industries etc.
- manufacture of heat exchangers
- manufacture of machinery for liquefying air or gas
- manufacture of gas generators
- manufacture of calendering or other rolling machines and cylinders thereof (except for metal and glass)
- manufacture of centrifuges (except cream separators and clothes dryers)
- manufacture of gaskets and similar joints made of a combination of materials or layers of the same material
- manufacture of automatic goods vending machines
- manufacture of parts for general-purpose machinery

This class excludes:
- *manufacture of agricultural spraying machinery, see 2921*
- *manufacture of metal or glass rolling machinery and cylinders thereof, see 2923, 2929*
- *manufacture of agricultural dryers, machinery for filtering or purifying food, see 2925*
- *manufacture of cream separators, see 2925*
- *manufacture of industrial clothes dryers, see 2929*
- *manufacture of domestic refrigerating or freezing equipment, see 2930*
- *manufacture of domestic fans, see 2930*
- *manufacture of sensitive balances, see 3312*

292   Manufacture of special-purpose machinery

2921   Manufacture of agricultural and forestry machinery

This class includes:
- manufacture of tractors used in agriculture and forestry
- manufacture of walking (pedestrian-controlled) tractors
- manufacture of mowers, including lawnmowers
- manufacture of agricultural self-loading or self-unloading trailers or semi-trailers
- manufacture of agricultural machinery for soil preparation, planting or fertilizing:
  - ploughs, manure spreaders, seeders, harrows etc.
- manufacture of harvesting or threshing machinery:
  - harvesters, threshers, sorters etc.
- manufacture of milking machines
- manufacture of spraying machinery for agricultural use
- manufacture of diverse agricultural machinery:
  - poultry-keeping machinery, bee-keeping machinery, equipment for preparing fodder etc.
  - machines for cleaning, sorting or grading eggs, fruit etc.

This class excludes:
- *manufacture of non-power-driven agricultural hand tools, see 2893*
- *manufacture of conveyors for farm use, see 2915*
- *manufacture of power-driven hand tools, see 2922*
- *manufacture of cream separators, see 2925*
- *manufacture of machinery to clean, sort or grade seed, grain or dried leguminous vegetables, see 2925*
- *manufacture of road tractors for semi-trailers, see 3410*
- *manufacture of road trailers or semi-trailers, see 3420*

2922   Manufacture of machine tools

This class includes:
- manufacture of machine tools for working metals and other materials (wood, bone, stone, hard rubber, hard plastics, cold glass etc.), including those using a laser beam, ultrasonic waves, plasma arc, magnetic pulse etc.
- manufacture of machine tools for turning, drilling, milling, shaping, planning, boring, grinding etc.
- manufacture of stamping or pressing machine tools
- manufacture of punch presses, hydraulic presses, hydraulic brakes, drop hammers, forging machines etc.
- manufacture of draw-benches, thread rollers or machines for working wires
- manufacture of machines for nailing, stapling, glueing or otherwise assembling wood, cork, bone, hard rubber or plastics etc.
- manufacture of gas or electric welding, brazing or soldering machines
- manufacture of hand tools, with self-contained electric or non-electric motor or pneumatic drive
- manufacture of rotary or rotary percussion drills, chainsaws, filing machines, riveters, sheet metal cutters etc.
- manufacture of presses for the manufacture of particle board and the like

This class also includes:
- manufacture of parts and accessories for the machine tools listed above: work holders, dividing heads and other special attachments for machine tools

This class excludes:
- *manufacture of interchangeable tools for hand tools or machine tools (drills, punches, dies, taps, milling cutters, turning tools, saw blades, cutting knives etc.), see 2893*

- *manufacture of machinery used in metal mills or foundries, see 2923*
- *manufacture of machinery for mining and quarrying, see 2924*

2923   Manufacture of machinery for metallurgy

This class includes:
- manufacture of machines and equipment for handling hot metals:
  - converters, ingot moulds, ladles, casting machines
- manufacture of metal-rolling mills and rolls for such mills

This class excludes:
- *manufacture of draw-benches, see 2922*
- *manufacture of moulding boxes and moulds (except ingot moulds), see 2929*
- *manufacture of machines for forming foundry moulds, see 2929*

2924   Manufacture of machinery for mining, quarrying and construction

This class includes:
- manufacture of continuous-action elevators and conveyors for underground use
- manufacture of boring, cutting, sinking and tunnelling machinery (whether or not for underground use)
- manufacture of machinery for treating minerals by screening, sorting, separating, washing, crushing etc.
- manufacture of concrete and mortar mixers
- manufacture of earth-moving machinery:
  - bulldozers, angle-dozers, graders, scrapers, levellers, mechanical shovels, shovel loaders etc.
- manufacture of piledrivers and pile-extractors, mortar spreaders, bitumen spreaders, concrete surfacing machinery etc.
- manufacture of tracklaying tractors and tractors used in construction or mining
- manufacture of bulldozer and angle-dozer blades

This class excludes:
- *manufacture of lifting and handling equipment, see 2915*
- *manufacture of other tractors, see 2921, 3410*
- *manufacture of machine tools for working stone, including machines for splitting or clearing stone, see 2922*
- *manufacture of concrete-mixer lorries, see 3410*

2925   Manufacture of machinery for food, beverage and tobacco processing

This class includes:
- manufacture of agricultural dryers
- manufacture of machinery for the dairy industry:
  - cream separators
  - milk processing machinery (homogenizers and irradiators)
  - milk converting machinery (butter chums, butter workers and moulding machines)
  - cheese-making machines (homogenizers, moulders, presses) etc.
- manufacture of machinery for the grain milling industry:
  - machinery to clean, sort or grade seeds, grain or dried leguminous vegetables (winnowers, sieving belts, separators, grain brushing machines etc.)
  - machinery to produce flour and meal etc. (grinding mills, feeders, sifters, bran cleaners, blenders, rice hullers, pea splitters)
- manufacture of presses, crushers etc. used to make wine, cider, fruit juices etc.
- manufacture of machinery for the bakery industry or for making macaroni, spaghetti or similar products:
  - bakery ovens, dough mixers, dough-dividers, moulders, slicers, cake depositing machines etc.

- manufacture of machines and equipment to process diverse foods:
  - machinery to make confectionery, cocoa or chocolate; to manufacture sugar; for breweries; to process meat or poultry, to prepare fruit, nuts or vegetables; to prepare fish, shellfish or other seafood
  - machinery for filtering and purifying
  - other machinery for the industrial preparation or manufacture of food or drink
- manufacture of machinery for the extraction or preparation of animal or vegetable fats or oils
- manufacture of machinery for the preparation of tobacco and for the making of cigarettes or cigars, or for pipe or chewing tobacco or snuff
- manufacture of machinery for the preparation of food in hotels and restaurants

This class excludes:
- *manufacture of packing, wrapping and weighing machinery, see 2919*
- *manufacture of cleaning, sorting or grading machinery for eggs, fruit or other crops (except seeds, grains and dried leguminous vegetables), see 2921*

2926   Manufacture of machinery for textile, apparel and leather production

This class includes:
- manufacture of textile machinery:
  - machines for preparing, producing, extruding, drawing, texturing or cutting man-made textile fibres, materials or yarns
  - machines for preparing textile fibres: cotton gins, bale breakers, garnetters, cotton spreaders, wool scouters, wool carbonizers, combs, carders, roving frames etc.
  - spinning machines
  - machines for preparing textile yarns: reelers, warpers and related machines
  - weaving machines (looms), including hand looms
  - knitting machines
  - machines for making knotted net, tulle, lace, braid etc.
- manufacture of auxiliary machines or equipment for textile machinery:
  - dobbies, jacquards, automatic stop motions, shuttle changing mechanisms, spindles and spindle flyers etc.
- manufacture of machinery for fabric processing:
  - machinery for washing, bleaching, dyeing, dressing, finishing, coating or impregnating textile fabrics
  - manufacture of machines for reeling, unreeling, folding, cutting or pinking textile fabrics
- manufacture of laundry machinery:
  - ironing machines, including fusing presses
  - commercial washing and drying machines
  - dry-cleaning machines
- manufacture of sewing machines, sewing machine heads and sewing machine needles (whether or not for household use)
- manufacture of machines for producing or finishing felt or non-wovens
- manufacture of leather machines:
  - machinery for preparing, tanning or working hides, skins or leather
  - machinery for making or repairing footwear or other articles of hides, skins, leather or fur skins

This class excludes:
- *manufacture of paper or paperboard cards for use on jacquard machines, see 2109*
- *manufacture of ironing machines of the calender type, see 2919*
- *manufacture of machines used in bookbinding, see 2929*
- *manufacture of textile printing machinery, see 2929*
- *manufacture of domestic washing and drying machines, see 2930*

2927   Manufacture of weapons and ammunition

This class includes:
- manufacture of tanks and other fighting vehicles
- manufacture of heavy weapons (artillery, mobile guns, rocket launchers, torpedo tubes, heavy machine guns)
- manufacture of small arms (revolvers, shotguns, light machine guns)
- manufacture of air or gas guns and pistols
- manufacture of war ammunition
- manufacture of military ballistic and guided missiles

This class also includes:
- manufacture of hunting, sporting or protective firearms and ammunition
- manufacture of explosive devices such as bombs, mines and torpedoes

This class excludes:
- *manufacture of percussion caps, detonators or signalling flares, see 2429*
- *manufacture of cutlasses, swords, bayonets etc., see 2893*
- *manufacture of armoured vehicles for the transport of banknotes or valuables, see 3410*

2929   Manufacture of other special-purpose machinery

This class includes manufacture of special-purpose machinery not elsewhere classified.

This class includes:
- manufacture of machinery for making paper pulp
- manufacture of paper and paperboard making machinery
- manufacture of dryers for wood, paper pulp, paper or paperboard
- manufacture of machinery producing articles of paper or paperboard
- manufacture of machinery for working soft rubber or plastics or for the manufacture of products of these materials:
    • extruders, moulders, pneumatic tyre making or retreading machines and other machines for making a specific rubber or plastic product
- manufacture of printing and bookbinding machines and machines for activities supporting printing, including machines for printing on textiles and other materials
- manufacture of moulding boxes for any material; mould bases; moulding patterns; moulds (except ingot moulds)
- machinery for producing tiles, bricks, shaped ceramic pastes, pipes, graphite electrodes, blackboard chalk, foundry moulds etc.
- manufacture of semi-conductor manufacturing machinery
- manufacture of industrial robots for multiple uses
- manufacture of diverse special machinery and equipment:
    • machines to assemble electric or electronic lamps, tubes (valves) or bulbs
    • machines for production or hot-working of glass or glassware, glass fibre or yarn
    • machinery or apparatus for isotopic separation
    • manufacture of industrial clothes dryers

This class excludes:
- *manufacture of machinery or equipment to work hard rubber, hard plastics or cold glass, see 2922*
- *manufacture of ingot moulds, see 2923*
- *manufacture of household appliances, see 2930*
- *manufacture of photocopy machines etc., see 3000*

293   **Manufacture of domestic appliances n.e.c.**

2930   **Manufacture of domestic appliances n.e.c.**

This class includes:
- manufacture of domestic electric appliances:
  - refrigerators and freezers, dishwashers, washing and drying machines, vacuum cleaners, floor polishers, waste disposers, grinders, blenders, juice squeezers, tin openers, electric shavers, electric toothbrushes, knife sharpeners, ventilating or recycling hoods
- manufacture of domestic electrothermic appliances:
  - electric water heaters; electric blankets, electric dryers, combs, brushes, curlers; electric smoothing irons; space heaters and household-type fans; electric ovens, microwave ovens, cookers, hotplates, toasters, coffee or tea makers, frypans, roasters, grills, hoods, electric heating resistors etc.
- manufacture of domestic non-electric cooking and heating equipment:
  - non-electric space heaters, cooking ranges, grates, stoves, water heaters, cooking appliances, plate warmers

This class excludes:
- *manufacture of industrial or commercial equipment, see groups 291 and 292*
- *manufacture of industrial refrigeration and freezing equipment, see 2919*
- *manufacture of machinery for the preparation of food in commercial kitchens, see 2925*
- *manufacture of commercial washing and drying machines, see 2926*
- *manufacture of sewing machines, see 2926*

30   **Manufacture of office, accounting and computing machinery**

The manufacture of office machinery (e.g. photocopiers, cash registers etc.) and computer equipment (e.g. computers, word processors and peripherals) is considered to include installation, but not maintenance (725), software design (722) or the manufacture of electronic components (321).

300   **Manufacture of office, accounting and computing machinery**

3000   **Manufacture of office, accounting and computing machinery**

This class includes:
- manufacture of manual or electric typewriters
- manufacture of word-processing machines
- manufacture of hectograph or stencil duplicating machines, addressing machines and sheet-fed office-type offset printing machines
- manufacture of calculating machines, cash registers, postage franking machines, special terminals for issuing of tickets and reservations etc.
- manufacture of photocopy machines
- manufacture of automatic data processing machines, including microcomputers:
  - digital machines
  - analog machines
  - hybrid machines
- manufacture of peripheral units:
  - terminals, printers, plotters etc.
  - input devices: keyboards, mice, joysticks, pens and graphic tablets etc.
  - magnetic or optical readers and writers
  - computer storage devices
- manufacture of diverse office machinery or equipment:
  - machines that sort, wrap or count coins; automatic banknote dispensers; machines that stuff envelopes, sort mail; pencil sharpening machines; perforating or stapling machines etc.

This class excludes:
- *manufacture of electronic components found in computing machinery, see 3210*
- *manufacture of electronic games, see 3694*
- *repair and maintenance of computer systems, see 7250*

31   Manufacture of electrical machinery and apparatus n.e.c.

This division includes the manufacture of products that generate, distribute and store electrical power. Also included is the manufacture of electrical lighting and signalling equipment.

This division excludes the manufacture of electronics products (division 32) and electric household appliances (division 29).

311   Manufacture of electric motors, generators and transformers

3110   Manufacture of electric motors, generators and transformers

This class includes:
- manufacture of alternating current (AC) motors or generators
- manufacture of direct current (DC) motors or generators
- manufacture of universal AC/DC motors
- manufacture of AC or DC generator sets
- manufacture of electric rotary or static converters
- manufacture of electrical transformers

This class excludes:
- *manufacture of vehicle generators and cranking motors, see 3190*
- *manufacture of diodes, see 3210*

312   Manufacture of electricity distribution and control apparatus

3120   Manufacture of electricity distribution and control apparatus

This class includes:
- manufacture of electrical apparatus for switching or protecting electrical circuits, or for making connections to or in electrical circuits:
  - switches, fuses, lightning arresters, voltage limiters, surge suppressors, plugs, junction boxes, relays, sockets, lamp holders
- manufacture of electric control or distribution boards, panels, consoles, desks, cabinets and other bases

This class also includes:
- manufacture of boards and panels equipped with devices classified in class 3312

This class excludes:
- *manufacture of parts of these apparatus, made of moulded plastics, glass or ceramic material, see 2520, 2610, 2691*
- *manufacture of fuse wire or strip, see 2720*
- *manufacture of carbon or graphite electrodes, see 3190*
- *manufacture of boards, panels, consoles etc. for use in line telephony or line telegraphy, see 3220*

313   Manufacture of insulated wire and cable

3130   Manufacture of insulated wire and cable

This class includes:
- manufacture of insulated wire, cable, strip and other insulated conductors, whether or not fitted with connectors

- manufacture of optical fibre cables for coded data transmission: telecommunications, video, control, data etc.

This class excludes:
- *manufacture of uninsulated non-ferrous metal wire, see 2720*
- *manufacture of uninsulated metal cable or insulated cable not capable of being used as a conductor of electricity, see 2899*
- *manufacture of wiring sets, see 3190*
- *manufacture of optical fibres and optical fibre cables for live transmission of images: endoscopy, lighting, live images, see 3320*

314 Manufacture of accumulators, primary cells and primary batteries

3140 Manufacture of accumulators, primary cells and primary batteries

This class includes:
- manufacture of primary cells and primary batteries
  • cells containing manganese dioxide, mercuric dioxide, silver oxide etc.
- manufacture of electric accumulators, including parts thereof:
  • separators, containers, covers
  • lead-acid, nickel-cadmium, nickel-iron accumulators etc.

315 Manufacture of electric lamps and lighting equipment

3150 Manufacture of electric lamps and lighting equipment

This class includes:
- manufacture of electric filament or discharge lamps:
  • ultraviolet or infrared lamps
  • arc lamps
  • flashbulbs, flash cubes etc.
- manufacture of electric lamps and lighting fittings:
  • chandeliers, table, desk, bedside or floor-standing lamps, even non-electric
  • portable electric lamps
  • illuminated signs and nameplates etc., including neon signs
  • outdoor and road lighting
  • lighting sets of a kind used for Christmas trees

This class also includes:
- manufacture of non-electric lighting equipment:
  • gas lamps
  • miners' carbide lights
- manufacture of lighting equipment for vehicles, except motor vehicles and cycles

This class excludes:
- *manufacture of lighting equipment for motor vehicles and cycles, see 3190*
- *manufacture of electronic discharge lamps and photo flash apparatus, see 3320*

319 Manufacture of other electrical equipment n.e.c.

3190 Manufacture of other electrical equipment n.e.c.

This class includes:
- manufacture of electrical ignition or starting equipment for internal combustion engines: ignition magnetos, magneto-dynamos, ignition coils, sparking plugs, glow plugs, starter motors, generators (dynamos, alternators), voltage regulators etc.
- manufacture of wiring sets and wiring harnesses
- manufacture of windscreen wipers and electrical defrosters and demisters for motor vehicles

and motorcycles
- manufacture of defrosters and demisters with electrical resistors for aircraft, ships, trains etc.
- manufacture of dynamos for cycles
- manufacture of electrical lighting and sound or visual signalling equipment for cycles and motor vehicles: lamps, horns, sirens etc.
- manufacture of electrical signalling, safety or traffic control equipment for motorways, roads or streets, railways and tramways, inland waterways, ports and harbours and airports
- manufacture of diverse electrical sound or visual signalling apparatus:
    • bells, sirens, indicator panels, burglar and fire alarms etc.
- manufacture of electromagnets, including electromagnetic or permanent magnet chucks, clutches, brakes, couplings, clamps or lifting heads
- manufacture of electrical insulators and insulating fittings, except of glass or ceramics
- manufacture of insulating fittings for electrical machines or equipment, except of ceramics or plastics
- manufacture of carbon or graphite electrodes
- manufacture of electrical conduit tubing and joints for such tubing, of base metal lined with insulating material
- manufacture of diverse electrical machines and apparatus:
    • particle accelerators, signal generators, mine detectors etc.

This class excludes:
- *manufacture of glass envelopes for lamps, see 2610*
- *manufacture of hand-held electrically operated spray guns, see 2919*
- *manufacture of electric lawnmowers, see 2921*
- *manufacture of electric household appliances, see 2930*
- *manufacture of electronic valves and tubes (including cold cathode valves), see 3210*
- *manufacture of electrically operated hand-held medical or dental instruments, see 3311*

32   Manufacture of radio, television and communication equipment and apparatus

This division covers the manufacture of electronic equipment for broadcasting and transmission, data communications equipment, receivers, recorders and reproduction equipment. The division covers all intermediate products from professional equipment to that for the general public.

It should be pointed out that the installation and repair of professional equipment are also covered by this division. On the other hand, the repair of household equipment falls under 5260, and the installation of wiring, aerials or alarms falls under construction (4530).

321   Manufacture of electronic valves and tubes and other electronic components

3210   Manufacture of electronic valves and tubes and other electronic components

This class includes:
- manufacture of thermionic, cold cathode or photocathode valves or tubes:
    • television picture tubes, television camera tubes, image converters and intensifiers, microwave tubes, receiver or amplifier valves or tubes etc.
- manufacture of diodes, transistors and similar semiconductor devices
- manufacture of photosensitive semiconductor devices, including photovoltaic cells and single solar cells
- manufacture of mounted piezoelectric crystals
- manufacture of electronic integrated circuits and micro-assemblies:
    • monolithic integrated circuits, hybrid integrated circuits and electronic micro-assemblies of moulded module, micromodule or similar types
- manufacture of printed circuit boards, bare boards
- manufacture of electrical capacitors (or condensers), including power capacitors
- manufacture of resistors, including rheostats and potentiometers
- manufacture of electronic components for use on printed circuits, except transformers
- manufacture of liquid crystal displays (LCDs)

This class excludes:
- *manufacture of loaded printed circuit assemblies (classified in the same class as the manufacture of the complete machine)*
- *manufacture of transformers, see 3110*
- *manufacture of switches, see 3120*

322   Manufacture of television and radio transmitters and apparatus for line telephony and line telegraphy

3220   Manufacture of television and radio transmitters and apparatus for line telephony and line telegraphy

This class includes:
- manufacture of apparatus for television transmission, including manufacture of relay transmitters and television transmitters for industrial use
- manufacture of television cameras
- manufacture of transmission apparatus for radio-broadcasting
- manufacture of transmission apparatus for radio-telephony:
  • fixed transmitters and transmitter-receivers, radio-telephony apparatus for transport equipment, radio-telephones, other transponders etc.
- manufacture of apparatus for line telephony:
  • telephone sets, fax machines, automatic and non-automatic switchboards and exchanges, telex and teleprinter apparatus etc.
- manufacture of mobile telephones
- manufacture of data communications equipment:
  • routers, gateways, hubs, bridges

This class also includes:
- installation of telecommunications equipment

This class excludes:
- *manufacture of electronic components, see 3210*
- *installation of electrical or telecommunications wiring in buildings, see 4530*
- *repair of mobile telephones, see 5260*

323   Manufacture of television and radio receivers, sound or video recording or reproducing apparatus, and associated goods

3230   Manufacture of television and radio receivers, sound or video recording or reproducing apparatus, and associated goods

This class includes:
- manufacture of television receivers, including video monitors and video projectors
- manufacture of video recording or reproducing apparatus, including camcorders
- manufacture of digital cameras
- manufacture of radio-broadcasting receivers
- manufacture of magnetic tape recorders and other sound recording apparatus, including telephone answering machines, cassette-type recorders etc.
- manufacture of turntables (record decks), record players, cassette players
- manufacture of CD players, DVD players etc.
- manufacture of microphones, loudspeakers, headphones, earphones, amplifiers and sound amplifier sets
- manufacture of specialized parts for equipment in this class:
  • pick-ups, tone arms, sound-heads, tables for turntables, aerials, aerial reflectors and aerial rotors, cable converters, TV decoders

This class also includes:
- manufacture of sound electro-acoustic apparatus, conference systems, portable sound systems

This class excludes:
- *publishing and reproduction of pre-recorded audio and video discs and tapes, see groups 221 and 223, 9211*
- *manufacture of prepared unrecorded media, see 2429*

33 Manufacture of medical, precision and optical instruments, watches and clocks

This division covers not only scientific and technical instruments (e.g. electro-diagnostic apparatus, avionic equipment etc.) but also photographic and cinematographic equipment, industrial process control equipment, and personal goods (e.g. watches, spectacles etc.).

This division also includes the installation and repair of such industrial equipment, although the repair of personal goods falls under group 526.

331 Manufacture of medical appliances and instruments and appliances for measuring, checking, testing, navigating and other purposes, except optical instruments

3311 Manufacture of medical and surgical equipment and orthopaedic appliances

This class includes:
- manufacture of instruments and appliances used for medical, surgical, dental or veterinary purposes:
  - electro-diagnostic apparatus such as electrocardiographs, ultrasonic diagnostic equipment, scintillation scanners, nuclear magnetic resonance apparatus, dental drill engines, sterilizers, ophthalmic instruments
- manufacture of syringes, needles used in medicine
- manufacture of mirrors, reflectors, endoscopes etc.
- manufacture of apparatus based on the use of X-rays or alpha, beta or gamma radiation, whether or not for use in human or animal medicine:
  - X-ray tubes, high-tension generators, control panels, desks, screens etc.
- manufacture of medical, surgical, dental or veterinary furniture:
  - operating tables, hospital beds with mechanical fittings, dentists' chairs, barbers' chairs
- manufacture of mechanotherapy appliances, massage apparatus, psychological testing apparatus, ozone therapy, oxygen therapy, artificial respiration apparatus, gas masks etc.

This class also includes:
- manufacture of orthopaedic appliances:
  - crutches, surgical belts and trusses, splints, artificial teeth, artificial limbs and other artificial parts of the body, hearing aids, pacemakers, orthopaedic shoes etc.

This class excludes:
- *manufacture of surgical dressings, medicated wadding, fracture bandages etc., see 2423*
- *manufacture of cement used in dentistry, see 2423*
- *manufacture of thermometers, see 3312*
- *manufacture of corrective spectacle lenses and of their frames or of optical microscopes, see 3320*
- *denture fitting by dentists or spectacles fitting by optometrists, see 8512, 8519*

3312 Manufacture of instruments and appliances for measuring, checking, testing, navigating and other purposes, except industrial process control equipment

This class includes:
- manufacture of laboratory-type sensitive balances
- manufacture of drawing, marking-out or mathematical calculating instruments:

113

- measuring rods and tapes, micrometers, callipers and gauges etc.
- manufacture of microscopes other than optical microscopes and diffraction apparatus
- manufacture of apparatus for measuring and checking electrical quantities:
  - oscilloscopes, spectrum analyzers, crosstalk meters, instruments for checking current, voltage, resistance etc.
- manufacture of apparatus for measuring or checking non-electrical quantities:
  - radiation detectors and counters, apparatus for testing and regulating vehicle motors etc.
- manufacture of navigational, meteorological, geophysical and related instruments and apparatus:
  - surveying instruments, oceanographic or hydrologic instruments, seismometers, range-finders, automatic pilots, sextants, ultrasonic sounding instruments etc.
  - air navigation instruments and systems, radar apparatus, radio navigational aid apparatus
- manufacture of electricity supply meters and supply meters for water, gas, petrol etc.
- manufacture of machines and appliances for testing the mechanical properties of materials
- manufacture of instruments and apparatus for carrying out physical or chemical analyses:
  - polarimeters, photometers, refractometers, colorimeters, spectrometers, pH-meters, viscometers, surface tension instruments etc.
- manufacture of instruments and apparatus for measuring or checking the flow, level, pressure or other variables of liquids or gases:
  - flow meters, level gauges, manometers, heat meters etc.
- manufacture of diverse measuring, checking or testing instruments, apparatus or machines:
  - hydrometers, thermometers, barometers, revolution counters, taximeters, pedometers, tachometers, balancing machines, test benches, comparators etc.
- manufacture of automatic regulating or controlling instruments and apparatus (except industrial process control equipment):
  - thermostats, pressure controller, humidity regulators
  - regulators of electrical quantities

This class excludes:
- *manufacture of pumps incorporating measuring devices, see 2912*
- *manufacture of medical and surgical instruments, see 3311*
- *manufacture of industrial process control equipment, see 3313*
- *manufacture of binoculars, monoculars and similar optical devices, see 3320*
- *manufacture of optical microscopes, see 3320*

3313   Manufacture of industrial process control equipment

This class includes:
- manufacture of instruments and apparatus used for automatic continuous measurement and control of variables such as temperature, pressure, viscosity and the like of materials or products as they are being manufactured or otherwise processed

332   Manufacture of optical instruments and photographic equipment

3320   Manufacture of optical instruments and photographic equipment

This class includes:
- manufacture of optical elements mounted or not:
  - prisms, lenses, optical mirrors, colour filters, polarizing elements etc. of glass or other material
  - optical fibres and optical fibre cables for live transmission of images: endoscopy, lighting, live images
  - spectacle lenses and contact lenses
  - spectacle frames and frames fitted with lenses, whether or not the lenses are optically worked: sunglasses, protective glasses, corrective glasses etc.
  - unworked optical elements other than of glass

- manufacture of optical instruments:
  - optical microscopes, equipment for microphotography and microprojection, magnifying glasses, reading glasses, thread counters etc.
  - binoculars, sight telescopes, telescopic sights and observation telescopes, astronomical equipment etc.
  - lasers, excluding laser diodes etc.
  - mounted, optically worked glass mirrors, door eyes etc.
- manufacture of photographic and cinematographic equipment:
  - cameras
  - image projectors, enlargers and reducers
  - cinematographic projectors, including those incorporating sound reproducing apparatus
  - photo flash apparatus
  - apparatus and equipment for photographic and cinematographic laboratories, apparatus for the projection of circuit patterns on sensitized semiconductor materials, projection screens

This class excludes:
- *manufacture of photochemical products, see 2429*
- *manufacture of unworked glass optical elements, see 2610*
- *manufacture of photocopy machines, see 3000*
- *manufacture of optical fibre cables for coded data transmission, see 3130*
- *manufacture of photographic flashbulbs, see 3150*
- *manufacture of television cameras, see 3220*
- *manufacture of video cameras, see 3230*
- *manufacture of medical and surgical instruments containing optical elements (e.g. endoscopes), see 3311*
- *manufacture of microscopes other than optical, see 3312*
- *manufacture of measuring or checking appliances containing optical elements, see 3312*

333   Manufacture of watches and clocks

3330   Manufacture of watches and clocks

This class includes:
- manufacture of watches and clocks of all kinds, including instrument panel clocks; watch and clock cases, including cases of precious metals
- manufacture of time-recording equipment and equipment for measuring, recording and otherwise displaying intervals of time with a watch or clock movement or with synchronous motor, e.g. parking meters, process timers
- manufacture of time switches and other releases with a watch or clock movement or with synchronous motor
- manufacture of components for clocks and watches:
  - movements of all kinds for watches and clocks
  - springs, jewels, dials, hands, plates, bridges and other parts
- manufacture of metal watch straps, watch bands and watch bracelets, including those of precious metal

This class excludes:
- *manufacture of non-metallic watch bands, see 1912*

34   Manufacture of motor vehicles, trailers and semi-trailers

This class includes the manufacture of motor vehicles for transporting people or goods. The manufacture of various parts and accessories, as well as manufacture of trailers and semi-trailers, is included here.

The maintenance and repair of vehicles produced in this division are classified in 5020.

341   Manufacture of motor vehicles

3410   Manufacture of motor vehicles

This class includes:
- manufacture of passenger cars
- manufacture of commercial vehicles:
  - vans, lorries, over-the-road tractors for semi-trailers etc.
- manufacture of buses, trolley-buses and coaches
- manufacture of motor vehicle engines
- manufacture of chassis fitted with engines
- manufacture of other motor vehicles:
  - snowmobiles, golf carts, amphibious vehicles
  - fire engines, street sweepers, travelling libraries, armoured cars etc.
  - concrete-mixer lorries

This class excludes:
- *manufacture of agricultural tractors, see 2921*
- *manufacture of tractors used in construction or mining, see 2924*
- *manufacture of electrical parts for motor vehicles, see 3190*
- *manufacture of bodies for motor vehicles, see 3420*
- *manufacture of parts and accessories for motor vehicles, see 3430*
- *maintenance, repair and alteration of motor vehicles, see 5020*

342   Manufacture of bodies (coachwork) for motor vehicles; manufacture of trailers and semi-trailers

3420   Manufacture of bodies (coachwork) for motor vehicles; manufacture of trailers and semi-trailers

This class includes:
- manufacture of bodies, including cabs for motor vehicles
- outfitting of all types of motor vehicles, trailers and semi-trailers
- manufacture of trailers and semi-trailers:
  - for transport of goods: tankers, removal trailers etc.
  - for transport of passengers: caravan trailers etc.
- manufacture of containers for carriage by one or more modes of transport

This class excludes:
- *manufacture of trailers and semi-trailers specially designed for use in agriculture, see 2921*
- *manufacture of parts and accessories of bodies for motor vehicles, see 3430*
- *manufacture of vehicles drawn by animals, see 3599*

343   Manufacture of parts and accessories for motor vehicles and their engines

3430   Manufacture of parts and accessories for motor vehicles and their engines

This class includes:
- manufacture of diverse parts and accessories for motor vehicles:
  - brakes, gearboxes, axles, road wheels, suspension shock absorbers, radiators, silencers, exhaust pipes, catalysers, clutches, steering wheels, steering columns and steering boxes
- manufacture of parts and accessories of bodies for motor vehicles:
  - safety belts, airbags, doors, bumpers

This class also includes:
- manufacture of inlet and exhaust valves of internal combustion engines

This class excludes:
- *manufacture of pumps for motor vehicles and engines, see 2912*
- *manufacture of batteries for vehicles, see 3140*
- *manufacture of electrical equipment for motor vehicles, see 3190*
- *maintenance, repair and alteration of motor vehicles, see 5020*

35   Manufacture of other transport equipment

351   Building and repairing of ships and boats

3511   Building and repairing of ships

This class includes the building and repairing of ships, except vessels for sports or recreation, and construction and repair of floating structures.

This class includes:
- building of commercial vessels: passenger vessels, ferry-boats, cargo ships, tankers, tugs etc.
- building of warships
- building of fishing boats and fish-processing factory vessels

This class also includes:
- construction of hovercraft (except recreation-type hovercraft)
- construction of drilling platforms, floating or submersible
- construction of floating structures:
  - floating docks, pontoons, coffer-dams, floating landing stages, buoys, floating tanks, barges, lighters, floating cranes, non-recreational inflatable rafts etc.
- manufacture of sections for ships and floating structures

This class excludes:
- *manufacture of parts of vessels, other than major hull assemblies:*
  - *manufacture of sails, see 1721*
  - *manufacture of ships' propellers, see 2899*
  - *manufacture of iron or steel anchors, see 2899*
  - *manufacture of marine engines, see 2911*
- *manufacture of navigational instruments, see 3312*
- *manufacture of amphibious motor vehicles, see 3410*
- *manufacture of inflatable boats or rafts for recreation, see 3512*
- *ship-breaking, see 3710*

3512   Building and repairing of pleasure and sporting boats

This class includes:
- manufacture of inflatable boats and rafts
- building of sailboats with or without auxiliary motor
- building of motor boats
- building of recreation-type hovercraft
- building of other pleasure and sporting boats:
  - canoes, kayaks, rowing boats, skiffs
- maintenance, repair or alteration of pleasure boats

This class excludes:
- *manufacture of parts of pleasure and sporting boats:*
  - *manufacture of sails, see 1721*
  - *manufacture of iron or steel anchors, see 2899*
  - *manufacture of marine engines, see 2911*
- *manufacture of sailboards, see 3693*

352   Manufacture of railway and tramway locomotives and rolling stock

3520   Manufacture of railway and tramway locomotives and rolling stock

This class includes:
- manufacture of electric, diesel, steam and other rail locomotives
- manufacture of self-propelled railway or tramway coaches, vans and trucks, maintenance or service vehicles
- manufacture of railway or tramway rolling stock, not self-propelled:
  - passenger coaches, goods vans, tank wagons, self-discharging vans and wagons, workshop vans, crane vans, tenders etc.
- manufacture of specialized parts of railway or tramway locomotives or of rolling stock:
  - bogies, axles and wheels, brakes and parts of brakes; hooks and coupling devices, buffers and buffer parts; shock absorbers; wagon and locomotive frames; bodies; corridor connections etc.

This class also includes:
- manufacture of mechanical and electromechanical signalling, safety and traffic control equipment for railways, tramways, roads, inland waterways, parking facilities or airfields

This class excludes:
- *manufacture of unassembled rails, see 2710*
- *manufacture of engines and turbines, see 2911*
- *manufacture of electric motors, see 3110*
- *manufacture of electrical signalling, safety or traffic-control equipment, see 3190*

353   Manufacture of aircraft and spacecraft

3530   Manufacture of aircraft and spacecraft

This class includes:
- manufacture of aeroplanes for the transport of goods or passengers, for use by the defence forces, for sport or other purposes
- manufacture of helicopters
- manufacture of gliders, hang-gliders
- manufacture of dirigibles and balloons
- manufacture of spacecraft and spacecraft launch vehicles, satellites, planetary probes, orbital stations, shuttles
- manufacture of parts and accessories of the aircraft of this class:
  - major assemblies such as fuselages, wings, doors, control surfaces, landing gear, fuel tanks, nacelles etc.
  - airscrews, helicopter rotors and propelled rotor blades
  - motors and engines of a kind typically found on aircraft
  - parts of turbojets and turbopropellers for aircraft
- manufacture of aircraft launching gear, deck arresters etc.
- manufacture of ground flying trainers

This class also includes:
- maintenance, repair and alteration of aircraft or aircraft engines

This class excludes:
- *manufacture of parachutes, see 1721*
- *manufacture of military ballistic missiles, see 2927*
- *manufacture of ignition parts and other electrical parts for internal combustion engines, see 3190*
- *manufacture of aircraft instrumentation and aeronautical instruments, see 3312*
- *manufacture of air navigation systems, see 3312*

359   Manufacture of transport equipment n.e.c.

3591   Manufacture of motorcycles

This class includes:
- manufacture of motorcycles, mopeds and cycles fitted with an auxiliary engine
- manufacture of engines for motorcycles
- manufacture of sidecars
- manufacture of parts and accessories for motorcycles

This class excludes:
- *manufacture of bicycles, see 3592*
- *manufacture of invalid carriages, see 3592*

3592   Manufacture of bicycles and invalid carriages

This class includes:
- manufacture of non-motorized bicycles and other cycles, including delivery tricycles, tandems, children's bicycles
- manufacture of parts and accessories of bicycles
- manufacture of invalid carriages with or without motor
- manufacture of parts and accessories of invalid carriages

This class excludes:
- *manufacture of bicycles with auxiliary motor, see 3591*
- *manufacture of children's cycles other than bicycles, see 3694*

3599   Manufacture of other transport equipment n.e.c.

This class includes:
- manufacture of wheelbarrows, luggage trucks, handcarts, sledges etc.
- manufacture of vehicles drawn by animals

36   Manufacture of furniture; manufacturing n.e.c.

It should be noted that division 36 is a residual division. The usual criteria for grouping classes into divisions have not been applied here.

Repair of products from division 36 generally fall under group 526 (Repair of personal and household goods), except repair of office furniture, musical instruments, professional sports equipment, automatic bowling alley equipment and the like.

361   Manufacture of furniture

3610   Manufacture of furniture

This class covers manufacture of furniture of any kind, any material (except stone, concrete or ceramic) for any place and various purposes.

This class includes:
- manufacture of chairs and seats for offices, workrooms, hotels, restaurants, public and domestic premises
- manufacture of chairs and seats for theatres, cinemas and the like
- manufacture of chairs and seats for transport equipment
- manufacture of sofas, sofabeds and sofa sets
- manufacture of garden chairs and seats
- manufacture of special furniture for shops: counters, display cases, shelves etc.
- manufacture of office furniture
- manufacture of furniture for churches, schools, restaurants

- manufacture of kitchen furniture
- manufacture of furniture for bedrooms, living rooms, gardens etc.
- manufacture of cabinets for sewing machines, televisions etc.

This class also includes:
- restoring of furniture
- finishing such as upholstery of chairs and seats
- finishing of furniture such as spraying, painting, French polishing and upholstering
- manufacture of mattress supports
- manufacture of mattresses:
  - mattresses fitted with springs or stuffed or internally fitted with a supporting material
  - uncovered cellular rubber or plastic mattresses

This class excludes:
- *manufacture of pillows, pouffes, cushions, quilts and eiderdowns, see 1721*
- *manufacture of inflatable rubber mattresses, see 2519*
- *manufacture of furniture of ceramics, concrete and stone, see 2691, 2695, 2696*
- *manufacture of lighting fittings or lamps, see 3150*
- *manufacture of medical, surgical, dental or veterinary furniture, see 3311*

369   Manufacturing n.e.c.

3691   Manufacture of jewellery and related articles

This class includes:
- manufacture of coins, including coins for use as legal tender, whether or not of precious metal
- production of worked pearls
- production of precious and semi-precious stones in the worked state. Included is the working of industrial quality stones and synthetic or reconstructed precious or semi-precious stones
- working of diamonds
- manufacture of jewellery of precious metal or of base metals clad with precious metals, or precious or semi-precious stones, or of combinations of precious metal and precious or semi-precious stones or of other materials
- manufacture of goldsmiths' articles of precious metals or of base metals clad with precious metals:
  - dinnerware, flatware, hollowware, toilet articles, office or desk articles, articles for religious use etc.
- manufacture of technical or laboratory articles of precious metal (except instruments and parts thereof): crucibles, spatulas, electroplating anodes etc.

This class excludes:
- *manufacture of articles of base metal plated with precious metal, see division 28*
- *manufacture of watch cases and metal straps, see 3330*
- *manufacture of imitation jewellery, see 3699*

3692   Manufacture of musical instruments

This class includes:
- manufacture of stringed instruments
- manufacture of keyboard stringed instruments, including automatic pianos
- manufacture of keyboard pipe organs, including harmoniums and similar keyboard instruments with free metal reeds
- manufacture of accordions and similar instruments, including mouth organs
- manufacture of wind instruments
- manufacture of percussion musical instruments
- manufacture of musical instruments, the sound of which is produced electronically
- manufacture of musical boxes, fairground organs, calliopes etc.

- manufacture of instrument parts and accessories:
  - metronomes, tuning forks, pitch pipes, cards, discs and rolls for automatic mechanical instruments etc.

This class also includes:
- manufacture of whistles, call horns and other mouth-blown sound signalling instruments
- restoring of organs and other historic musical instruments

This class excludes:
- *publishing and reproduction of pre-recorded sound and video tapes and discs, see groups 221 and 223, 9211*
- *manufacture of microphones, amplifiers, loudspeakers, headphones and similar components, see 3230*
- *manufacture of record players, tape recorders and the like, see 3230*
- *manufacture of toy instruments, see 3694*
- *piano tuning, see 5260*

3693   Manufacture of sports goods

This class includes:
- manufacture of articles and equipment for sports, outdoor and indoor games, of any material:
  - hard, soft and inflatable balls
  - rackets, bats and clubs
  - skis, bindings and poles
  - sailboards
  - requisites for sport fishing, including landing nets
  - requisites for hunting, mountain climbing etc.
  - leather sports gloves and sports headgear
  - ice skates, roller skates etc.
  - bows and crossbows
  - gymnasium, fitness centre or athletic equipment

This class excludes:
- *manufacture of boat sails, see 1721*
- *manufacture of sports clothing, see 1810*
- *manufacture of saddlery and harness, see 1912*
- *manufacture of sports footwear, see 1920*
- *manufacture of weapons and ammunition, see 2927*
- *manufacture of sports vehicles other than toboggans and the like, see divisions 34 and 35*
- *manufacture of boats, see 3512*
- *manufacture of billiard tables and bowling equipment, see 3694*
- *manufacture of whips and riding crops, see 3699*

3694   Manufacture of games and toys

This class includes manufacture of games and toys of any material:
- manufacture of dolls and doll garments and accessories
- manufacture of toy animals
- manufacture of wheeled toys designed to be ridden, including tricycles
- manufacture of toy musical instruments
- manufacture of articles for funfair, table or parlour games
- manufacture of playing cards
- manufacture of pin-tables, coin-operated games, billiards, special tables for casino games, automatic bowling alley equipment etc.
- manufacture of electronic games: video game consoles, chess etc.
- manufacture of reduced-size ("scale") models and similar recreational models, electrical trains, construction sets etc.
- manufacture of puzzles etc.

This class excludes:
- *manufacture of bicycles, see 3592*
- *manufacture of festive, carnival or other entertainment articles, see 3699*
- *writing and publishing of software for video game consoles, see 7221, 7229*

3699   Other manufacturing n.e.c.

This class includes:
- manufacture of brooms and brushes, including brushes constituting parts of machines, hand-operated mechanical floor sweepers, mops and feather dusters, paint brushes, paint pads and rollers, squeegees and other brushes, brooms, mops etc.
- manufacture of shoe and clothes brushes
- manufacture of pens and pencils of all kinds whether or not mechanical
- manufacture of pencil leads
- manufacture of date, sealing or numbering stamps, hand-operated devices for printing, or embossing labels, hand printing sets, prepared typewriter ribbons and inked pads
- manufacture of baby carriages
- manufacture of umbrellas, sun-umbrellas, walking sticks, seat-sticks, whips, riding crops, buttons, press-fasteners, snap-fasteners, press-studs, slide fasteners
- manufacture of cigarette lighters and matches
- manufacture of articles of personal use: smoking pipes, combs, hair slides, scent sprays, vacuum flasks and other vacuum vessels for personal or household use, wigs, false beards, eyebrows
- manufacture of roundabouts, swings, shooting galleries and other fairground amusements
- manufacture of linoleum and hard non-plastic surface floor coverings
- manufacture of imitation jewellery
- manufacture of miscellaneous articles: candles, tapers and the like, artificial flowers, fruit and foliage, jokes and novelties, hand sieves and hand riddles; tailors' dummies, burial caskets etc.
- taxidermy activities

This class excludes:
- *manufacture of lighter wicks, see 1729*

37   Recycling

This division includes:
- processing of waste and scrap and other articles, whether used or not, into secondary raw material. A transformation process is required, either mechanical or chemical. It is typical that, in terms of commodities, input consists of waste and scrap, the input being sorted or unsorted but normally unfit for further direct use in an industrial process, whereas the output is made fit for direct use in an industrial manufacturing process. The resulting secondary raw material is to be considered an intermediate good, with a value, but is not a final new product.

This division excludes:
- *manufacture of new final products from (whether or not self-manufactured) secondary raw material, see divisions 14 to 36*
- *wholesale of waste and scrap, including collecting, sorting, separating, stripping of used goods such as cars in order to obtain reusable parts, (re-)packing, storage and delivery, but without a real transformation process, see divisions 50, 51 and 52*
- *wholesale or retail sale of second-hand goods, see divisions 50 and 51, 5240*
- *treatment of waste, not for further use in an industrial manufacturing process, but with the aim of disposal, see 9000*

371   Recycling of metal waste and scrap

3710   Recycling of metal waste and scrap

This class includes:
- processing of metal waste and scrap and of metal articles into secondary raw material. Examples of mechanical or chemical transformation processes are:
  - mechanical crushing of metal waste such as used cars, washing machines, bikes etc. with subsequent sorting and separation
  - mechanical reduction of large iron pieces such as railway wagons
  - shredding of metal waste, end-of-life vehicles etc.
  - other methods of mechanical treatment as cutting, pressing to reduce the volume
- ship-breaking

This class excludes:
- *manufacture of new final metals or new final metal products from (whether or not self-manufactured) secondary metal raw materials, see divisions 27 and 28*
- *car dismantling sites, demolition of machinery, computers in order to obtain reusable parts etc., including trade in second-hand spare parts, see divisions 50, 51 and 52*
- *disposal of used goods such as refrigerators to eliminate harmful waste, see 9000*

372   Recycling of non-metal waste and scrap

3720   Recycling of non-metal waste and scrap

This class includes:
- processing of non-metal waste and scrap and of non-metal articles into secondary raw material. Examples of transformation processes are:
  - reclaiming of rubber such as used tires to produce secondary raw material
  - sorting and pelleting of plastics to produce secondary raw material for tubes, flower pots, pallets and the like
  - processing (cleaning, melting, grinding) of plastic or rubber waste to granulates
  - reclaiming of chemicals from chemical waste
  - crushing, cleaning and sorting of glass
  - crushing, cleaning and sorting of other waste such as demolition waste to obtain secondary raw material
  - mechanical crushing and grinding of waste from the construction and demolition of buildings (including wood), asphalt
  - processing of used cooking oils and fats into secondary raw materials for pet food or feed for farm animals
  - processing of other food, beverage and tobacco waste and residual substances into secondary raw material
  - reclaiming metals out of photographic waste, e.g. fixer solution or photographic films and paper

This class excludes:
- *production of new final products from (whether or not self-manufactured) secondary raw materials such as spinning of yarn from garnetted stock or making pulp from waste paper or retreading tyres. Such activities should be classified in the appropriate class of manufacturing, see divisions 14 to 36*
- *treatment of food residual substances to manufacture food products, see division 15*
- *treatment of slaughter waste to produce animal feeds, see 1533*
- *reprocessing of nuclear fuels and treatment of nuclear waste, see 2330*
- *composting of organic waste, see 2412*
- *wholesale in non-metal waste and scrap, including collecting, sorting, packing, dealing etc., but without a real transformation process, see 5149*
- *wholesale or retail sale trade in second-hand goods, see division 50 and 51, 5240*

- *incineration, dumping, burying etc. of waste, see 9000*
- *treatment and disposal of transition radioactive waste from hospitals etc., see 9000*
- *treatment and disposal of toxic, contaminated waste, see 9000*
- *disposal of food, beverages and tobacco waste, see 9000*

E   Electricity, gas and water supply

This section covers the activity of providing electric power, natural gas, steam supply, and water supply through a permanent infrastructure (network) of lines, mains and pipes. The dimension of the network is not decisive; also included are electricity, gas, steam and water supply and the like in industrial parks or blocks of flats.

Production, infrastructure management, and supplying end-users may be handled by the same or a different unit. Units engaged in the supply of electricity and/or gas and/or steam and hot water and/or water have to be classified according to their principal activity.

40   Electricity, gas, steam and hot water supply

401   Production, transmission and distribution of electricity

4010   Production, transmission and distribution of electricity

This class includes:
- operation of generation facilities that produce electric energy; including thermal, nuclear, hydroelectric, gas turbine, diesel and renewable
- operation of transmission systems that convey the electricity from the generation facility to the distribution system;
- operation of distribution systems (i.e., consisting of lines, poles, meters, and wiring) that convey electric power received from the generation facility or the transmission system to the final consumer
- sale of electricity to the user
- activities of electric power brokers or agents that arrange the sale of electricity via power distribution systems operated by others.

402   Manufacture of gas; distribution of gaseous fuels through mains

4020   Manufacture of gas; distribution of gaseous fuels through mains

This class includes:
- production of gas for the purpose of gas supply by carbonation of coal, from by-products of agriculture or from waste
- manufacture of gaseous fuels with a specified calorific value, by purification, blending and other processes from gases of various types including natural gas
- transportation, distribution and supply of gaseous fuels of all kinds through a system of mains
- sale of gas to the user through mains
- activities of gas brokers or agents that arrange the sale of gas over gas distribution systems operated by others

This class excludes:
- *operation of coke ovens, see 2310*
- *manufacture of refined petroleum products, see 2320*
- *manufacture of industrial gases, see 2411*
- *bulk sale of gaseous fuels, or its sale in canisters (see 5110, 5141, 5239 and group 525)*
- *transportation of gases by pipelines (other than mains), see 6030*

403   Steam and hot water supply

4030   Steam and hot water supply

This class includes:
- production, collection and distribution of steam and hot water for heating, power and other purposes

This class also includes:
- production and distribution of chilled water or ice for cooling purposes

41   Collection, purification and distribution of water

410   Collection, purification and distribution of water

4100   Collection, purification and distribution of water

This class also includes:
- purification of water for water supply purposes
- desalting of sea water to produce water as the principal product of interest

This class excludes:
- *irrigation system operation for agricultural purposes, see 0140*
- *(long-distance) transport of water via pipelines, see 6030*
- *treatment of waste water in order to prevent pollution, see 9000*

F   Construction

45   Construction

This division includes general construction and special trade construction for buildings and civil engineering, building installation and building completion. It includes new work, repair, additions and alterations, the erection of prefabricated buildings or structures on the site and also construction of a temporary nature.

General construction is the construction of entire dwellings, office buildings, stores and other public and utility buildings, farm buildings etc., or the construction of heavy constructions such as motorways, streets, bridges, tunnels, railways, airfields, harbours and other water projects, irrigation systems, sewerage systems, industrial facilities, pipelines and electric lines, sports facilities etc. This work can be carried out on own account or on a fee or contract basis. Portions of the work and sometimes even the whole practical work can be subcontracted out to trade contractors.

Special trade construction includes the construction of parts of buildings and civil engineering works or preparation therefor. It is usually specialized in one aspect common to different structures, requiring specialized skills or equipment. Activities such as pile-driving, foundation work, water well drilling, carcass work, concrete work, bricklaying, stone setting, scaffolding, roof covering etc., are covered. The erection of steel structures is included provided that the parts are not produced by the same unit. Special trade construction is carried out mostly under subcontract, but in repair construction especially it is done directly for the owner of the property.

Building installation activities include the installation of all kind of utilities that make the construction function as such. These activities are usually performed at the site of the construction, although parts of the job may be carried out in a special shop. Included are activities such as plumbing, installation of heating and air-conditioning systems, antennas, alarm systems and other electrical work, sprinkler systems, elevators and escalators etc. Also included are insulation work (water, heat, sound), sheet metal work, commercial refrigerating work, the installation of illumination and signalling systems for roads, railways, airports, harbours etc. Also included is repair of the same type as the above-mentioned installation activities.

Building completion encompasses activities that contribute to the completion or finishing of a construction such as glazing, plastering, painting and decorating, floor and wall tiling or covering with other materials like parquet, carpets, wallpaper etc., floor sanding, finish carpentry, acoustical work, cleaning of the exterior etc. Also included is repair of the same type as the above-mentioned activities.

This division excludes:
- *manufacture of building materials, see sections C and D*
- *erecting or installing industrial equipment, see section D (e.g. installation of industrial furnaces, turbines etc.)*
- *erection of complete prefabricated buildings or structures from self-manufactured parts, which is classified in the relevant category in manufacturing, depending on the material chiefly used, except if the chief material is concrete, in which case it remains classified here*
- *erection of metal structures from self-manufactured parts, see 2811*
- *installation of self-manufactured carpentry or joinery, which is classified in the relevant category in manufacturing, depending on the material used (e.g. wood, see 2022)*
- *architectural and engineering activities, 7421*
- *project management for constructions, see 7421*
- *landscape planning and design, lawn and garden installation and maintenance and tree surgeons' activities, see 0140*
- *construction activities directly related to extraction of oil and natural gas, see 1120. (However, the construction of buildings, roads etc., on the mining site remains in this class.)*
- *cleaning of windows, inside as well as outside, chimneys, boilers, interiors etc., see 7493*

451   Site preparation

4510   Site preparation

This class includes:
- demolition or wrecking of buildings and other structures
- clearing of building sites
- earth moving: excavation, landfill, levelling and grading of construction sites, trench digging, rock removal, blasting etc.
- stripping work of contaminated topsoil as part of construction activities
- site preparation for mining:
  • overburden removal and other development and preparation of mineral properties and sites, except oil and gas sites
- test drilling, test boring and core sampling for construction, geophysical, geologic or similar purposes

This class also includes:
- building site drainage
- drainage of agricultural or forestry land
- clearing of mines and the like (including detonation) from construction sites

This class excludes:
- *drilling of production oil or gas wells, see 1110 (when on own account) or 1120 (when on a fee or contract basis)*
- *water well drilling, see 4520*
- *shaft sinking, see 4520*
- *oil and gas field exploration, geophysical, geologic and seismic surveying, see 7421*
- *decontamination of soil, see 9000*

452   Building of complete constructions or parts thereof; civil engineering

4520   Building of complete constructions or parts thereof; civil engineering

This class includes:
- construction of all types of buildings
- construction of civil engineering constructions:
  - bridges, including those for elevated highways, viaducts, tunnels and subways
  - long-distance pipelines, communication and power lines
  - urban pipelines, urban communication and power lines; ancillary urban works
- construction of:
  - waterways, harbour and river works, pleasure ports (marinas), locks etc.
  - dams and dykes
  - sewer systems, including repair
- construction of motorways, streets, roads, other vehicular and pedestrian ways
- construction of railways
- construction of airfield runways
- construction work, other than on buildings, for stadiums, swimming pools, gymnasiums, tennis courts, golf courses and other sports installations
- assembly and erection of prefabricated constructions on the site
- erection of roofs
- roof covering
- surface work on elevated motorways, bridges and tunnels
- installation of crash barriers, traffic signs and the like
- dredging
- subsurface work
- construction activities specializing in one aspect common to different kind of structures, requiring specialized skill or equipment:
  - construction of foundations, including pile driving
  - water well drilling and construction, shaft sinking
  - erection of non-self-manufactured steel elements
  - steel bending
  - bricklaying and stone setting
  - scaffolds and work platform erecting and dismantling, including renting of scaffolds and work platforms
  - erection of chimneys and industrial ovens
  - work with specialist access requirements necessitating climbing skills and the use of related equipment, e.g. working at height on tall structures

This class also includes:
- development on own account involving construction

This class excludes:
- *service activities incidental to oil and gas extraction, see 1120*
- *erection of complete prefabricated constructions from self-manufactured parts not of concrete, see divisions 20, 26 and 28*
- *preliminary earth moving, see 4510*
- *building installation, see 4530*
- *building completion, see 4540*
- *architectural and engineering activities, see 7421*
- *project management for construction, see 7421*
- *renting of scaffolds without erection and dismantling, see 7122*

453   Building installation

4530   Building installation

This class includes:
- installation in buildings or other construction projects of:
  - electrical wiring and fittings
  - telecommunications wiring
  - electrical heating systems, including electric solar energy collector residential antennas and aerials
  - fire alarms
  - burglar alarm systems
  - lifts and escalators
  - lightning conductors etc.
- installation in buildings or other construction projects of:
  - thermal, sound or vibration insulation
  - plumbing and sanitary equipment
  - gas fittings
  - heating, ventilation, refrigeration or air-conditioning equipment and ducts
  - non-electric solar energy collectors
  - sprinkler systems
- installation of illumination and signalling systems for roads, railways, airports and harbours
- installation in buildings or other construction projects of fittings and fixtures n.e.c.
- general technical repair and maintenance of building installations

This class excludes:
- *installation of telecommunication systems, see 3220*

454   Building completion

4540   Building completion

This class includes:
- application in buildings or other construction projects of interior and exterior plaster or stucco, including related lathing materials
- installation of not self-manufactured doors, windows, door and window frames, fitted kitchens, staircases, shop fittings and the like, of wood or other materials
- interior completion such as ceilings, wooden wall coverings, movable partitions etc.
- laying, tiling, hanging or fitting in buildings or other construction projects of:
  - ceramic, concrete or cut stone wall or floor tiles, ceramic stove fitting
  - parquet and other wood floor coverings
  - carpets and linoleum floor coverings, including of rubber or plastic
  - terrazzo, marble, granite or slate floor or wall coverings
  - wallpaper
- interior and exterior painting of buildings
- painting of civil engineering structures
- installation of glass, mirrors etc.
- installation of private swimming pools
- steam cleaning, sandblasting and similar activities for building exteriors
- cleaning of new buildings after construction
- other building completion and finishing work n.e.c.

This class excludes:
- *installation of self-manufactured carpentry or joinery, which is classified in the relevant category in manufacturing, depending on the material used (e.g. if made of wood, see 2022)*
- *interior cleaning of buildings and other structures, see 7493*
- *activities of interior decoration designers, see 7499*

455   Renting of construction or demolition equipment with operator

4550   Renting of construction or demolition equipment with operator

This class includes:
- renting of cranes, with operator
- renting of bulldozers, mortar spreaders, concrete surfacing machinery etc. with operator

This class excludes:
- *renting of construction or demolition machinery and equipment without operators, see 7122*

G   Wholesale and retail trade; repair of motor vehicles, motorcycles and personal and household goods

This section includes wholesale and retail sale (sale without transformation) of any type of goods, and rendering services incidental to the sale of merchandise. Wholesaling and retailing are the final steps in the distribution of merchandise. Also included in this section are the repair of motor vehicles and the installation and repair of personal and household goods.

Sale without transformation is considered to include the usual operations (*or manipulations*) associated with trade, for example sorting, grading and assembling of goods, mixing (blending) of goods (for example wine or sand), bottling (with or without preceding bottle cleaning), packing, breaking bulk and repacking for distribution in smaller lots, storage (whether or not frozen or chilled), cleaning and drying of agricultural products, cutting out of wood fibreboards or metal sheets on own account.

Wholesale is the resale (sale without transformation) of new and used goods to retailers, to industrial, commercial, institutional or professional users, or to other wholesalers, or involves acting as an agent or broker in buying merchandise for, or selling merchandise to, such persons or companies. The principal types of businesses included are merchant wholesalers, i.e. wholesalers who take title to the goods they sell, such as wholesale merchants or jobbers, industrial distributors, exporters, importers, and cooperative buying associations, sales branches and sales offices (but not retail stores) that are maintained by manufacturing or mining units apart from their plants or mines for the purpose of marketing their products and that do not merely take orders to be filled by direct shipments from the plants or mines. Also included are merchandise and commodity brokers, commission merchants and agents and assemblers, buyers and cooperative associations engaged in the marketing of farm products. Wholesalers frequently physically assemble, sort and grade goods in large lots, break bulk, repack and redistribute in smaller lots, for example pharmaceuticals; store, refrigerate, deliver and install goods, engage in sales promotion for their customers and label design.

Retailing is the resale (sale without transformation) of new and used goods mainly to the general public for personal or household consumption or utilization, by shops, department stores, stalls, mail-order houses, hawkers and peddlers, consumer cooperatives, auction houses etc. Most retailers take title to the goods they sell, but some act as agents for a principal and sell either on consignment or on a commission basis.

50   Sale, maintenance and repair of motor vehicles and motorcycles; retail sale of automotive fuel

This division includes:
- all activities (except manufacture and renting) related to motor vehicles and motorcycles, including lorries and trucks:
  - wholesale and retail sale of new and second-hand vehicles
  - maintenance and repair
  - wholesale and retail sale of parts and accessories
  - activities of commission agents involved in wholesale or retail sale of vehicles
  - washing, polishing and towing of vehicles etc.

This division also includes:
- retail sale of automotive fuel and lubricating or cooling products

This division excludes:
- *renting of motor vehicles and motorcycles without driver, see 7111*
- *renting of private cars with drivers, see 6022*
- *renting of trucks with driver, see 6023*

501   Sale of motor vehicles

5010   Sale of motor vehicles

This class includes:
- wholesale and retail sale of new and used vehicles:
  - passenger motor vehicles, including specialized passenger motor vehicles such as ambulances and minibuses etc.
  - lorries, trailers and semi-trailers
  - camping vehicles such as caravans and motor homes

This class also includes:
- wholesale and retail sale of off-road motor vehicles (jeeps etc.)
- wholesale and retail sale by commission agents
- car auctioning

This class excludes:
- *wholesale and retail sale of parts and accessories for motor vehicles, see 5030*

502   Maintenance and repair of motor vehicles

5020   Maintenance and repair of motor vehicles

This class includes:
- maintenance and repair of motor vehicles:
  - mechanical repairs
  - electrical repairs
  - electronic injection systems repair
  - ordinary servicing
  - bodywork repair
  - repair of motor vehicle parts
  - washing, polishing etc.
  - spraying and painting
  - repair of screens and windows
  - repair of seats
- tyre and tube repair, fitting or replacement
- anti-rust treatment
- installation of parts and accessories not as part of the manufacturing process
- towing
- roadside assistance

This class excludes:
- *retreading and rebuilding of tyres, see 2511*

503   Sale of motor vehicle parts and accessories

5030   Sale of motor vehicle parts and accessories

This class includes:
- wholesale and retail sale of all kinds of parts, components, supplies, tools and accessories for motor vehicles (when not combined with sale of motor vehicles)

504 Sale, maintenance and repair of motorcycles and related parts and accessories

5040 Sale, maintenance and repair of motorcycles and related parts and accessories

This class includes:
- wholesale and retail sale of motorcycles, including mopeds
- wholesale and retail sale, including mail order, of parts and accessories for motorcycles
- activities of commission agents
- maintenance and repair of motorcycles

This class excludes:
- *sale, maintenance and repair of bicycles and related parts and accessories, see 5110, 5139, 5239, 5260*

505 Retail sale of automotive fuel

5050 Retail sale of automotive fuel

This class includes:
- retail sale of fuel for motor vehicles, motorcycles etc.:
  - motor spirit
  - gasoline
  - petrol
  - liquefied petroleum gas

This class also includes:
- retail sale of similar fuels used in boats
- retail sale of lubricating products and cooling products for motor vehicles

This class excludes:
- *wholesale of fuels, see 5141*
- *retail sale of liquefied petroleum gas for cooking or heating, see 5239*

51 Wholesale trade and commission trade, except of motor vehicles and motorcycles

This division includes:
- resale (sale without transformation) of new and used goods to retailers, to industrial, commercial, institutional or professional users, or to other wholesalers; or acting as agent in buying merchandise for, or selling merchandise to, such persons or companies:
  - activities of wholesale merchants, jobbers, industrial distributors, exporters, importers, co-operative buying associations, merchandise and commodity brokers, commission merchants and agents and assemblers, buyers and cooperative associations engaged in the marketing of farm products

This division also includes:
- the usual manipulations involved in wholesale such as assembling, sorting and grading of goods in large lots, breaking bulk, repacking and bottling, redistribution in smaller lots, e.g. pharmaceuticals; storage, refrigeration, delivery and installation of goods on own account
- packing of solid goods and bottling of liquid or gaseous goods, including blending and filtering on own account

This division excludes:
- *wholesale of motor vehicles, caravans and motorcycles, see 5010, 5040*
- *wholesale of motor accessories, see 5030, 5040*
- *renting and leasing of goods, see division 71*
- *packing of solid goods and bottling of liquid or gaseous goods, including blending and filtering for third parties, see 7495*

511   Wholesale on a fee or contract basis

5110   Wholesale on a fee or contract basis

This class includes:
- activities of commission agents, commodity brokers and all other wholesalers who trade on behalf and on the account of others
- activities of those involved in bringing sellers and buyers together or undertaking commercial transactions on behalf of a principal, including on the Internet

This class also includes:
- activities of wholesale auctioneering houses

This class excludes:
- *wholesale trade in own name, see 512 to 519*
- *retail sale by agents, see division 52*
- *activities of insurance agents, see 6720*
- *activities of real estate agents, see 7020*

512   Wholesale of agricultural raw materials, live animals, food, beverages and tobacco

5121   Wholesale of agricultural raw materials and live animals

This class includes:
- wholesale of grains and seeds
- wholesale of oleaginous fruits
- wholesale of flowers and plants
- wholesale of unmanufactured tobacco
- wholesale of live animals
- wholesale of hides and skins
- wholesale of leather
- wholesale of agricultural material, waste, residues and by-products used for animal feed

This class excludes:
- *wholesale of textile fibres, see 5149*

5122   Wholesale of food, beverages and tobacco

This class includes:
- wholesale of fruit and vegetables
- wholesale of dairy products
- wholesale of eggs and egg products
- wholesale of edible oils and fats of animal or vegetable origin
- wholesale of meat and meat products
- wholesale of fishery products
- wholesale of sugar, chocolate and sugar confectionery
- wholesale of bakery products
- wholesale of beverages
- wholesale of coffee, tea, cocoa and spices
- wholesale of tobacco products

This class also includes:
- buying of wine in bulk and bottling without transformation
- wholesale of feed for pet animals

This class excludes:
- *blending of wine or distilled spirits, see 1551*

513   Wholesale of household goods

5131   Wholesale of textiles, clothing and footwear

This class includes:
- wholesale of yarn
- wholesale of fabrics
- wholesale of household linen etc.
- wholesale of haberdashery: needles, sewing thread etc.
- wholesale of clothing, including sports clothes
- wholesale of clothing accessories such as gloves, ties and braces
- wholesale of footwear
- wholesale of fur articles
- wholesale of umbrellas

This class excludes:
- *wholesale of jewellery and leather goods, see 5139*
- *wholesale of textile fibres, see 5149*

5139   Wholesale of other household goods

This class includes:
- wholesale of household furniture
- wholesale of household appliances
- wholesale of lighting equipment
- wholesale of cutlery
- wholesale of glassware and woodenware
- wholesale of wallpaper and floor coverings
- wholesale of pharmaceutical and medical goods
- wholesale of perfumeries, cosmetics and soaps
- wholesale of bicycles and their parts and accessories
- wholesale of stationery, books, magazines and newspapers, photographic and optical goods, leather goods and travel accessories, watches, clocks and jewellery, musical instruments, games and toys, sports goods, woodenware, wickerwork and corkware etc.

This class excludes:
- *wholesale of office furniture, see 5159*

514   Wholesale of non-agricultural intermediate products, waste and scrap

5141   Wholesale of solid, liquid and gaseous fuels and related products

This class also includes:
- wholesale of automotive fuels, greases, lubricants, oils etc.

5142   Wholesale of metals and metal ores

This class includes:
- wholesale of ferrous and non-ferrous metal ores
- wholesale of ferrous and non-ferrous metals in primary forms
- wholesale of ferrous and non-ferrous semi-finished metal products n.e.c.
- wholesale of gold and other precious metals

This class excludes:
- *wholesale of waste and scrap, see 5149*

5143 **Wholesale of construction materials, hardware, plumbing and heating equipment and supplies**

This class includes:
- wholesale of wood in the rough
- wholesale of products of primary processing of wood
- wholesale of paint and varnish
- wholesale of construction materials:
  • sand, gravel
- wholesale of flat glass
- wholesale of hardware and locks
- wholesale of fittings and fixtures
- wholesale of hot water heaters
- wholesale of sanitary equipment:
  • baths, washbasins, toilets and other sanitary porcelain
- wholesale of sanitary installation equipment:
  • tubes, pipes, fittings, taps, T-pieces, connections, rubber pipes etc.
- wholesale of tools such as hammers, saws, screwdrivers and other hand tools

5149 **Wholesale of other intermediate products, waste and scrap**

This class includes:
- wholesale of industrial chemicals:
  • aniline, printing ink, essential oils, industrial gases, chemical glues, colouring matter, synthetic resin, methanol, paraffin, scents and flavourings, soda, industrial salt, acids and sulphurs, starch derivates etc.
- wholesale of fertilizers and agrochemical products
- wholesale of plastic materials in primary forms
- wholesale of rubber
- wholesale of textile fibres etc.
- wholesale of paper in bulk
- wholesale of precious stones
- wholesale of metal and non-metal waste and scrap and materials for recycling, including collecting, sorting, separating, stripping of used goods such as cars in order to obtain reusable parts, packing and repacking, storage and delivery, but without a real transformation process. Additionally, the purchased and sold waste have a remaining value.
- dismantling of end-of-life vehicles (dismantling of cars; wholesale in car wrecks; sale of parts from car wrecks to private persons and professional users).

This class excludes:
- *processing of waste and scrap and other articles into secondary raw material when a real transformation process is required. The resulting secondary raw material is fit for direct use in an industrial manufacturing process and is not a final product, see 3710 and 3720*
- *ship-breaking, see 3710*
- *shredding of cars by means of a mechanical process, see 3710*
- *retail sale of second-hand goods, see 5240*
- *treatment of waste, not for a further use in an industrial manufacturing process, but with the aim of disposal, see 9000*
- *collection and treatment of household and industrial waste, see 9000*

515 **Wholesale of machinery, equipment and supplies**

5151 **Wholesale of computers, computer peripheral equipment and software**

This class includes:
- wholesale of computers and computer peripheral equipment
- wholesale of software

This class excludes:
- *wholesale of electronic parts, see 5152*
- *wholesale of copy machines and other office equipment, see 5159*
- *wholesale of computer-controlled machinery, see 5159*

5152   Wholesale of electronic and telecommunications parts and equipment

This class includes:
- wholesale of electronic valves and tubes
- wholesale of semiconductor devices
- wholesale of microchips and integrated circuits
- wholesale of printed circuits
- wholesale of blank audio and video tapes and diskettes, magnetic and optical disks
- wholesale of telephone and communications equipment

This class excludes:
- *wholesale of computers and computer peripheral equipment, see 5151*

5159   Wholesale of other machinery, equipment and supplies

This class includes:
- wholesale of office machinery and equipment, except computers and computer peripheral equipment
- wholesale of office furniture
- wholesale of transport equipment except motor vehicles, motorcycles and bicycles
- wholesale of production-line robots
- wholesale of wires and switches and other installation equipment for industrial use
- wholesale of other electrical material such as electrical motors, transformers
- wholesale of other machinery n.e.c. for use in industry, trade and navigation and other services

This class also includes:
- wholesale of computer-controlled machine tools
- wholesale of computer-controlled machinery for the textile industry and of computer-controlled sewing and knitting machines
- wholesale of measuring instruments and equipment
- wholesale of lawnmowers however operated

This class excludes:
- *wholesale of motor vehicles, trailers and caravans, see 5010*
- *wholesale of motor vehicle parts, see 5030*
- *wholesale of motorcycles, see 5040*
- *wholesale of bicycles, see 5139*
- *wholesale of computers and peripheral equipment, see 5151*
- *wholesale of electronic parts and telephone and communications equipment, see 5152*

519   Other wholesale

5190   Other wholesale

This class includes:
- specialized wholesale not covered in one of the previous categories
- wholesale of a variety of goods without any particular specialization

52   Retail trade, except of motor vehicles and motorcycles; repair of personal and household goods

This division includes the resale (sale without transformation) of new and used goods mainly to the general public for personal or household consumption or utilization, by shops, department stores, stalls, mail-order houses, hawkers and peddlers, consumer cooperatives etc.

Retail trade is classified first by type of sale outlet (retail trade in stores: groups 521 to 524; retail trade not in stores: group 525). Retail trade in stores is further subdivided into retail sale of new goods (groups 521 to 523) and retail sale of used goods (group 524). For retail sale of new goods in stores, there exists a further distinction between specialized retail sale (groups 522 to 523) and non-specialized retail sale (group 521). The above groups are further subdivided by the range of products sold. Sale not via stores lists the forms of trade (e.g. mail order, markets, door-to-door, by vending machines etc.).

The goods sold in this division are for obvious reasons limited to the so-called consumer goods and therefore exclude goods not normally entering retail trade, such as cereal grains, ores, industrial machinery and equipment etc.

This division also includes establishments engaged in selling to the general public, from displayed merchandise, products such as typewriters, stationery, paint or lumber, although these sales may not be for personal or household goods.

Some processing of goods may be involved, but only incidental to selling.

This division also includes the retail sale by commission agents, activities of retail auctioning houses and the repair and installation of personal or household goods whether or not done in combination with retail sale.

This division excludes:
- *sale of farmers' products by farmers, see division 01*
- *manufacture and sale of goods (e.g. food), which is generally classified as manufacturing in divisions 15-37*
- *sale of motor vehicles, motorcycles and their parts and of fuel for these articles, see division 50*
- *trade in cereal grains, ores, crude petroleum, industrial chemicals, iron and steel and industrial machinery and equipment, see division 51*
- *sale of food and drinks for consumption on the premises and sale of takeaway food, see 5520*
- *renting and hiring of personal and household goods to the general public, see 7130*

521   Non-specialized retail trade in stores

5211   Retail sale in non-specialized stores with food, beverages or tobacco predominating

This class includes stores engaged in:
- retail sale of a large variety of goods of which, however, food products, beverages or tobacco should be predominant:
  - activities of general stores that have, apart from their main sales of food products, beverages or tobacco, several other lines of merchandise such as wearing apparel, furniture, appliances, hardware, cosmetics etc.

5219   Other retail sale in non-specialized stores

This class includes stores engaged in:
- retail sale of a large variety of goods of which food products, beverages or tobacco are not predominant
- activities of department stores carrying a general line of merchandise, including wearing apparel, furniture, appliances, hardware, cosmetics, jewellery, toys, sports goods etc.

522   Retail sale of food, beverages and tobacco in specialized stores

5220   Retail sale of food, beverages and tobacco in specialized stores

This class includes stores specialized in the sale of any the following merchandise lines:
- fresh or preserved fruit and vegetables
- dairy products and eggs
- meat and meat products (including poultry)

- fish, other seafood and products thereof
- bakery products
- sugar confectionery
- beverages (not for consumption on the premises)
- tobacco products
- other food products

523   Other retail trade of new goods in specialized stores

This group includes stores that are specialized in the retail sale of specific lines of products.

5231   Retail sale of pharmaceutical and medical goods, cosmetic and toilet articles

This class includes stores specialized in:
- retail sale of pharmaceuticals
- retail sale of medical and orthopaedic goods
- retail sale of perfumery and cosmetic articles

5232   Retail sale of textiles, clothing, footwear and leather goods

This class includes stores specialized in:
- retail sale of fabrics
- retail sale of knitting yarn
- retail sale of basic materials for rug, tapestry or embroidery making
- retail sale of textiles
- retail sale of haberdashery: needles, sewing thread etc.
- retail sale of articles of clothing
- retail sale of articles of fur
- retail sale of clothing accessories such as gloves, ties, braces etc.
- retail sale of footwear
- retail sale of leather goods
- retail sale of travel accessories of leather and leather substitutes

5233   Retail sale of household appliances, articles and equipment

This class includes stores specialized in:
- retail sale of household furniture
- retail sale of articles for lighting
- retail sale of household utensils and cutlery, crockery, glassware, china and pottery
- retail sale of curtains and net curtains
- retail sale of household articles of textile materials
- retail sale of wood, cork goods and wickerwork goods
- retail sale of household articles and equipment n.e.c.
- retail sale of household appliances
- retail sale of radio and television equipment and other household audio-visual equipment
- retail sale of musical records, audio and video tapes, compact discs and cassettes
- retail sale of musical instruments and scores

This class excludes:
- *retail sale of cork floor tiles, see 5239*
- *retail sale of antiques, see 5240*
- *renting of tapes and records, see 7130*

5234   Retail sale of hardware, paints and glass

This class includes stores specialized in:
- retail sale of hardware
- retail sale of paints, varnishes and lacquers

- retail sale of flat glass
- retail sale of other building material such as bricks, wood, sanitary equipment
- retail sale of do-it-yourself material and equipment

This class also includes:
- retail sale of lawnmowers, however operated
- retail sale of saunas

5239   Other retail sale in specialized stores

This class includes stores specialized in:
- retail sale of office equipment, computers and non-customized software
- retail sale of office supplies such as pens, pencils, paper etc.
- retail sale of books, newspapers and stationery
- retail sale of photographic, optical and precision equipment
- retail sale of telecommunication equipment
- activities of opticians
- retail sale of wallpaper and floor coverings
- retail sale of carpets and rugs
- retail sale of watches, clocks and jewellery
- retail sale of sports goods, fishing gear, camping goods, boats and bicycles
- retail sale of games and toys
- retail sale of flowers, plants, seeds, fertilizers, pet animals and pet food
- retail sale of souvenirs, craftwork and religious articles
- retail sale of household fuel oil, bottled gas, coal and fuelwood
- retail sale of cleaning materials
- retail sale of weapons and ammunition
- retail sale of stamps and coins
- retail sale of non-food products n.e.c.

This class excludes:
- *retail sale of second-hand or antique books, see 5240*

524   Retail sale of second-hand goods in stores

5240   Retail sale of second-hand goods in stores

This class includes:
- retail sale of second-hand books
- retail sale of other second-hand goods
- retail sale of antiques
- activities of auctioning houses (retail)

This class excludes:
- *retail sale of second-hand motor vehicles, see 5010*
- *activities of Internet auctions and other non-store auctions (retail), see 5259*
- *activities of pawn shops, see 6592*

525   Retail trade not in stores

5251   Retail sale via mail order houses

This class includes:
- retail sale of any kind of product by mail order. Goods are sent to the buyer, who made his choice on the basis of advertisements, catalogues, models or any other means of advertising

This class also includes:
- direct sale via television, radio, telephone and Internet

5252   **Retail sale via stalls and markets**

This class includes:
- retail sale of any kind of product in a usually movable stall either along a public road or at a fixed marketplace

5259   **Other non-store retail sale**

This class includes:
- retail sale of any kind of product in any way that is not included in previous classes:
  - by direct sales or door-to-door sales persons
  - through vending machines etc.
- retail sale on a fee or contract basis
- activities of Internet auctions and other non-store auctions (retail)

This class excludes:
- *delivery of new products by stores, see groups 521-523*

526   **Repair of personal and household goods**

This group includes:
- repair of personal and household goods when not carried out in combination with manufacture, wholesale or retail sale of these goods. If carried out in combination, the repair is included in the retailing, wholesaling or manufacturing activity

This group excludes:
- *repair of motor vehicles and motorcycles, see division 50*

5260   **Repair of personal and household goods**

This class includes:
- repair of household appliances
- repair of consumer electronics:
  - television, radio, video cassette recorders (VCR), CD players etc.
  - telephones, including mobile phones
- repair of boots, shoes, luggage and the like
- repair of bicycles
- repair and alteration of clothing
- repair and alteration of jewelry
- repair of watches
- piano-tuning
- "while-you-wait" services

H   Hotels and restaurants

55   **Hotels and restaurants**

The sector comprises units providing customers with short-term lodging and/or preparing meals, snacks, and beverages for immediate consumption. The section includes both accommodation and food services because the two activities are often combined at the same unit.

There may be some overlap between activities in section H. A restaurant activity is a specific activity, but may also be implicitly included in lodging.

Lodging units provide lodging or short-term accommodations for travellers, vacationers and others. There is a wide range of units. Some provide lodging only; while others provide meals and recreational facilities, as well as lodging. The type of complementary services provided may vary from unit to unit.

Units belonging to the restaurant group provide complete meals fit for immediate consumption. Those units can be traditional restaurants, self-service or takeaway restaurants as well as permanent or temporary fish-and-chips stands and the like with or without seating. What is decisive is the fact that meals fit for immediate consumption are offered, not the kind of facility providing them. Excluded is the production of meals not fit for immediate consumption, of meals not planned to be consumed immediately and of prepared food that is not considered to be a meal (see division 15). Also excluded is the sale of not self-manufactured food that is not considered to be a meal and of meals that are not fit for immediate consumption (see section G).

551   Hotels; camping sites and other provision of short-stay accommodation

5510   Hotels; camping sites and other provision of short-stay accommodation

This class includes:
- provision of short-stay lodging in:
  · hotels, motels and inns
  · hotels with conference facilities
  · resorts
  · holiday chalets, cottages and flats
  · student houses, boarding schools
  · hostels for migrant workers
  · camping space and camping facilities, trailer camps
  · other short-stay lodging facilities such as guest houses, farmhouses, youth hostels, mountain refuges (shelters) etc.

This class also includes:
- operation of sleeping cars when carried out by separate units

This class excludes:
- *rental of long-stay accommodation, see 7010*
- *operation of sleeping cars as integrated activities of railway companies or other passenger transport facilities, see 6010*

552   Restaurants, bars and canteens

5520   Restaurants, bars and canteens

This class includes:
- sale of meals for consumption generally on the premises, as well as sale of drinks accompanying the meals, possibly accompanied by some form of entertainment, by:
  · restaurants
  · self-service restaurants such as cafeterias
  · fast-food outlets such as burger bars
  · takeaway restaurants
  · fish-and-chips stands and the like
  · ice cream parlours
- sale of drinks for consumption on the premises, possibly accompanied by some form of entertainment, by:
  · pubs, bars, nightclubs, beer halls etc.
- sale of meals and drinks, usually at reduced prices to groups of clearly defined persons who are mostly linked by ties of a professional nature:
  · activities of sport, factory or office canteens
  · activities of school canteens and kitchens
  · activities of university dining halls
  · activities of messes and canteens for members of the armed forces etc.

This class also includes:
- catering, i.e. activities of contractors supplying meals prepared in a central food preparation unit for consumption on other premises such as the supply of prepared meals to:
  - airlines
  - "meals on wheels"
  - banquets, corporate hospitality
  - weddings, parties and other celebrations or functions
- operation of dining cars when carried out by separate units
- restaurant and bar activities on board ships when carried out by separate units

This class excludes:
- *sale through vending machines, see 5259*
- *sale of drinks not for immediate consumption, see division 52*
- *operation of dining cars as integrated activities of railway companies or other passenger transport facilities, see 6010*

I Transport, storage and communications

This section includes:
- activities related to providing passenger or freight transport, whether scheduled or not, by rail, pipeline, road, water or air
- supporting activities such as terminal and parking facilities, cargo handling, storage etc.
- postal activities and telecommunication
- renting of transport equipment with driver or operator

This section excludes:
- *major repair or alteration of transport equipment, except motor vehicles, see division 35*
- *construction, maintenance and repair of roads, railroads, harbours, airfields, see 4520*
- *maintenance and repair of motor vehicles, see 5020*
- *renting of transport equipment without driver or operator, see group 711*

60 Land transport; transport via pipelines

This division includes the transport of passengers and freight via road and rail, as well as freight transport via pipelines.

601 Transport via railways

6010 Transport via railways

This class includes:
- passenger transport by inter-urban railways
- freight transport by inter-urban, suburban and urban railways

This class also includes:
- related activities such as switching and shunting
- operation of sleeping cars or dining cars as an integrated operation of railway companies

This class excludes:
- *operation of sleeping cars or dining cars when operated by separate units, see 5510, 5520*
- *passenger transport by urban and suburban transit systems, see 6021*
- *passenger and freight terminal activities, cargo handling, storage and other auxiliary activities, see division 63*
- *maintenance and minor repair of rolling stock, see 6303*
- *operation of railroad infrastructure, see 6303*

602 Other land transport

6021   Other scheduled passenger land transport

This class includes:
- activities providing urban, suburban or inter-urban transport of passengers on scheduled routes normally following a fixed time schedule, entailing the picking up and setting down of passengers at normally fixed stops. They may be carried out with motor bus, tramway, streetcar, trolley bus, underground and elevated railways etc.

This class also includes:
- operation of school buses, town-to-airport or town-to-station lines, funicular railways, aerial cableways etc.

This class excludes:
- *passenger transport by inter-urban railways, see 6010*

6022   Other non-scheduled passenger land transport

This class includes:
- other non-scheduled passenger road transport:
  • charters, excursions and other occasional coach services
  • taxi operation

This class also includes:
- other rental of private cars with operator
- passenger transport by man- or animal-drawn vehicles

This class excludes:
- *ambulance transport, see 8519*

6023   Freight transport by road

This class includes:
- all freight transport operations by road:
  • logging haulage
  • stock haulage
  • refrigerated haulage
  • heavy haulage
  • bulk haulage, including haulage in tanker trucks including milk collection at farms
  • haulage of automobiles
  • transport of waste and waste materials, without collection or disposal

This class also includes:
- furniture removal
- renting of trucks with driver
- freight transport by man or animal-drawn vehicles

This class excludes:
- *log hauling within the forest, as part of logging operations, see 0200*
- *operation of terminal facilities for handling freight, see 6303*
- *crating and packing services for transport, see 6309*
- *post and courier activities, see 641*
- *waste transport as integrated part of waste collection activities carried out by specialized enterprises, see 9000*

603   Transport via pipelines

6030   Transport via pipelines

This class includes:
- transport of gases, liquids, water, slurry and other commodities via pipelines

This class also includes:
- maintenance of pipelines
- operation of pump stations

This class excludes:
- *distribution of natural or manufactured gas, water or steam, see 4020, 4030, 4100*

61 Water transport

This division includes the transport of passengers or freight over water, whether scheduled or not. Also included are the operation of towing or pushing boats, excursion, cruise or sightseeing boats, ferries, water taxis etc.

This division excludes restaurant and bar activities on board ships (see class 5520), except when delivered as an integral part of transportation.

611 Sea and coastal water transport

6110 Sea and coastal water transport

This class includes:
- transport of passengers or freight over seas and coastal waters, whether scheduled or not:
  - operation of excursion, cruise or sightseeing boats
  - operation of ferries, water taxis etc.
  - transport by towing or pushing of barges, oil rigs etc.
- rental of ships and boats with crew for sea and coastal water transport

This class also includes:
- transport of passengers or freight via great lakes, requiring similar types of vessels
- rental of pleasure boats with crew for sea and coastal water transport

This class excludes:
- *restaurant and bar activities on board ships, except when integral part of transportation, see 5520*
- *cargo handling, storage of freight, harbour operation and other auxiliary activities such as docking, pilotage, lighterage, vessel salvage, see division 63*
- *operation of gambling cruises, see 9249*

612 Inland water transport

6120 Inland water transport

This class includes:
- transport of passenger or freight via rivers, canals, lakes and other inland waterways, including inside harbours and ports

This class also includes:
- rental of pleasure boats with crew for inland water transport

62 Air transport

This division includes:
- transport of passengers or freight by air or via space

This division excludes:
- *crop spraying, see 0140*
- *overhaul of aircraft or aircraft engines, see 3530*
- *aerial advertising, see 7430*
- *aerial photography, see 7494*

621   Scheduled air transport

6210   Scheduled air transport

This class includes:
- transport of passengers or freight by air over regular routes and on regular schedules

This class excludes:
- *regular charter flights, see 6220*

622   Non-scheduled air transport

6220   Non-scheduled air transport

This class includes:
- non-scheduled transport of passengers or freight by air
- scenic and sightseeing flights
- launching of satellites and space vehicles
- space transport of physical goods and passengers

This class also includes:
- regular charter flights
- renting of air-transport equipment with operator

63   Supporting and auxiliary transport activities; activities of travel agencies

This division includes activities related to handling freight immediately before or after transport or between transport segments. The operation and maintenance of all transport facilities are included. This division also includes activities assisting passengers, such as those of travel agencies.

630   Supporting and auxiliary transport activities; activities of travel agencies

6301   Cargo handling

This class includes:
- loading and unloading of goods or passengers' luggage irrespective of the mode of transport used for transportation
- stevedoring

This class excludes:
- *operation of terminal facilities, see 6303*

6302   Storage and warehousing

This class includes:
- operation of storage and warehouse facilities for all kind of goods:
  • operation of grain silos, general merchandise warehouses, refrigerated warehouses, storage tanks etc.

This class also includes:
- storage of goods in foreign trade zones

This class excludes:
- *parking facilities for motor vehicles, see 6303*

6303   Other supporting transport activities

This class includes:
- activities related to land transport of passengers, animals or freight:
  • operation of terminal facilities such as railway stations, bus stations, stations for the handling of goods

- operation of railroad infrastructure
- operation of roads, bridges, tunnels, car parks or garages, bicycle parkings
- activities related to water transport of passengers, animals or freight:
  - operation of terminal facilities such as harbours and piers
  - operation of waterway locks etc.
  - navigation, pilotage and berthing activities
  - lighterage, salvage activities
  - lighthouse activities
- activities related to air transport of passengers, animals or freight:
  - operation of terminal facilities such as airway terminals etc.
  - airport and air-traffic-control activities
  - ground service activities on airfields etc.

This class also includes:
- firefighting and fire-prevention services at airports
- maintenance and minor repair of rolling stock

This class excludes:
- *cargo handling, see 6301*
- *operation of flying schools, see 8090*
- *operation of docking facilities related to pleasure boats (marinas), see 9249*

6304   Activities of travel agencies and tour operators; tourist assistance activities n.e.c.

This class includes:
- travel agency activities:
  - furnishing of travel information, advice and planning
  - arranging of made-to-measure tours, accommodation and transportation for travellers and tourists
  - sale of packaged tours etc.
  - furnishing of tickets
- activities of local tourist information offices and accommodation offices
- activities of tourist guides

6309   Activities of other transport agencies

This class includes:
- forwarding of freight
- arranging or organizing of transport operations by road, sea or air
- organization of group and individual consignments (including pickup and delivery of goods and grouping of consignments)
- issue and procurement of transport documents and waybills
- bill auditing and freight rate information
- activities of customs agents
- activities of sea-freight forwarders and air-cargo agents
- brokerage for ship and aircraft space
- goods-handling operations, e.g. temporary crating for the sole purpose of protecting the goods during transit, uncrating, sampling, weighing of goods

This class excludes:
- *courier activities, see 6412*
- *activities related to the arrangement of freight insurance, see 6720*

64   **Post and telecommunications**

641   **Post and courier activities**

6411   **National post activities**

This class includes:
- pickup, transport and delivery (domestic or international) of mail and parcels
- collection of mail and parcels from public letter-boxes or from post offices
- distribution and delivery of mail and parcels
- mailbox rental, poste restante etc.
- mail sorting
- sale of postage stamps

This class excludes:
- *postal giro and postal savings activities and other financial activities carried out in combination with postal activities, see 6519*

6412   **Courier activities other than national post activities**

This class includes:
- pickup, transport and delivery of letters and mail-type parcels and packages by firms other than national post. One or more modes of transport may be involved and the activity may be carried out with either self-owned (private) transport or via public transport.

This class also includes:
- home delivery services

This class excludes:
- *similar activities carried out by the national postal authority, see 6411*

642   **Telecommunications**

6420   **Telecommunications**

This class includes:
- transmission of sound, images, data or other information via cables, broadcasting, relay or satellite:
  - telephone, telegraph and telex communication
  - transmission (transport) of radio and television programmes
- maintenance of the network
- Internet access provision
- public pay-telephone services

This class excludes:
- *dissemination of information through web sites (Internet publishing), see 7240*
- *production of radio and television programmes, whether or not combined with broadcasting, see 9213*

J   **Financial intermediation**

This sector comprises units primarily engaged in financial transactions, i.e. transactions involving the creation, liquidation or change of ownership of financial assets. Also included are insurance and pension funding (division 66) and activities facilitating financial transactions (division 67). Units charged with monetary control, the monetary authorities, are included here.

This sector does not include compulsory social security (see 7530).

65   **Financial intermediation, except insurance and pension funding**

This division includes:
- the activity of obtaining and redistributing funds other than for the purpose of insurance or pension funding or compulsory social security

Note: National institutional arrangements are likely to play a significant role in determining the classification of units within this division.

Credit-card activities are classified according to type of operator.

651   **Monetary intermediation**

This group includes:
- the obtaining of funds in the form of transferable deposits, i.e. funds that are fixed in money terms, and obtained on a day-to-day basis and, apart from central banking, from non-financial sources.

6511   **Central banking**

This class includes:
- taking deposits that are used for clearance between financial institutions
- supervising banking operations
- holding the country's exchange reserves
- issuing and managing the country's currency:
    - monitoring and control of the money supply
- acting as banker to the government

The activities of central banks will vary for institutional reasons.

6519   **Other monetary intermediation**

This class includes:
- monetary intermediation of monetary institutions other than central banks, such as:
    - banks
    - savings banks
    - discount houses
    - credit unions

This class also includes:
- postal giro and postal savings bank activities
- specialized institutions granting credit for house purchase that also take deposits

This class excludes:
- *non-depository institutions granting credit for house purchase, see 6592*

659   **Other financial intermediation**

This group includes:
- financial intermediation other than that conducted by monetary institutions

This class excludes:
- *insurance and pension funding, see division 66*

6591   **Financial leasing**

This class includes:
- leasing where the term approximately covers the expected life of the asset and the lessee acquires substantially all the benefits of its use and takes all the risks associated with its ownership. The asset may or may not eventually be transferred.

This class excludes:
- *operational leasing, see division 71, according to type of goods leased*

6592   Other credit granting

This class includes:
- financial intermediation primarily concerned with making loans by institutions not involved in monetary intermediation:
  • granting of consumer credit
  • provision of long-term finance to industry
  • money lending outside the banking system
  • credit granting for house purchase by specialized non-depository institutions
  • pawnshops and pawnbrokers

This class excludes:
- *credit granting for house purchase by specialized institutions that also take deposits, see 6519*
- *operational leasing, see division 71, according to type of goods leased*

6599   Other financial intermediation n.e.c.

This class includes:
- other financial intermediation primarily concerned with distributing funds other than by making loans:
  • investment in securities, e.g. shares, bonds, bills, unit trust units etc.
  • dealing for own account by securities dealers
  • investment in property where this is carried out primarily for other financial intermediaries (e.g. property unit trusts)
  • writing of swaps, options and other hedging arrangements
- activities of financial holding companies

This class excludes:
- *financial leasing, see 6591*
- *security dealing on behalf of others, see 6712*
- *trade, leasing and renting of property, see division 70*
- *operational leasing, see division 71*

66   Insurance and pension funding, except compulsory social security

This division includes units engaged in setting up and managing insurance funds for all kinds of insurance types (life and non-life) and units engaged in the provision of retirement incomes. In either case, activities involving the collection and investment of funds are included. The activities include long- and short-term risk spreading with or without a savings element.

This division differentiates between pension funding and life and non-life insurance as the primary breakdown.

This division excludes:
- *compulsory social security, see 7530*
- *activities auxiliary to insurance and pension funding, see 6720*

660   Insurance and pension funding, except compulsory social security

6601   Life insurance

This class includes:
- life insurance and life reinsurance with or without a substantial savings element

6602 **Pension funding**

This class includes:
- the provision of retirement incomes

This class excludes:
- *compulsory social security schemes, see 7530*

6603 **Non-life insurance**

This class includes:
- insurance and reinsurance of non-life insurance business:
  . accident and fire insurance
  . health insurance
  . property insurance
  . motor, marine, aviation and transport insurance
  . pecuniary loss and liability insurance

67 **Activities auxiliary to financial intermediation**

This division includes the provision of services involved in or closely related to financial intermediation, but not themselves involving financial intermediation. The primary breakdown of this division is according to the type of financial transaction or funding served.

671 **Activities auxiliary to financial intermediation, except insurance and pension funding**

6711 **Administration of financial markets**

This class includes:
- operation and supervision of financial markets other than by public authorities:
  . activities of stock exchanges, commodity exchanges etc.

6712 **Security dealing activities**

This class includes:
- dealing in financial markets on behalf of others (e.g. stockbroking) and related activities

This class excludes:
- *dealing in markets on own account, see 6599*

6719 **Activities auxiliary to financial intermediation n.e.c.**

This class includes:
- activities auxiliary to financial intermediation n.e.c.:
  . financial advisers
  . mortgage advisers and brokers
  . "bureaux de change" etc.

This class excludes:
- *activities of insurance agents, see 6720*
- *activities closely related to insurance and pension funding, see 6720*

672 **Activities auxiliary to insurance and pension funding**

6720 **Activities auxiliary to insurance and pension funding**

This class includes:
- activities involved in or closely related to insurance and pension funding other than financial intermediation:
  . activities of insurance agents
  . average and loss adjusters

- activities of insurance risk and damage evaluators
- investigation in connection with insurance
- actuaries
- salvage administration

This class excludes:
- *marine salvage activities, see 6303*

K   Real estate, renting and business activities

This section includes activities that focus mainly on the business sector with the obvious exception of real estate activities. However, more or less all activities covered in this section can also be provided to private households, for example, renting of personal and household goods, database activities, legal activities, investigation and security services, interior decoration and photographic activities.

70   Real estate activities

701   Real estate activities with own or leased property

7010   Real estate activities with own or leased property

This class includes:
- buying, selling, renting and operating of self-owned or leased real estate:
  - apartment buildings and dwellings
  - non-residential buildings, including exhibition halls
  - land

This class also includes:
- subdividing real estate into lots
- development and sale of land
- operation of residential mobile home sites

This class excludes:
- *development on own account involving construction, see 4520*
- *operation of hotels, rooming houses, camps, trailer camps and other non-residential or short-stay lodging places, see 5510*

702   Real estate activities on a fee or contract basis

7020   Real estate activities on a fee or contract basis

This class includes:
- activities of real estate agents and brokers
- intermediation in buying, selling and renting of real estate on a fee or contract basis
- managing of real estate on a fee or contract basis
- appraisal services for real estate
- real estate escrow agents

71   Renting of machinery and equipment without operator and of personal and household goods

This division includes renting and operational leasing. The length of the rental may be short- or long-term. The machinery and equipment may be provided with or without maintenance.

This division excludes:
- *financial leasing, which is normally a special form of credit granting, see 6591*

711   Renting of transport equipment

7111   Renting of land transport equipment

This class includes:
- renting and operational leasing of land-transport equipment without drivers:
  - automobiles
  - trucks, haulage tractors, trailers and semi-trailers
  - motorcycles, caravans and campers etc.
  - railroad vehicles

This class also includes:
- renting of containers
- renting of pallets

This class excludes:
- *renting or leasing of vehicles or trucks with driver, see 6022, 6023*
- *financial leasing, see 6591*
- *renting of accommodation or office containers, see 7129*
- *renting of bicycles, see 7130*

7112   Renting of water transport equipment

This class includes:
- renting and operational leasing of water-transport equipment without operator:
  - commercial boats and ships

This class excludes:
- *renting of water-transport equipment with operator, see 6110, 6120*
- *financial leasing, see 6591*
- *renting of pleasure boats, see 7130*

7113   Renting of air transport equipment

This class includes:
- renting and operational leasing of air transport equipment without operator:
  - airplanes
  - hot-air balloons

This class excludes:
- *renting of air-transport equipment with operator, see 6220*
- *financial leasing, see 6591*

712   Renting of other machinery and equipment

7121   Renting of agricultural machinery and equipment

This class includes:
- renting and operational leasing of agricultural and forestry machinery and equipment without operator:
  - renting of products produced by class 2921, such as agricultural tractors etc.

This class excludes:
- *renting of this machinery or equipment with operator, see 0140*
- *financial leasing, see 6591*

7122   Renting of construction and civil engineering machinery and equipment

This class includes:
- renting and operational leasing of construction and civil-engineering machinery and equipment

without operator:
- crane lorries
- scaffolds and work platforms, without erection and dismantling

This class excludes:
- *renting of this machinery or equipment with operator, see 4550*
- *financial leasing, see 6591*

7123   Renting of office machinery and equipment (including computers)

This class includes:
- renting and operational leasing of office machinery and equipment without operator:
  - computers and computer peripheral equipment
  - duplicating machines, typewriters and word-processing machines
  - accounting machinery and equipment: cash registers, electronic calculators etc.

This class excludes:
- *financial leasing, see 6591*

7129   Renting of other machinery and equipment n.e.c.

This class includes:
- renting and operational leasing, without operator, of other machinery and equipment that are generally used as capital goods by industries:
  - engines and turbines
  - machine tools
  - mining and oilfield equipment
  - professional radio, television and communication equipment
  - motion picture production equipment
  - measuring and controlling equipment
  - other scientific, commercial and industrial machinery

This class also includes:
- renting of accommodation or office containers

This class excludes:
- *financial leasing, see 6591*
- *renting of agricultural machinery and equipment, see 7121*
- *renting of construction and civil-engineering machinery and equipment, see 7122*
- *renting of office machinery and equipment, including computers, see 7123*

713   Renting of personal and household goods n.e.c.

7130   Renting of personal and household goods n.e.c.

This class includes:
- the renting of all kinds of household or personal goods, to households or industries:
  - textiles, wearing apparel and footwear
  - furniture, pottery and glass, kitchen and tableware, electrical appliances and house wares
  - pleasure boats
  - bicycles
  - sports equipment
  - jewellery, musical instruments, scenery and costumes
  - books, journals and magazines
  - videotapes, records, CDs, DVDs etc.
  - do-it-yourself machinery and equipment, hand tools
  - flowers and plants

This class excludes:
- *renting of passenger cars, small vans, motorcycles, caravans and trailers without operator, see 7111*
- *renting of leisure and pleasure equipment as an integral part of recreational facilities, see 9249*
- *provision of linen, work uniforms and related items by laundries, see 9301*

72   Computer and related activities

This division includes activities related to the design, set-up, operation and maintenance of computer systems and networks, as well as custom software development and software publishing. Included are data-processing activities of various kinds and the storage and online distribution of electronic content. Also included are the maintenance and repair of other office, accounting and computing machinery.

721   Hardware consultancy

7210   Hardware consultancy

This class includes:
- consultancy on type and configuration of hardware with or without associated software applications by analysing the users' needs and problems and presenting the best solution

This class excludes:
- *hardware consultancy carried out by computer producing or selling units, see 3000, 5151, 5239*

722   Software publishing, consultancy and supply

7221   Software publishing

This class includes:
- production, supply and documentation of ready-made (non-customized) software:
  • operating systems
  • business and other applications
  • computer games for all platforms

This class excludes:
- *reproduction of software, see 2230*
- *retail sale of non-customized software, see 5239*
- *production of customized software, see 7229*

7229   Other software consultancy and supply

This class includes:
- analysis, design and programming of custom software, including:
  • analysis of the user's needs and problems, consultancy on the best solution
  • production of custom software to realize this solution
- development, production, supply and documentation of made-to-order software based on orders from specific users
- writing of software of any kind following directives of the user
- software maintenance
- web page design

This class excludes:
- *reproduction of software, see 2230*
- *software consultancy in conjunction with hardware consultancy, see 7210*
- *publishing of software, see 7221*

153

723   **Data processing**

7230   **Data processing**

This class includes:
- processing of data employing either the customer's or a proprietary program:
  - complete processing of data supplied by the customer
  - data entry services
  - scanning of documents
- management and operation on a continuing basis of data-processing facilities belonging to others
- timeshare computer services
- web-hosting

This class excludes:
- *renting and leasing of computers and computer peripheral equipment, see 7123*

724   **Database activities and online distribution of electronic content**

7240   **Database activities and online distribution of electronic content**

The online distribution in this class refers to units exclusively engaged in the online distribution of content, but not to units where online publishing is done in addition to traditional forms of publishing. In this respect, this is an exception to the general rule on classifying units according to the share of value added.

This class includes:
- assembly of compilations of data from one or more sources
- provision of online access to proprietary databases
- online database publishing
- online directory and mailing list publishing
- other online publishing, including e-books
- web search portals
- Internet search sites, Internet game sites, Internet entertainment sites

This class excludes:
- *online publishing combined with traditional publishing, see 221*
- *retail sale activities conducted over the Internet, see 5251*
- *publishing of database software, see 7221*
- *creation of database software or systems, see 7229*
- *operation of Internet gambling web sites, see 9249*

725   **Maintenance and repair of office, accounting and computing machinery**

7250   **Maintenance and repair of office, accounting and computing machinery**

This class includes:
- maintenance and repair of:
  - computer and computer peripheral equipment
  - typewriters, manual or electric
  - photocopy and thermocopy machines
  - electronic calculating machines, hand-held or desktop
  - cash registers

729   **Other computer-related activities**

7290   **Other computer-related activities**

This class includes:
- computer disaster recovery

- software installation services
- other computer-related services n.e.c.

73   Research and development

This division includes three types of research and development (R&D):
- basic research:
  - experimental or theoretical work undertaken primarily to acquire new knowledge of the underlying foundations of phenomena and observable facts, without particular application or use in view
- applied research:
  - original investigation undertaken in order to acquire new knowledge, directed primarily towards a specific practical aim or objective
- experimental development:
  - systematic work, drawing on existing knowledge gained from research and/or practical experience, directed to producing new materials, products and devices, to installing new processes, systems and services, and to improving substantially those already produced or installed

This division excludes:
- *governmental administration of R&D and of associated funds in the various natural or social sciences, see division 75*
- *administration and support of defence-related applied research and experimental development, see 7522*
- *education combined with R&D, see division 80*
- *raising and management of R&D funds for medical or other socially related R&D by charities, see 8532*

731   Research and experimental development on natural sciences and engineering (NSE)

7310   Research and experimental development on natural sciences and engineering (NSE)

This class includes:
- systematic studies and creative work in the three types of research and development defined above, in natural sciences (mathematics, physics, astronomy, chemistry, life sciences, medical sciences, earth sciences, agriculture, engineering and technology etc.). They are intended to increase the stock of knowledge and to devise new applications.

This class also includes:
- multidisciplinary research and development

732   Research and experimental development on social sciences and humanities (SSH)

7320   Research and experimental development on social sciences and humanities (SSH)

This class includes:
- systematic studies and creative efforts in the three types of research and development defined above, in social sciences and humanities (economics, psychology, sociology, archaeology, legal sciences, linguistics and languages, arts etc.). They are intended to increase the stock of knowledge and to devise new applications.

This class excludes:
- *market research, see 7413*

74   Other business activities

This division includes all business activities, except computer- and research-related activities, which are covered in divisions 72 and 73 of this sector. Some of the activities covered here are often carried out by ancillary units of larger businesses, while others are more likely to be carried out by independent units. Outsourcing is a major factor in changing the way these activities are accounted for. The majority of these activities are carried out for commercial clients, except for legal activities (7411), parts of labour recruitment and provision of personnel (7491) and photographic activities (7494), which are also provided for individuals.

741   Legal, accounting, bookkeeping and auditing activities; tax consultancy; market research and public opinion polling; business and management consultancy

7411   Legal activities

This class includes:
- legal representation of one party's interest against another party, whether or not before courts or other judicial bodies by, or under supervision of, persons who are members of the bar:
  - advice and representation in civil cases
  - advice and representation in criminal actions
  - advice and representation in connection with labour disputes
- general counselling and advising, preparation of legal documents:
  - articles of incorporation, partnership agreements or similar documents in connection with company formation
  - patents and copyrights
  - preparation of deeds, wills, trusts etc.
- other activities of notaries public, civil law notaries, bailiffs, arbitrators, examiners and referees

This class excludes:
- *law court activities, see 7523*

7412   Accounting, bookkeeping and auditing activities; tax consultancy

This class includes:
- recording of commercial transactions from businesses or others
- preparation of financial accounts, examination of such accounts and certification of their accuracy
- preparation of personal and business income tax returns
- advisory activities and representation (other than legal representation) on behalf of clients before tax authorities

This class excludes:
- *data-processing and tabulation activities, see 7230*
- *management consultancy such as design of accounting systems, cost accounting programmes, budgetary control procedures, see 7414*
- *bill collection, see 7499*

7413   Market research and public opinion polling

This class includes:
- investigation into market potential, acceptance and familiarity of products and buying habits of consumers for the purpose of sales promotion and development of new products, including statistical analyses of the results
- investigation into collective opinions of the public about political, economic and social issues and statistical analysis thereof

7414   Business and management consultancy activities

This class includes:
- provision of advice, guidance or operational assistance to businesses and the public service:
  - public relations and communication
  - design of accounting methods or procedures, cost accounting programmes, budgetary control procedures

- advice and help to businesses and public services in planning, organization, efficiency and control, management information etc.
- management consultancy such as by agronomists and agricultural economists to farms etc.

This class also includes:
- activities of management holding companies

This class excludes:
- *design of computer software for accounting systems, see 7229*
- *legal advice and representation, see 7411*
- *accounting, bookkeeping and auditing activities, tax consulting, see 7412*
- *market research and public opinion polling, see 7413*
- *architectural, engineering and other technical advisory activities, see 7421*
- *advertising activities, see 7430*

742 Architectural, engineering and other technical activities

7421 Architectural and engineering activities and related technical consultancy

This class includes:
- architectural consulting activities:
  - building design and drafting
  - supervision of construction
  - town and city planning and landscape architecture
- machinery and industrial plant design
- engineering, project management and technical activities:
  - projects involving civil engineering, hydraulic engineering, traffic engineering
  - projects elaboration and realization relative to electrical and electronic engineering, mining engineering, chemical engineering, mechanical, industrial and systems engineering, safety engineering
- elaboration of projects using air conditioning, refrigerating, sanitary and pollution control engineering, acoustical engineering etc.
- geologic and prospecting activities:
  - oil and gas field exploration, geophysical, geologic and seismic surveying
  - exploration of mineral deposits and of groundwater
- weather forecasting activities
- geodetic surveying activities:
  - land and boundary surveying activities
  - hydrologic surveying activities
  - subsurface surveying activities
  - cartographic and spatial information activities, including aerial photography thereof

This class also includes:
- activities of technical consultants other than engineers

This class excludes:
- *test drilling in connection with petroleum or gas extraction, see 1120*
- *test drilling and test hole boring, except for petroleum and gas extraction, see 4510*
- *activities of computer consultants, see 7210, 7229*
- *research and development activities, see 7310, 7320*
- *technical testing, see 7422*
- *aerial photography, see 7494*
- *interior decorating, see 7499*

7422 Technical testing and analysis

This class includes:
- testing and inspection of all types of materials and products:

- testing of composition and purity of minerals etc.
- testing activities in the field of food hygiene, including veterinary testing and control in relation to food production
- testing of physical characteristics and performance of materials, such as strength, thickness, durability, radioactivity etc.
- qualification and reliability testing
- performance testing of complete machinery: motors, automobiles, electronic equipment etc.
- radiographic testing of welds and joints
- failure analysis
- testing and measuring of environmental indicators: air and water pollution etc.
- certification of products, including consumer goods, motor vehicles, aircraft, pressurized containers, nuclear plants etc.
- periodic road-safety testing of motor vehicles
- testing with use of models or mock-ups (e.g. of aircraft, ships, dams etc.)

This class excludes:
- *testing and analysis of medical and dental specimens, see 8519*
- *testing of animal specimens, see 8520*

743   Advertising

7430   Advertising

This class includes:
- creation and realization of advertising campaigns:
  - creating and placing advertising in newspapers, periodicals, radio, television, the Internet and other media
  - creating and placing of outdoor advertising, e.g. billboards, panels, bulletins and frames, window dressing, showroom design, car and bus carding etc.
  - media representation, i.e. sale of time and space for various media soliciting advertising
  - aerial advertising
  - distribution or delivery of advertising material or samples
  - provision of advertising space on billboards etc.

This class excludes:
- *printing of advertising material, see 2221*
- *market research, see 7413*
- *public-relations activities, see 7414*
- *advertising photography, see 7494*
- *direct mailing activities (addressing, pre-sorting etc.), see 7499*
- *production of commercial messages for radio, television and film, see 9211, 9213*

749   Business activities n.e.c.

7491   Labour recruitment and provision of personnel

This class includes:
- personnel search, selection referral and placement in connection with employment supplied to the potential employer or to the prospective employee:
  - formulation of job descriptions
  - screening and testing of applicants
  - investigation of references etc.
- executive search and placement activities (headhunters)
- labour-contracting activities:
  - supply to others, chiefly on a temporary basis, of personnel hired by, and whose emoluments are paid by, the agency

This class excludes:
- *activities of farm labour contractors, see 0140*
- *activities of personal theatrical or artistic agents or agencies, see 7499*
- *motion picture, television and other theatrical casting activities, see 9249*

7492   Investigation and security activities

This class includes:
- surveillance, guard and other protective activities:
  - transport of valuables
  - bodyguard activities
  - street patrol, guard and watchman activities for apartment buildings, offices, factories, construction sites, hotels, theatres, dance halls, sport stadiums, shopping centres etc.
  - security activities in the field of public transportation such as luggage and passenger inspection at airports as well as patrol activities in trains and subways
  - store detective activities
  - remote-controlled supervision/inspection of technical equipment, buildings etc.
  - pre-qualification of alarms (deciding whether it is a false alarm or not) and calling police, fire brigade and ambulances if necessary
- consultancy in the field of industrial, household and public service security including security screening
- activities of private investigators

This class also includes:
- training of dogs for security reasons

This class excludes:
- *installation of alarm systems, see 4530*
- *investigation in connection with insurance, see 6720*

7493   Building-cleaning and industrial-cleaning activities

This class includes:
- interior cleaning of buildings of all types, including offices, factories, shops, institutions and other business and professional premises and multi-unit residential buildings
- window cleaning
- chimney cleaning and cleaning of fireplaces, stoves, furnaces, incinerators, boilers, ventilation ducts and exhaust units
- cleaning of industrial machinery
- sterilization of objects and premises
- bottle cleaning

This class also includes:
- disinfecting and exterminating activities for buildings, ships, trains etc.
- cleaning of trains, buses, planes etc.
- cleaning of inside of road and sea tankers

This class excludes:
- *agricultural pest control, see 0140*
- *steam-cleaning, sandblasting and similar activities for building exteriors, see 4540*
- *cleaning of new buildings after construction, see 4540*
- *carpet and rug shampooing, drapery and curtain cleaning, see 9301*

7494   Photographic activities

This class includes:
- commercial and consumer photograph production:
  - portrait photography for passports, schools, weddings etc.

- photography for commercials, publishers, fashion, real estate or tourism purposes
- aerial photography
- videotaping of events: weddings, meetings etc.
- film processing:
  - developing, printing and enlarging from client-taken negatives or cine-films
  - mounting of slides
  - copying and restoring or transparency retouching in connection with photographs

This class also includes:
- microfilming of documents

This class excludes:
- *cartographic and spatial information activities, see 7421*
- *processing motion picture film related to the motion picture and television industries, see 9211*

7495   Packaging activities

This class includes:
- packaging activities on a fee or contract basis, whether or not these involve an automated process:
  - filling of aerosols
  - bottling of liquids, including beverages and food
  - packaging of solids (blister packaging, foil-covered etc.)
  - security packaging of pharmaceutical preparations
  - labelling, stamping and imprinting
  - parcel-packing and gift-wrapping

This class excludes:
- *packing activities incidental to transport, see 6309*

7499   Other business activities n.e.c.

This class includes a great variety of service activities generally delivered to commercial clients.

This class includes:
- stenographic and mailing activities:
  - typing
  - other secretarial activities such as transcribing from tapes or discs
  - copying, blueprinting, multigraphing and similar activities
  - envelope addressing, stuffing, sealing and mailing, mailing list compilation etc., including for advertising material
- translation and interpretation
- bill collecting, credit rating in connection with an individual's or firm's creditworthiness or business practices
- business brokerage activities, i.e. arranging for the purchase and sale of small and medium-sized businesses, including professional practices
- patent brokerage activities (arranging for the purchase and sale of patents)
- appraisal activities other than for real estate and insurance
- fashion design related to textiles, wearing apparel, shoes, jewellery, furniture and other interior decoration and other fashion goods as well as other personal or household goods
- services of graphic designers
- activities of interior decorators
- activities of fair, exhibition and congress organizers
- activities of stand designers
- activities of self-employed auctioneers
- activities of consultants other than technical and engineering
- operation of enterprises on account of others
- trading stamp activities

This class also includes:
- proof-reading
- telephone answering activities
- call centre activities
- activities carried on by agents and agencies on behalf of individuals usually involving the obtaining of engagements in motion picture, theatrical production or other entertainment or sports attractions and the placement of books, plays, artworks, photographs etc., with publishers, producers etc.
- reading of gas, water and electricity meters

This class excludes:
- *wholesale of used motor vehicles by auctioning, see 5010*
- *activities of auctioning houses (retail), see 5240*
- *online auction activities (retail), see 5259*
- *credit card activities, see division 65*
- *database activities, see 7240*
- *bookkeeping activities, see 7412*
- *machinery and industrial design, see 7421*
- *display of advertisement and other advertising design, see 7430*

L   Public administration and defence; compulsory social security

See description of division 75.

75   Public administration and defence; compulsory social security

This division includes activities normally carried out by the public administration. However, the legal or institutional status is not, in itself, the determining factor. This division includes units that are part of local or central public bodies that enable the administration of the community to function properly.

This division includes:
- general administration (e.g. executive, legislative, financial administration etc. at all levels of government) and supervision in the field of social and economic life (group 751)
- defence, justice, police, foreign affairs etc. (group 752)
- management of compulsory social security schemes (group 753)

Activities classified elsewhere in ISIC do not fall under division 75 even if carried out by public administrations. For example, administration of the school system (i.e. regulations, checks, curricula) falls under division 75, but teaching itself does not (see division 80), and a prison or military hospital is classified to health (see division 85). Similarly, some activities described in division 75 may be carried out by non-government units.

751   Administration of the State and the economic and social policy of the community

7511   General (overall) public service activities

This class includes:
- executive and legislative administration of central, regional and local bodies
- administration and supervision of fiscal affairs:
  - operation of taxation schemes
  - duty/tax collection on goods and tax violation investigation
  - customs administration
- budget implementation and management of public funds and public debt:
  - raising and receiving of moneys and control of their disbursement
- administration of overall (civil) R&D policy and associated funds
- administration and operation of overall economic and social planning and statistical services at the various levels of government

This class excludes:
- *administration of R&D policies intended to increase personal well-being and of associated funds, see 7512*
- *administration of R&D policies intended to improve economic performance and competitiveness, see 7513*
- *administration of defence-related R&D policies and of associated funds, see 7522*

7512   **Regulation of the activities of agencies that provide health care, education, cultural services and other social services, excluding social security**

This class includes:
- public administration of programmes aimed to increase personal well-being:
  - health
  - education
  - culture
  - sport
  - recreation
  - environment
  - housing
  - social services
- public administration of R&D policies and associated funds for these areas

This class also includes:
- sponsoring of recreational and cultural activities
- distribution of grants to artists
- administration of potable water supply programmes
- administration of waste collection and disposal operations
- administration of environmental protection programmes
- administration of housing programmes

This class excludes:
- *compulsory social security activities, see 7530*
- *education activities, see division 80*
- *human health-related activities, see group 851*
- *sewage and refuse disposal and sanitation, see 9000*
- *activities of libraries, public archives, museums and other cultural institutions, see 923*
- *sporting or other recreational activities, see 924*

7513   **Regulation of and contribution to more efficient operation of business**

This class includes:
- public administration and regulation, including subsidy allocation, for different economic sectors:
  - agriculture
  - land use
  - energy and mining resources
  - infrastructure
  - transport
  - communication
  - hotels and tourism
  - wholesale and retail trade
- administration of R&D policies and associated funds to improve economic performance
- administration of general labour affairs
- implementation of regional development policy measures, e.g. to reduce unemployment

This class excludes:
- *research and experimental development activities, see division 73*

7514   Supporting service activities for the government as a whole

This class includes:
- general personnel and other general service activities:
  • administration and operation of general personnel services, whether or not connected with a specific function
  • development and implementation of general personnel policies and procedures covering selection and promotion, rating methods, job description, evaluation and classification, administration of civil service regulations etc.
- administration, operation and support of overall general services:
  • centralized supply and purchasing services
  • maintenance and storage of government records and archives
  • operation of government-owned or -occupied buildings
  • operation of central offices and other general services not connected with a specific function

752   Provision of services to the community as a whole

7521   Foreign affairs

This class includes:
- administration and operation of the ministry of foreign affairs and diplomatic and consular missions stationed abroad or at offices of international organizations
- administration, operation and support for information and cultural services intended for distribution beyond national boundaries
- aid to foreign countries, whether or not routed through international organizations
- provision of military aid to foreign countries
- management of foreign trade, international financial and foreign technical affairs
- international assistance, e.g. refugee or hunger relief programmes

7522   Defence activities

This class includes:
- administration, supervision and operation of military defence affairs and land, sea, air and space defence forces such as:
  • combat forces of army, navy and airforce
  • engineering, transport, communications, intelligence, material, personnel and other non-combat forces and commands
  • reserve and auxiliary forces of the defence establishment
  • provision of equipment, structures, supplies etc.
  • health activities for military personnel in the field
- administration, operation and support of civil defence forces
- support for the working out of contingency plans and the carrying out of exercises in which civilian institutions and populations are involved
- administration of defence-related R&D policies and related funds

This class excludes:
- *research and experimental development activities, see division 73*
- *provision of military aid to foreign countries, see 7521*
- *activities of military tribunals, see 7523*
- *provision of supplies for domestic emergency use in case of peacetime disasters, see 7523*
- *educational activities of military schools, colleges and academies, see division 80*
- *activities of military hospitals, see 8511*

7523   Public order and safety activities

This class includes:
- administration and operation of regular and auxiliary police forces supported by public authorities and of port, border, coastguards and other special police forces, including traffic

163

regulation, alien registration, operation of police laboratories and maintenance of arrest records
- firefighting and fire prevention:
  • administration and operation of regular and auxiliary fire brigades supported by public authorities in fire prevention, firefighting, rescue of persons and animals, assistance in civic disasters, floods, road accidents etc.
- administration and operation of administrative civil and criminal law courts, military tribunals and the judicial system, including legal representation and advice on behalf of the government or when provided by the government in cash or services
- rendering of judgements and interpretations of the law
- arbitration of civil actions
- prison administration and provision of correctional services, including rehabilitation services
- provision of supplies for domestic emergency use in case of peacetime disasters

This class excludes:
- *forestry fire-protection services, see 0200*
- *private firefighting and fire-prevention services in factories, see section D*
- *firefighting and fire-prevention services at airports, see 6303*
- *advice and representation in civil, criminal and other cases, see 7411*
- *administration and operation of military armed forces, see 7522*
- *activities of prison schools, see division 80*
- *activities of prison hospitals, see 8511*

753   Compulsory social security activities

7530   Compulsory social security activities

This class includes:
- funding and administration of government-provided social security programmes:
  • sickness, work-accident and unemployment insurance
  • retirement pensions
  • programmes covering losses of income due to maternity, temporary disablement, widowhood etc.

This class excludes:
- *non-compulsory social security, see 6602*
- *provision of welfare services and social work, see 8531, 8532*

M   Education

See description of division 80.

80   Education

This division includes public as well as private education at any level or for any profession, oral or written as well as by radio and television or other means of communication. It includes education by the different institutions in the regular school system at its different levels as well as adult education, literacy programmes etc. Also included are military schools and academies, prison schools etc. at their respective levels.

For each level of initial education, the classes include special education for physically or mentally handicapped pupils.

The breakdown of the categories in this division is based on the level of education offered as defined by the levels of ISCED 1997.

This division excludes:
- *education primarily concerned with recreational activities such as bridge or golf, see division 92*

801   Primary education

8010   Primary education

This class includes:
- pre-primary education (education preceding the first level)
- primary education (education at the first level)

Education can be provided in classrooms or through radio, television broadcast, Internet or correspondence.

This class also includes:
- special education for handicapped students at this level
- provision of literacy programmes for adults

This class excludes:
- *child day-care activities, see 8532*

802   Secondary education

8021   General secondary education

This class includes:
- general school education in the first stage of the secondary level corresponding more or less to the period of compulsory school attendance
- general school education in the second stage of the secondary level giving, in principle, access to higher education

Education can be provided in classrooms or through radio, television broadcast, Internet or correspondence.

Subject specialization at this level often begins to have some influence even on the educational experience of those pursuing a general programme. Such programmes are designated to qualify students either for technical and vocational education or for entrance to higher education without any special subject prerequisite.

This class also includes:
- special education for handicapped students at this level

This class excludes:
- *adult education as defined in 8090*

8022   Technical and vocational secondary education

This class includes:
- technical and vocational education below the level of higher education as defined in 8030

Typically, the programmes emphasize subject-matter specialization and instruction in both theoretical background and practical skills generally associated with present or prospective employment. The aim of a programme can vary from preparation for a general field of employment to a very specific job.

Education can be provided in classrooms or through radio, television broadcast, Internet or correspondence.

This class also includes:
- special education for handicapped students at this level

This class excludes:
- *technical and vocational education at post-secondary and university levels, see 8030*

803   Higher education

8030   Higher education

This class includes:
- first, second and third stages of higher education:
  - post-secondary education not leading to a university degree or equivalent
  - post-secondary education leading to a university degree or equivalent

A great variety of subject-matter programmes are offered at this level, some emphasizing more theoretical instruction and others, more practical instruction.

Education can be provided in classrooms or through radio, television broadcast, Internet or correspondence.

This class also includes:
- special education for handicapped students at this level

809   Other education

8090   Other education

This class is reserved for specialized training, generally for adults, not comparable to the general education in groups 801-803.

This class includes:
- adult education, i.e. education for people who are not in the regular school and university system. Instruction may be given in day or evening classes in schools or in special institutions providing for adults: driving schools, flying schools, art schools, cooking schools etc.
- instructions on general and vocational subjects
- education that is not definable by level

Education can be provided in classrooms or through radio, television broadcast, Internet or correspondence.

This class excludes:
- *higher education, see 8030*
- *activities of dance schools, see 9219*
- *instruction in sport and games, see 9241*

N   Health and social work

See description of division 85.

85   Health and social work

This sector includes the provision of health care by diagnosis and treatment and the provision of residential care for medical and social reasons, as well as the provision of social assistance, such as counselling, welfare, child protection, community housing and food services, vocational rehabilitation and childcare to those requiring such assistance. Also included is the provision of veterinary services.

851   Human health activities

8511   Hospital activities

This class includes:
- short- or long-term hospital activities of general and specialized hospitals, sanatoriums, preventoria, medical nursing homes, asylums, mental hospital institutions, rehabilitation

centres, leprosariums and other health institutions that have accommodation facilities, including military-base and prison hospitals:

- medical and surgical technical care activities such as diagnosis, treatment, operations, analyses, emergency activities etc.

The activities are chiefly directed to inpatients, carried out under the direct supervision of medical doctors and comprise:
- services of medical and paramedical staff
- services of laboratory and technical facilities, including radiologic and anaesthesiologic services
- emergency room services
- food and other hospital facilities

This class excludes:
- *health activities for military personnel in the field, see 7522*
- *private consultants' services to inpatients, see 8512*
- *dental activities without accommodation, see 8512*
- *ambulance activities, see 8519*
- *veterinary activities, see 8520*

8512   Medical and dental practice activities

This class includes:
- medical consultation and treatment in the field of general and specialized medicine by general practitioners and medical specialists and surgeons
- dental practice activities of a general or specialized nature
- orthodontic activities

The activities can be carried out in private practice, group practices and in hospital outpatient clinics, and in clinics such as those attached to firms, schools, homes for the aged, labour organizations and fraternal organizations, as well as in patients' homes.

This class also includes:
- dental activities in operating rooms
- private consultants' services to inpatients

This class excludes:
- *production of artificial teeth, denture and prosthetic appliances by dental laboratories, see 3311*
- *inpatient hospital activities, see 8511*
- *paramedical activities such as those of midwives, nurses and physiotherapists, see 8519*

8519   Other human health activities

This class includes:
- activities for human health not performed by hospitals or by medical doctors or dentists:
- activities of nurses, midwives, physiotherapists or other paramedical practicioners in the field of optometry, hydrotherapy, medical massage, occupational therapy, speech therapy, chiropody, homeopathy, chiropractice, acupuncture etc.

These activities may be carried out in health clinics such as those attached to firms, schools, homes for the aged, labour organizations and fraternal organizations and in residential health facilities other than hospitals, as well as in own consulting rooms, patients' homes or elsewhere.

This class also includes:
- activities of dental paramedical personnel such as dental therapists, school dental nurses and dental hygienists, who may work remote from, but are periodically supervised by, the dentist
- activities of medical laboratories
- activities of blood banks, sperm banks, transplant organ banks etc.

- ambulance transport of patients by any mode of transport including airplanes
- residential health facilities, except hotels

This class excludes:
- *production of artificial teeth, denture and prosthetic appliances by dental laboratories, see 3311*
- *testing activities in the field of food hygiene, see 7422*
- *hospital activities, see 8511*
- *medical and dental practice activities, see 8512*

852   Veterinary activities

8520   Veterinary activities

This class includes:
- animal health care and control activities for farm animals
- animal health care and control activities for pet animals

These activities are carried out by qualified veterinarians when working in veterinary hospitals as well as when visiting farms, kennels or homes, in own consulting and surgery rooms or elsewhere.

This class also includes:
- activities of veterinary assistants or other auxiliary veterinary personnel
- clinico-pathological and other diagnostic activities pertaining to animals
- animal ambulance activities

This class excludes:
- *farm animal boarding activities without health care, see 0140*
- *pet animal boarding activities without health care, see 9309*

853   Social work activities

8531   Social work activities with accommodation

This class includes:
- activities provided on a round-the-clock basis directed to provide social assistance to children, the aged and special categories of persons with some limits on ability for self-care, but where medical treatment or education are not important elements:
  - orphanages
  - children's boarding homes and hostels
  - residential nurseries
  - homes for the aged
  - homes for the physically or mentally handicapped, including the blind, deaf and dumb
  - rehabilitation homes (without medical treatment) for people addicted to drugs or alcohol
  - homes for the homeless
  - institutions that take care of unmarried mothers and their children

The activities may be carried out by government offices or private organizations.

This class excludes:
- *funding and administration of compulsory social security programmes, see 7530*
- *adoption activities, see 8532*
- *short-term shelter activities for disaster victims, see 8532*

8532   Social work activities without accommodation

This class includes:
- social, counselling, welfare, refugee, referral and similar activities, the services of which are delivered to individuals and families in their homes or elsewhere and carried out by government offices or by private organizations, disaster relief organizations and national or

local self-help organizations and by specialists providing counselling services:
  - welfare and guidance activities for children and adolescents
  - adoption activities, activities for the prevention of cruelty to children and others
  - old-age and sick visiting
  - household budget counselling, marriage and family guidance
  - community and neighbourhood activities
  - activities for disaster victims, refugees, immigrants etc., including temporary or extended shelter for them
  - vocational rehabilitation and habilitation activities for handicapped or unemployed persons provided that the education component is limited
- eligibility determination in connection with welfare aid, rent supplements or food stamps
- child day-care activities, including day-care activities for handicapped children
- day-care activities for handicapped adults
- day facilities for the homeless and other socially weak groups
- charitable activities like fund-raising or other supporting activities aimed at social work

This class excludes:
- *funding and administration of compulsory social security programmes, see 7530*
- *activities similar to those described in this class, but including accommodation, see 8531*

O Other community, social and personal service activities

This section includes services provided by businesses and government units to individuals, other businesses or the community as a whole, not covered in previous parts of the classification.

90 **Sewage and refuse disposal, sanitation and similar activities**

This division includes:
- collection and treatment of household and industrial waste, not for a further use in an industrial manufacturing process, but with the aim of disposal and resulting in a product with little or no value.

This division also includes:
- other activities such as street cleaning and snow removal etc.

This division excludes:
- *processing of waste and scrap and other articles into secondary raw material fit for direct use in an industrial manufacturing process, see 3710 and 3720*
- *wholesale (purchase and sale) in waste and scrap, including collecting, sorting, packing, dealing etc., but without a real transformation process, see 5149*

900 **Sewage and refuse disposal, sanitation and similar activities**

9000 **Sewage and refuse disposal, sanitation and similar activities**

This class includes:
- collecting and transporting of human waste water from one or several users, as well as rain water by means of sewerage networks, collectors, tanks and other means of transport (sewage vehicles etc.) and their treatment and disposal
- treatment of waste water by means of physical, chemical and biological processes like dilution, screening, filtering, sedimentation etc.
- treatment of waste water from swimming pools and from industry
- maintenance and cleaning of sewers and drains
- emptying and cleaning of cesspools and septic tanks, sinks and pits from sewage, servicing of chemical toilets
- collection of waste from households and enterprises by means of refuse bins, wheeled bins, containers etc.

- collection of refuse in litter-bins in public places
- collection of hazardous waste, used batteries, used cooking oils and fats etc.
- collection of used oil from shipment or garages
- collection of construction and demolition waste
- operation of waste collection centres
- waste disposal by incineration or by other means:
  • dumping of refuse on land or in water, burial or ploughing-under of refuse
  • treatment and disposal of transition radioactive waste, i.e. radioactive waste decaying within the period of transport, from hospitals etc.
- treatment and disposal of toxic live or dead animals and other contaminated waste
- disposal of used goods such as refrigerators to eliminate harmful waste
- decontamination of soils and groundwater at the place of pollution, either in situ or ex situ, using e.g. mechanical, chemical or biological methods
- decontamination and cleaning up of surface water following accidental pollution, e.g. through collection of pollutants or through application of chemicals
- cleaning up oil spills on land, in surface water, in ocean and seas, including coastal seas
- outdoor sweeping and watering of streets, squares, paths, markets, public gardens, parks etc.
- snow and ice clearing on highways, airport runways, including spreading of salt or sand etc.
- specialized other pollution-control activities

This class excludes:
- *cleaning of ditches and pest control for the benefit of agriculture, see 0140*
- *treatment of residual food substances for manufacture of food products, see division 15*
- *treatment of slaughter waste to produce animal feeds, see 1533*
- *reprocessing of nuclear fuels and treatment of radioactive nuclear waste, see 2330*
- *composting of organic waste, see 2412*
- *processing food, beverages and tobacco waste into secondary raw material, see 3720*
- *purification of water for water supply purposes, see 4100*
- *stripping work of contaminated topsoil as part of construction activities, see 4510*
- *clearing of mines and the like (including detonation) from construction sites, see 4510*
- *construction and repair of sewer systems, see 4520*
- *treatment of waste and scrap without a real mechanical or chemical transformation process and for sale to third parties, such as dismantling of cars, machinery or computers or such as sorting or pressing of paper, textile, plastics, wood waste etc., see divisions 50-52*
- *collection of waste as part of wholesale of waste, see 5149*
- *transporting of polluted soil, already stripped off by third parties, see 6023*
- *technical testing and analysis, see 7422*
- *disinfecting and exterminating activities in buildings, see 7493*

91   Activities of membership organizations n.e.c.

This division includes activities of organizations representing interests of special groups or promoting ideas to the general public. These organizations usually have a constituency of members, but their activities may involve and benefit non-members as well. The primary breakdown of this division is determined by the purpose that these organizations serve, namely interests of employers, self-employed individuals and the scientific community (group 911), interests of employees (group 912) or promotion of religious, political, cultural, educational or recreational ideas and activities (group 919).

911   Activities of business, employers and professional organizations

9111   Activities of business and employers organizations

This class includes:
- activities of organizations whose members' interests centre on the development and prosperity of enterprises in a particular line of business or trade, including farming, or on the

economic growth and climate of a particular geographical area or political subdivision without regard for the line of business.
- activities of federations of such associations
- activities of chambers of commerce, guilds and similar organizations
- dissemination of information, representation before government agencies, public relations and labour negotiations

This class excludes:
- *activities of trade unions, see 9120*

9112   Activities of professional organizations

This class includes:
- activities of organizations whose members' interests centre chiefly on a particular scholarly discipline or professional practice or technical field
- activities of associations of specialists engaged in scientific, academic or cultural activities, such as associations of writers, painters, performers of various kinds, journalists etc.
- dissemination of information, the establishment and supervision of standards of practice, representation before government agencies and public relations

This class also includes:
- activities of learned societies

This class excludes:
- *education provided by these organizations, see division 80*

912   Activities of trade unions

9120   Activities of trade unions

This class includes:
- activities of associations whose members are employees interested chiefly in the representation of their views concerning the salary and work situation and in concerted action through organization
- activities of single plant unions, of unions composed of affiliated branches and of labour organizations composed of affiliated unions on the basis of trade, region, organizational structure or other criteria

This class excludes:
- *education provided by such organizations, see division 80*

919   Activities of other membership organizations

9191   Activities of religious organizations

This class includes:
- activities of religious organizations or individuals providing services directly to worshippers in churches, mosques, temples, synagogues or other places
- activities of organizations furnishing monastery and convent services
- religious retreat activities

This class also includes:
- religious funeral service activities

This class excludes:
- *education provided by such organizations, see division 80*
- *health activities by such organizations, see group 851*
- *social work activities by such organizations, see group 853*

171

ISIC Rev.3.1

9192 Activities of political organizations

This class includes:
- activities of political organizations and auxiliary organizations such as young people's auxiliaries associated with a political party. These organizations chiefly engage in influencing decision-taking in public governing bodies by placing members of the party or those sympathetic to the party in political office and involve the dissemination of information, public relations, fund-raising etc.

9199 Activities of other membership organizations n.e.c.

This class includes:
- activities of organizations not directly affiliated to a political party furthering a public cause or issue by means of public education, political influence, fund-raising etc.:
  - citizens initiative or protest movements
  - environmental and ecological movements
  - organizations supporting community and educational facilities n.e.c.
  - organizations for the protection and betterment of special groups, e.g. ethnic and minority groups
  - associations for patriotic purposes, including war veterans' associations
- special interest groups such as touring clubs and automobile associations and consumer associations
- associations for the purpose of social acquaintanceship such as rotary clubs, lodges etc.
- associations of youth, young persons' associations, student associations, clubs and fraternities etc.
- associations for the pursuit of a cultural or recreational activity or hobby (other than sports or games), e.g. poetry, literature and book clubs, historical clubs, gardening clubs, film and photo clubs, music and art clubs, craft and collectors' clubs, social clubs, carnival clubs etc.
- associations for the protection of animals

This class excludes:
- activities of professional associations, see 9112

92 Recreational, cultural and sporting activities

This division includes the operation of facilities and provision of services to meet the cultural, entertainment, recreational and sports interest of their customers. This includes the production and promotion of, and participation in, live performances, events or exhibits intended for public viewing, the provision of artistic, creative or technical skills for the production of artistic products and live performances, the preservation and exhibition of objects and sites of historical, cultural or educational interest and the operation of facilities and the provision of services that enable customers to participate in sports or recreational activities or pursue amusement, hobbies and leisure-time interests.

921 Motion picture, radio, television and other entertainment activities

9211 Motion picture and video production and distribution

This class includes:
- production of theatrical and non-theatrical motion pictures whether on film, videotape or disc for direct projection in theatres or for broadcasting on television:
  - production in a motion picture studio, or in special laboratories for animated films or cartoons, of full-length films, documentaries, shorts etc., for public entertainment, for advertising, education, training or news information
  - processing of motion picture film
  - publishing of motion picture film
- supporting activities such as film editing, cutting, dubbing etc.

172

- activities of sound-recording studios
- distribution of motion pictures and videotapes to other industries but not to the general public, including sale or rental of movies or tapes to other industries, as well as activities allied to the distribution of films and videotapes such as film and tape booking, delivery, storage etc.
- buying and selling of motion picture and video distribution rights

This class excludes:
- *film duplicating (except reproduction of motion picture film for theatrical distribution) as well as audio and video tape, CD or DVD reproduction from master copies, see 2230*
- *retail trade of tapes, see groups 521, 523, 525*
- *wholesale of blank videotapes, see 5152*
- *wholesale of recorded videotapes, see 5139*
- *renting of tapes to the general public, see 7130*
- *film processing other than for the motion picture industry, see 7494*
- *activities of personal theatrical or artistic agents or agencies, see 7499*
- *activities of own account actors, cartoonists, directors, stage designers and technical specialists, see 9214*

9212   Motion picture projection

This class includes:
- motion picture or videotape projection in cinemas, in the open air or in other projection facilities

This class also includes:
- activities of cine-clubs

9213   Radio and television activities

This class includes:
- production of radio and television programmes, whether live or taped, whether or not combined with broadcasting
- broadcasting of radio and television programmes

The programmes produced and broadcast may be for entertainment, promotion, education or training or news dissemination such as sports, weather etc. The production of programmes may result in a permanent tape which may be sold, rented or stored for broadcast or rebroadcast.

This class excludes:
- *radio and television transmission via cable networks, see 6420*
- *radio and television transmission by relay or satellite, see 6420*
- *news agencies, see 9220*

9214   Dramatic arts, music and other arts activities

This class includes:
- production of live theatrical presentations, concerts and opera or dance productions and other stage productions:
  - activities of groups or companies, orchestras or bands
  - activities of individual artists such as actors, directors, musicians, authors, lecturers or speakers, sculptors, painters, cartoonists, engravers, etchers, stage-set designers and builders etc.
- operation of concert and theatre halls and other arts facilities
- operation of ticket agencies
- restoring of works of art such as paintings etc.

This class excludes:
- *restoring of furniture, see 3610*
- *restoring of organs and other historical musical instruments, see 3692*

ISIC Rev.3.1

> - *restoring of buildings, see division 45*
> - *activities of personal theatrical or artistic agents or agencies, see 7499*
> - *operation of cinemas, see 9212*
> - *casting activities, see 9249*

9219 Other entertainment activities n.e.c.

This class includes:
- production of entertainment n.e.c.:
  - activities of ballrooms and discotheques
  - activities of dancing schools and dance instructors
  - circus production
  - activities of amusement parks and amusement fairs
  - puppet shows, rodeos, activities of shooting galleries, firework display, model railway installations etc.

This class excludes:
- *other recreational activities, see 9249*

922 News agency activities

9220 News agency activities

This class includes:
- news syndicate and news agency activities furnishing news, pictures and features to the media
- activities of independent journalists

923 Library, archives, museums and other cultural activities

9231 Library and archives activities

This class includes:
- documentation and information activities of libraries of all kinds, reading, listening and viewing rooms, public archives providing service to the general public or to a special clientele, such as students, scientists, staff, members:
  - organization of a collection, whether specialized or not
  - cataloguing collections
  - lending and storage of books, maps, periodicals, films, records, tapes, works of art etc.
  - retrieval activities in order to comply with information requests etc.

This class excludes:
- *renting of videotapes, see 7130*
- *database activities, see 7240*

9232 Museums activities and preservation of historic sites and buildings

This class includes:
- operation of museums of all kinds:
  - art museums, museums of jewellery, furniture, costumes, ceramics, silverware
  - natural history, science and technological museums, historical museums, including military museums and historic houses
  - other specialized museums
  - open-air museums
- operation and preservation of historic sites and buildings

9233 Botanical and zoological gardens and nature reserves activities

This class includes:
- operation of botanical and zoological gardens, including children's zoos
- operation of nature reserves, including wildlife preservation etc.

924   Sporting and other recreational activities

9241   Sporting activities

This class includes:
- operation of facilities for outdoor or indoor sports events (open, closed or covered, with or without spectator seating):
  - football, hockey, cricket, baseball stadiums
  - track and field stadiums
  - swimming pools and stadiums
  - ice hockey arenas
  - boxing arenas
  - golf courses
  - bowling lanes
  - winter sports arenas and stadiums
- organization and operation of outdoor or indoor sports events for professionals or amateurs by organizations with or without own facilities:
  - football clubs, bowling clubs, swimming clubs, golf clubs, boxing, wrestling, health or body-building clubs, winter sports clubs, chess, draughts, domino or card clubs, field and track clubs, shooting clubs etc.
- activities related to promotion and production of sporting events
- activities of individual own-account sportsmen and athletes, judges, timekeepers, instructors, teachers, coaches etc.
- activities of sport and game schools
- activities of racing stables, kennels and garages
- activities of riding academies
- operation of sport fishing preserves
- support activities for sport or recreational hunting and fishing
- related service activities

This class excludes:
- *renting of sports equipment, see 7130*
- *park and beach activities, see 9249*

9249   Other recreational activities

This class includes activities related to recreation not elsewhere classified in this division:
- activities of recreation parks and beaches, including renting of facilities such as bathhouses, lockers, chairs etc.
- operation of recreational transport facilities, e.g. marinas
- motion picture, television and other theatrical casting activities
- gambling and betting activities:
  - sale of lottery tickets
  - operation (exploitation) of coin-operated gambling machines
  - operation (exploitation) of coin-operated games
  - operation of gambling cruises
  - operation of virtual gambling web sites
- fairs and shows of a recreational nature

This class also includes:
- renting of leisure and pleasure equipment as an integral part of recreational facilities

This class excludes:
- *activities of personal theatrical or artistic agents or agencies, see 7499*
- *other entertainment activities, e.g. circus production or activities of ballrooms, see 9219*

93   Other service activities

This division includes all service activities not elsewhere classified.

930   Other service activities

9301   Washing and (dry-)cleaning of textile and fur products

This class includes:
- laundering and dry-cleaning, pressing etc., of all kinds of clothing (including fur) and textiles, provided by mechanical equipment, by hand or by self-service coin-operated machines, whether for the general public or for industrial or commercial clients
- laundry collection and delivery
- carpet and rug shampooing and drapery and curtain cleaning, whether on clients' premises or not
- provision of linens, work uniforms and related items by laundries
- diaper supply services

This class also includes:
- repair and minor alteration of garments or other textile articles when done in connection with cleaning

This class excludes:
- *repair and alteration of clothing etc., as an independent activity, see 5260*
- *renting of clothing other than work uniforms, even if cleaning of these goods is an integral part of the activity, see 7130*

9302   Hairdressing and other beauty treatment

This class includes:
- hair washing, trimming and cutting, setting, dyeing, tinting, waving, straightening and similar activities for men and women
- shaving and beard trimming
- facial massage, manicure and pedicure, make-up etc.

This class excludes:
- *manufacture of wigs, see 3699*

9303   Funeral and related activities

This class includes:
- burial and incineration of human or animal corpses and related activities:
  - preparing the dead for burial or cremation and embalming and morticians' services
  - providing burial or cremation services
  - rental of equipped space in funeral parlours
- rental or sale of graves
- maintenance of graves and mausoleums

This class excludes:
- *religious funeral service activities, see 9191*

9309   Other service activities n.e.c.

This class includes:
- activities of Turkish baths, sauna and steam baths, solariums, reducing and slendering salons, massage salons etc.
- astrological and spiritualists' activities
- social activities such as escort services, dating services, services of marriage bureaux
- pet care services such as boarding, grooming, sitting and training pets

- genealogical organizations
- shoeshiners, porters, valet car parkers etc.
- coin-operated personal service machines (photo booths, weighing machines, machines for checking blood pressure, coin-operated lockers etc.)

This class excludes:
- *public pay-telephone services, see 6420*
- *veterinary activities, see 8520*
- *activities of health clubs, see 9241*

P Activities of private households as employers and undifferentiated production activities of private households

This section includes activities within households, where the same household is the consumer of the products produced. This can be effected through the employment of domestic personnel (division 95) or through the production of goods or services for own use (division 96 and 97).

95 Activities of private households as employers of domestic staff

See description of class 9500.

950 Activities of private households as employers of domestic staff

9500 Activities of private households as employers of domestic staff

This class includes the activities of households as employers of domestic personnel such as maids, cooks, waiters, valets, butlers, laundresses, gardeners, gatekeepers, stable-lads, chauffeurs, caretakers, governesses, babysitters, tutors, secretaries etc. It allows the domestic personnel employed to state the activity of their employer in censuses or studies, even though the employer is an individual.

The product, which is self-consumed, is considered non-market and assessed according to the cost of the personnel in the national accounts. These services cannot be provided by companies.

96 Undifferentiated goods-producing activities of private households for own use

See description of class 9600.

960 Undifferentiated goods-producing activities of private households for own use

9600 Undifferentiated goods-producing activities of private households for own use

This class contains the undifferentiated subsistence goods-producing activities of households, that is to say, the activities of households that are engaged in a variety of activities that produce goods for their own subsistence. These activities include hunting and gathering, farming, the production of shelter and clothing and other goods produced by the household for its own subsistence. In application, if households are also engaged in the production of marketed goods, they are classified to the appropriate goods-producing industry of ISIC. If they are principally engaged in a specific goods-producing subsistence activity, they are classified to the appropriate goods-producing industry of ISIC.

97 Undifferentiated service-producing activities of private households for own use

See description of class 9700.

970   **Undifferentiated service-producing activities of private households for own use**

9700   **Undifferentiated service-producing activities of private households for own use**

This class contains the undifferentiated subsistence services-producing activities of households. These activities include cooking, teaching, caring for household members and other services produced by the household for its own subsistence. In application, if households are also engaged in the production of multiple goods for subsistence purposes, they are classified to the undifferentiated goods-producing subsistence activities of households.

Q   Extraterritorial organizations and bodies

This section allows the employees of extraterritorial organizations to state the activity of their employer in censuses or studies, even though the employer is considered to be outside the economic territory of a country (although within the geographical territory).

99   **Extraterritorial organizations and bodies**

See description of class 9900.

990   **Extraterritorial organizations and bodies**

9900   **Extraterritorial organizations and bodies**

This class includes:
- activities of international organizations such as the United Nations and the specialized agencies of the United Nations system, regional bodies etc., the International Monetary Fund, the World Bank, the World Customs Organization, the Organisation for Economic Co-operation and Development, the Organization the Petroleum Exporting Countries, the European Communities, the European Free Trade Association etc.

This class also includes:
- activities of diplomatic and consular missions when being determined by the country of their location rather than by the country they represent

This class excludes:
- *administration and operation of diplomatic and consular missions stationed abroad or at offices of international organizations, see 7521*

Part four

Alternate aggregations and special groupings

174. Any statistical classification reflects compromises between a number of theoretical principles and practical considerations. Thus, not all needs for aggregated data will be equally well served by simple aggregation through the various levels within the existing structure of ISIC. To meet specialized needs for standardized aggregates that are formed in more complex ways, ISIC, Rev.3.1, is supplemented by several alternate aggregations. Each alternate aggregation is intended to serve the needs of a group of users who wish to present data that are classified according to ISIC in terms of standard tabulation categories that are essentially user-defined and internationally recognized.

175. This part of the publication includes descriptions of alternate aggregations defining the information sector and the information and communications technologies (ICT) sector. Attention has been paid to the fact that these alternate aggregations are defined in terms of complete ISIC classes, therefore allowing aggregation of existing data into these aggregations. Use of partial ISIC classes would require additional knowledge about the size of the splits involved, which is usually not available to users or may even not be obtainable through regular business surveys.

176. Analysis of different phenomena may require statistical data that cannot be fully described in terms of complete ISIC classes. This may be due to the level of aggregation that had to be applied to ISIC as an international standard or it may be due to the fact that the information sought is based on a concept that is different from that in ISIC. In this case, it may still be possible to give a definition in terms of an alternate aggregation using partial ISIC classes, while the actual data conversion would need to be supplemented by additional information.

177. Other alternate aggregations, using complete or partial ISIC classes, have been defined in other existing frameworks and are also referenced in this part of the publication. In principle, the list of annexes is open-ended and the Statistical Commission may, in the future, request that additional annexes be prepared and issued to respond to evolving user needs.

A. Information sector

178. The expressions "information age" and "global information economy" are used with considerable frequency today. The general idea of an "information economy" includes both the notion of industries primarily producing, processing and distributing information, and the idea that every industry is using available information and information technology to reorganize and make itself more productive.

179. The information sector comprises units engaged in the following processes: (a) producing and distributing information and cultural products, (b) providing the means to transmit or distribute these products as well as data or communications and (c) processing data.

180. The main components of this sector are the publishing industries, including software publishing, the motion picture and sound recording industries, the broadcasting and telecommunications industries, and the information services and data-processing industries. Thus, activities included in this sector cut across traditionally defined areas in the economy, such as manufacturing, telecommunications, motion picture production and some service areas.

181. The distribution modes for information products produced in this sector may either eliminate the necessity for traditional manufacture, or reverse the conventional order of

manufacturing followed by distribution. A newspaper distributed online, for example, can be printed locally or by the final consumer. Similarly, it is anticipated that packaged software, which today is mainly bought through the traditional retail channels, will soon be available mainly online. The information sector is designed to make such economic changes transparent as they occur, or to facilitate designing surveys that will monitor the new phenomena and provide data to analyse the changes.

182. Many of the industries in the information sector are engaged in producing products protected by copyright law, or in distributing them (other than by traditional wholesale and retail methods). Examples are traditional publishing industries, software and database publishing industries, and film and sound industries. Broadcasting and telecommunications industries and information providers and processors are also included in the information sector, because their technologies are so closely linked to other industries in the information sector.

183. The information sector as defined here is compatible with the information sector of the North American Industry Classification System (NAICS) (sector 51).

184. The information sector as a whole can be defined through the following ISIC classes.

Group	Class	Description
221		PUBLISHING, PRINTING AND REPRODUCTION OF RECORDED MEDIA
	2211	Publishing of books, brochures and other publications
	2212	Publishing of newspapers, journals and periodicals
	2213	Publishing of music
	2219	Other publishing
		POST AND TELECOMMUNICATIONS
642	6420	Telecommunications
		COMPUTER AND RELATED ACTIVITIES
	7221	Software publishing
723	7230	Data processing
724	7240	Database activities and online distribution of electronic content
		RECREATIONAL, CULTURAL AND SPORTING ACTIVITIES
	9211	Motion picture and video production and distribution
	9212	Motion picture projection
	9213	Radio and television activities
922	9220	News agency activities
	9231	Library and archives activities

185. The list above corresponds to the definition of NAICS, sector 51. Representing more detailed categories of this sector will usually require the subdividing of existing ISIC classes. However, the following correlations can be established by using complete ISIC classes. Due to the allocation of activities in NAICS group 518 to three different ISIC classes, only the combination of NAICS groups 516, 517 and 518 can be linked to ISIC.

NAICS group		ISIC class	
511	Publishing industries (except Internet)	2211	Publishing of books, brochures and other publications
		2212	Publishing of newspapers, journals and periodicals
		2219	Other publishing
		7221	Software publishing
512	Motion picture and sound recording industries	2213	Publishing of music
		9211	Motion picture and video production and distribution
		9212	Motion picture projection
515	Broadcasting (except Internet)	9213	Radio and television activities
516	Internet publishing and broadcasting	6420	Telecommunications
+517	Telecommunications	7230	Data processing
+518	Internet service providers, web search portals and data processing services	7240	Database activities and online distribution of electronic content
519	Other information services	9220*	News agency activities
		9231	Library and archives activities

B. Information and communication technologies (ICT)

186. In recent years, there has been a growing demand for data related to information and communication technologies (ICT). While all activities related to ICT have been described by or been part of ISIC classes in a number of ISIC divisions, the interpretation of classes belonging to ICT and the boundaries of the ICT sector itself have been subject to discussion. The Organisation for Economic Co-operation and Development (OECD) has taken a leading role in standardizing the content of the ICT sector. The following table is consistent with the recommendations made by OECD.

187. The definition of this sector seeks to provide a statistical basis for the measurement in an internationally comparable way of that part of economic activity that is generated by the production of ICT goods and services.

188. The principles applied to the definition of the ICT sector are the following:
For manufacturing industries, the products of a candidate industry:
- must be intended to fulfil the function of information processing and communication including transmission and display, or
- must use electronic processing to detect, measure and/or record physical phenomena or to control a physical process;
For services industries, the products of a candidate industry:
- must be intended to enable the function of information processing and communication by electronic means.

---

* Independent journalists and photographers need to be excluded from this correspondence.

189.   The following table shows the divisions, groups and classes that are part of the ICT sector.

Group	Class	Description
Division 30		MANUFACTURE OF OFFICE, ACCOUNTING AND COMPUTING MACHINERY
300	3000	Manufacture of office, accounting and computing machinery
		MANUFACTURE OF ELECTRICAL MACHINERY AND APPARATUS N.E.C.
313	3130	Manufacture of insulated wire and cable
		MANUFACTURE OF RADIO, TELEVISION AND COMMUNICATION EQUIPMENT AND APPARATUS
321	3210	Manufacture of electronic valves and tubes and other electronic components
322	3220	Manufacture of television and radio transmitters and apparatus for line telephony and line telegraphy
323	3230	Manufacture of television and radio receivers, sound or video recording or reproducing apparatus, and associated goods MANUFACTURE OF MEDICAL APPLIANCES AND INSTRUMENTS AND APPLIANCES FOR MEASURING, CHECKING, TESTING, NAVIGATING AND OTHER PURPOSES, EXCEPT OPTICAL INSTRUMENTS
	3312	Manufacture of instruments and appliances for measuring, checking, testing, navigating and other purposes, except industrial process control equipment
	3313	Manufacture of industrial process control equipment
		WHOLESALE TRADE AND COMMISSION TRADE, EXCEPT OF MOTOR VEHICLES AND MOTORCYCLES
	5151	Wholesale of computers, computer peripheral equipment and software
	5152	Wholesale of electronic and telecommunications parts and equipment
		POST AND TELECOMMUNICATIONS
642	6420	Telecommunications
		RENTING OF MACHINERY AND EQUIPMENT WITHOUT OPERATOR AND OF PERSONAL AND HOUSEHOLD GOODS
	7123	Renting of office machinery and equipment (including computers)
Division 72		COMPUTER AND RELATED ACTIVITIES
721	7210	Hardware consultancy
722	7221	Software publishing
	7229	Other software consultancy and supply
723	7230	Data processing
724	7240	Database activities and online distribution of electronic content
725	7250	Maintenance and repair of office, accounting and computing machinery
729	7290	Other computer-related activities

ISIC Rev.3.1

C. Informal sector aggregates

190. The informal sector encompasses a wide range of different activities. In order to describe the heterogeneity of the informal sector, analyse the differences between the various segments regarding their income-generating potential, constraints and other characteristics, and devise appropriate actions for them, policy makers and analysts need data revealing the structure and composition of the informal sector. While kind of economic activity (or industry) is not a criterion by which to define the informal sector, it is an important variable with which to describe its characteristics. It is thus used as one of the standard variables for statistics on the informal sector. It is also often used as a variable for the stratification of informal sector survey samples.

191. Informal sector activities tend to be concentrated heavily in the following tabulation categories (sections): A, D, F, G, H, I and O. Because of this, it is suggested that, for statistics on the informal sector, an alternative highest level of aggregation be introduced, with a smaller number of categories obtained by and large through the aggregation of the existing ISIC, Rev.3.1 sections.

192. Within the informal sector, both repair services and trade are groups of activities that are numerically important, and they should not be grouped together at any level when presenting statistics for the informal sector by industry. Moreover, these two groups of activities are undertaken in the informal sector of developing countries by different units, which differ significantly in terms of the characteristics of the persons engaged in them, including sex.

193. At the highest aggregate level, the alternative structure of ISIC, Rev. 3.1, proposed for the informal sector consists of the following nine categories (designated by Roman numerals).

	Title	ISIC sections	ISIC divisions	ISIC groups
I.	Agriculture, hunting, forestry and fishing	A, B	01, 02, 05	011-050
II.	Mining and quarrying, manufacturing and electricity, gas and water supply	C, D, E	10-37, 40-41	101-410
III.	Construction	F	45	451-455
IV.	Wholesale and retail trade	G*	50*, 51, 52*	501, 503, 504*, 505-525
V.	Repair of motor vehicles, motorcycles and personal and household goods	G*	50*, 52*	502, 504*, 526
VI.	Hotels and restaurants	H	55	551-552
VII.	Transport, storage and communications	I	60-64	601-642
VIII.	Education, health and other social and personal services	M, N, O, P	80, 85, 90-93, 95	801-950
IX.	Other services	J, K, L, Q	65-67, 70-75, 99	651-753, 990

Note: An asterisk (*) denotes partial correspondence.

184

194.   The split between IV (Wholesale and retail trade) and V (Repair of motor vehicles, motorcycles and personal and household goods) requires a split of ISIC group 504, which includes the sale, maintenance and repair of motorcycles and related parts and accessories. All other portions of these two categories can be described in terms of full ISIC groups. Links to higher levels of ISIC require the appropriate splits in this case.

D.   Other alternate aggregations

195.   While the alternate aggregations presented in this publication are combinations only of complete ISIC classes, there is also a need to express other groupings within the economy that cannot be defined strictly in terms of ISIC. In some cases, this may simply be a result of the existing level of aggregation or disaggregation of ISIC, while in others, such a correspondence cannot be achieved owing to the different nature of the breakdown required.

196.   A number of other alternate aggregations have been developed, such as those included in previous versions of this publication. In the last 10 years, different frameworks have been developed, defining these areas of statistics, that sometimes contain aggregations of complete or partial ISIC classes, linking the scope of these frameworks to ISIC. Rather than repeat such aggregations, which may be subject to change depending on the further development of these frameworks, we will reference only the existing aggregations.

197.   A list of environmental activities described in terms of ISIC categories is included in the Handbook of National Accounting - Integrated Environmental and Economic Accounting (SEEA)[1].

198.   The list of tourism-related activities that appeared as annex II of ISIC, Rev.3,[2] has been superseded by the Tourism Satellite Account (TSA) which identifies tourism in terms of characteristic products purchased by visitors and the activities that produce them and lists them in terms of CPC and ISIC. The concepts, definitions and classifications to be used, as well as the recommended methodological framework, are described in *Tourism Satellite Account: Recommended Methodological Framework*.[3] Tourism characteristic products and tourism characteristic activities are listed in annex II of that publication.

199.   Other alternate aggregations may be discussed and proposed as international recommendations in the future. The classifications web site of the United Nations Statistics Division will be used to show the current state of development in this area.

---

[1]   *Handbook of National Accounting - Integrated Environmental and Economic Accounting 2003*, Statistical Papers, Series F, No. 61, Rev.1 (United Nations publication, forthcoming).
[2]   *International Standard Industrial Classification of All Economic Activities*, Statistical Papers, Series M, No. 4, Rev.3 (United Nations publication, Sales No. E.90.XVII.11).
[3]   Commission of the European Communities, Organisation for Economic Co-operation and Development, United Nations and World Tourism Organization, *Tourism Satellite Account: Recommended Methodological Framework*, Statistical Papers Series F, No. 80 (United Nations publication, Sales No. E.01.XVII.9).

Part five

Correspondence tables

A. Relationship between ISIC, Rev.3.1, and COFOG

200.   The following table shows the relationship between ISIC, Rev.3.1, and the Classification of the Functions of Government (COFOG) in terms of ISIC categories likely to be relevant to the general government sector.

201.   While ISIC and COFOG classify different objects - statistical units by activity for ISIC and transactions by purpose for COFOG - in practice they are very similar. In principle, the unit of classification in COFOG is the individual transaction, but for many types of outlays the unit will often be the same government unit as for ISIC. Moreover, the criteria of classification - function in the case of COFOG and activity for ISIC - are conceptually rather similar. However, COFOG is more appropriate than ISIC for classifying government expenditures because the COFOG list of functions is more detailed than the ISIC list of activities, having been drawn up specifically to take account of the range and diversity of government activities.

202.   It should be noted that, as set out in paragraph 92 above, ISIC itself does not try to identify the government as such. The institutional sectors of the System of National Accounts are not reflected in ISIC. Therefore, government units can practically be engaged in any activity classified in ISIC. However, there are certain ISIC categories that are more typical of government functions or more likely to be under governmental control or sponsorship and are therefore more likely to be closely related to government expenditures. These categories have been used in the following table.

203.   An asterisk in the table indicates that only a part of the corresponding COFOG class is used in the link. In these cases, a description of the relevant detail, rather than the name of the COFOG class, is given.

COFOG		ISIC, Rev.3.1	
01.1.1	Executive and legislative organs	7511	General (overall) public service activities
01.1.2	Financial and fiscal affairs	7511	General (overall) public service activities
01.1.3	External affairs	7521	Foreign affairs
01.2	Foreign economic aid	7521	Foreign affairs
01.3.1	General personnel services	7514	Supporting service activities for the government as a whole
01.3.2	Overall planning and statistical services	7511	General (overall) public service activities
01.3.3	Other general services	7514	Supporting service activities for the government as a whole
01.4 *	Basic research	73	Research and development
01.4 *	Administration of R&D policies and related funds, intended to increase personal well-being, related to basic research	7512	Regulation of the activities of agencies that provide health care, education, cultural services and other social services, excluding social security
01.4 *	Administration of R&D policies and related funds, intended to improve economic performance, related to basic research	7513	Regulation of and contribution to more efficient operation of business
01.5 *	R&D general public services	73	Research and development

188

COFOG

ISIC, Rev.3.1

01.5 *	Administration of R&D policies and related funds, intended to increase personal well-being, related to general public services	7512	Regulation of the activities of agencies that provide health care, education, cultural services and other social services, excluding social security
01.5 *	Administration of R&D policies and related funds, intended to improve economic performance, related to general public services	7513	Regulation of and contribution to more efficient operation of business
01.6	General public services n.e.c.	7511	General (overall) public service activities
01.7	Public debt transactions	7511	General (overall) public service activities
01.8	Transfers of a general character between different levels of government	7511	General (overall) public service activities
02.1	Military defence	7522	Defence activities
02.2	Civil defence	7522	Defence activities
02.3	Foreign military aid	7521	Foreign affairs
02.4 *	R&D defence (except administration of defence-related R&D policies and related funds)	73	Research and development
02.4 *	Administration of defence-related R&D policies and related funds	7522	Defence activities
02.5	Defence n.e.c	7522	Defence activities
03.1	Police services	7523	Public order and safety activities
03.2	Fire-protection services	7523	Public order and safety activities
03.3	Law courts	7523	Public order and safety activities
03.4	Prisons	7523	Public order and safety activities
03.5	R&D public order and safety	73	Research and development
03.6	Public order and safety n.e.c.	7523	Public order and safety activities
04.1.1 *	Operation of weather forecasting and geodesic surveys	7421	Architectural and engineering activities and related technical consultancy
04.1.1 *	General economic and commercial affairs (except foreign commercial affairs, operation of weather forecasting and geodesic surveys)	7513	Regulation of and contribution to more efficient operation of business
04.1.1 *	General foreign commercial affairs	7521	Foreign affairs
04.1.2	General labour affairs	7513	Regulation of and contribution to more efficient operation of business
04.2.1	Agriculture	7513	Regulation of and contribution to more efficient operation of business
04.2.2 *	Forest fire fighting and fire prevention services	0200	Forestry, logging and related service activities
04.2.2 *	Forestry (except forest fire fighting and fire prevention services)	7513	Regulation of and contribution to more efficient operation of business
04.2.3 *	Operation of fish hatcheries	0502	Aquaculture
04.2.3 *	Fishing and hunting (except operation of fish hatcheries)	7513	Regulation of and contribution to more efficient operation of business

COFOG		ISIC, Rev.3.1	
04.3.1	Coal and other solid mineral fuels	7513	Regulation of and contribution to more efficient operation of business
04.3.2	Petroleum and natural gas	7513	Regulation of and contribution to more efficient operation of business
04.3.3	Nuclear fuel	7513	Regulation of and contribution to more efficient operation of business
04.3.4	Other fuels	7513	Regulation of and contribution to more efficient operation of business
04.3.5 *	Operation of non-enterprise-type electricity supply systems	4010	Production, transmission and distribution of electricity
04.3.5 *	Electricity (except operation of non-enterprise-type electricity supply systems)	7513	Regulation of and contribution to more efficient operation of business
04.3.6 *	Operation of non-enterprise-type non-electricity supply systems	4030	Steam and hot water supply
04.3.6 *	Non-electric energy (except operation of non-enterprise-type non-electricity supply systems)	7513	Regulation of and contribution to more efficient operation of business
04.4	Mining, manufacturing and construction	7513	Regulation of and contribution to more efficient operation of business
04.5.1 *	Operation of non-enterprise-type road transport systems	602	Other land transport
04.5.1 *	Operation of non-enterprise-type road transport facilities	6303	Other supporting transport activities
04.5.1 *	Road transport (except operation of non-enterprise-type road transport systems and facilities)	7513	Regulation of and contribution to more efficient operation of business
04.5.2 *	Operation of non-enterprise-type water transport systems and facilities	61	Water transport
04.5.2 *	Supporting activities to water transport	6303	Other supporting transport activities
04.5.2 *	Water transport (except supporting activities to water transport and except operation of non-enterprise-type water transport systems and facilities)	7513	Regulation of and contribution to more efficient operation of business
04.5.3 *	Operation of non-enterprise-type railway transport systems	6010	Transport via railways
04.5.3 *	Operation of non-enterprise-type railway transport facilities	6303	Other supporting transport activities
04.5.3 *	Railway transport (except operation of non-enterprise-type railway transport systems and facilities)	7513	Regulation of and contribution to more efficient operation of business
04.5.4 *	Operation of non-enterprise-type air transport systems and facilities	62	Air transport
04.5.4 *	Support activities to air transport	6303	Other supporting transport activities
04.5.4 *	Air transport (except support activities to air transport and except operation of non-enterprise-type air transport systems and facilities)	7513	Regulation of and contribution to more efficient operation of business

190

COFOG		ISIC, Rev.3.1	
04.5.5 *	Operation of non-enterprise-type pipeline and other transport systems and facilities	6030	Transport via pipelines
04.5.5 *	Pipeline and other transport (except operation of non-enterprise-type pipeline and other transport systems and facilities)	7513	Regulation of and contribution to more efficient operation of business
04.6	Communication	7513	Regulation of and contribution to more efficient operation of business
04.7.1	Distributive trades, storage and warehousing	7513	Regulation of and contribution to more efficient operation of business
04.7.2	Hotels and restaurants	7513	Regulation of and contribution to more efficient operation of business
04.7.3 *	Tourist offices	6304	Activities of travel agencies and tour operators; tourist assistance activities n.e.c.
04.7.3 *	Tourism	7513	Regulation of and contribution to more efficient operation of business
04.7.4	Multi-purpose development projects	7513	Regulation of and contribution to more efficient operation of business
04.8	R&D economic affairs	73	Research and development
04.9	Economic affairs n.e.c	7513	Regulation of and contribution to more efficient operation of business
05.1 *	Administration of waste collection, treatment and disposal systems	7512	Regulation of the activities of agencies that provide health care, education, cultural services and other social services, excluding social security
05.1 *	Waste management	9000	Sewage and refuse disposal, sanitation and similar activities
05.2 *	Administration of waste-water treatment systems	7512	Regulation of the activities of agencies that provide health care, education, cultural services and other social services, excluding social security
05.2 *	Waste-water management	9000	Sewage and refuse disposal, sanitation and similar activities
05.3	Pollution abatement	7512	Regulation of the activities of agencies that provide health care, education, cultural services and other social services, excluding social security
05.4 *	Protection of biodiversity and landscape (except operation of natural parks and reserves)	7512	Regulation of the activities of agencies that provide health care, education, cultural services and other social services, excluding social security
05.4 *	Operation of natural parks and reserves	9233	Botanical and zoological gardens and nature reserves activities
05.5	R&D environmental protection	73	Research and development

COFOG		ISIC, Rev.3.1	
05.6	Environmental protection n.e.c.	7512	Regulation of the activities of agencies that provide health care, education, cultural services and other social services, excluding social security
06.1 *	Housing development (construction)	45	Construction
06.1 *	Housing development (except construction)	7512	Regulation of the activities of agencies that provide health care, education, cultural services and other social services, excluding social security
06.2	Community development	7512	Regulation of the activities of agencies that provide health care, education, cultural services and other social services, excluding social security
06.3 *	Water supply	4100	Collection, purification and distribution of water
06.3 *	Construction of non-enterprise type water supply systems	4520	Building of complete constructions or parts thereof; civil engineering
06.3 *	Administration of water supply affairs	7512	Regulation of the activities of agencies that provide health care, education, cultural services and other social services, excluding social security
06.4 *	Installation of street lighting	4530	Building installation
06.4 *	Street lighting	7512	Regulation of the activities of agencies that provide health care, education, cultural services and other social services, excluding social security
06.5	R&D housing and community amenities	73	Research and development
06.6	Housing and community amenities n.e.c	7512	Regulation of the activities of agencies that provide health care, education, cultural services and other social services, excluding social security
07.1	Medical products, appliances and equipment	7530	Compulsory social security activities
07.2	Outpatient services	8512	Medical and dental practice activities
07.3	Hospital services	8511	Hospital activities
07.4	Public-health services	8519	Other human health activities
07.5	R&D health	73	Research and development
07.6	Health n.e.c	7512	Regulation of the activities of agencies that provide health care, education, cultural services and other social services, excluding social security
08.1 *	Administration of recreational and sporting affairs	7512	Regulation of the activities of agencies that provide health care, education, cultural services and other social services, excluding social security
08.1 *	Operation of recreational and sporting facilities	92	Recreational, cultural and sporting activities

COFOG		ISIC, Rev.3.1	
08.2 *	Administration of cultural affairs	7512	Regulation of the activities of agencies that provide health care, education, cultural services and other social services, excluding social security
08.2 *	Operation of cultural facilities	92	Recreational, cultural and sporting activities
08.3 *	Operation of publishing services	22	Publishing, printing and reproduction of recorded media
08.3 *	Administration of broadcasting and publishing services	7512	Regulation of the activities of agencies that provide health care, education, cultural services and other social services, excluding social security
08.3 *	Operation of broadcasting services	92	Recreational, cultural and sporting activities
08.4 *	Administration of religious and other community services	7512	Regulation of the activities of agencies that provide health care, education, cultural services and other social services, excluding social security
08.4 *	Operation of religious services	9191	Activities of religious organizations
08.4 *	Operation of other community services	9199	Activities of other membership organizations n.e.c.
08.5	R&D recreation, culture and religion	73	Research and development
08.6	Recreation, culture and religion n.e.c	7512	Regulation of the activities of agencies that provide health care, education, cultural services and other social services, excluding social security
09.1 *	Inspection of schools providing pre-primary and primary education	7512	Regulation of the activities of agencies that provide health care, education, cultural services and other social services, excluding social security
09.1 *	Provision of pre-primary and primary education	8010	Primary education
09.2 *	Inspection of schools providing secondary education	7512	Regulation of the activities of agencies that provide health care, education, cultural services and other social services, excluding social security
09.2 *	Provision of secondary education	802	Secondary education
09.3 *	Inspection of institutions providing post-secondary non-tertiary education	7512	Regulation of the activities of agencies that provide health care, education, cultural services and other social services, excluding social security
09.3 *	Provision of post-secondary non-tertiary education	8030	Higher education
09.4 *	Inspection of universities and other institutions providing tertiary education	7512	Regulation of the activities of agencies that provide health care, education, cultural services and other social services, excluding social security

COFOG		ISIC, Rev.3.1	
09.4 *	Provision of tertiary education	8030	Higher education
09.5 *	Inspection of institutions providing education not definable by level	7512	Regulation of the activities of agencies that provide health care, education, cultural services and other social services, excluding social security
09.5 *	Provision of education not definable by level	8090	Other education
09.6 *	Inspection of subsidiary services to education	7512	Regulation of the activities of agencies that provide health care, education, cultural services and other social services, excluding social security
09.6 *	Subsidiary services to education	various	
09.7	R&D education	73	Research and development
09.8	Education n.e.c.	7512	Regulation of the activities of agencies that provide health care, education, cultural services and other social services, excluding social security
10.1 *	Sickness and disability (except benefits in kind)	7530	Compulsory social security activities
10.1 *	Benefits in kind concerning sickness and disability	85	Health and social work
10.2 *	Old age (except benefits in kind)	7530	Compulsory social security activities
10.2 *	Benefits in kind concerning old age	85	Health and social work
10.3 *	Survivors (except benefits in kind)	7530	Compulsory social security activities
10.3 *	Benefits in kind concerning survivors	85	Health and social work
10.4 *	Family and children (except benefits in kind)	7530	Compulsory social security activities
10.4 *	Benefits in kind concerning family and children	85	Health and social work
10.5 *	Unemployment (except benefits in kind)	7530	Compulsory social security activities
10.5 *	Benefits in kind concerning unemployment	85	Health and social work
10.6 *	Provision of low-cost or social housing	7010	Real estate activities with own or leased property
10.6 *	Housing (except provision of low-cost or social housing)	7530	Compulsory social security activities
10.7 *	Social exclusion n.e.c (except benefits in kind)	7530	Compulsory social security activities
10.7 *	Benefits in kind concerning social exclusion n.e.c.	85	Health and social work
10.8	R&D social protection	73	Research and development
10.9	Social protection n.e.c.	7512	Regulation of the activities of agencies that provide health care, education, cultural services and other social services, excluding social security

B. Correspondence between ISIC, Rev.3, and ISIC, Rev.3.1 (condensed)

204.   This table shows only ISIC classes that are affected by the changes made in ISIC Rev.3.1. All unlisted classes have the same scope and code in both classifications. An asterisk (*) next to the ISIC code indicates that only a part of the class is involved in this particular link.

Rev.3		Rev.3.1		Activity
A		**Agriculture, hunting and forestry**		
0112	*	0112		Growing of vegetables, horticultural specialties and nursery products, except olives
0112	*	0113	*	Growing of olives
0113		0113	*	Growing of fruit, nuts, beverage and spice crops
0140	*	0140		Agricultural and animal husbandry services, boarding of farm animals; except pet boarding
0140	*	9309	*	Pet boarding
0200	*	0113	*	Gathering of mushrooms, truffles, berries or nuts
0200	*	0200		Forestry, logging activities; gathering of forest products, except mushroom, truffles, berries or nuts
B		**Fishing**		
0500	*	0501		Fishing
0500	*	0502		Fish farming
D		**Manufacturing**		
1513		1513	*	Processing and preserving of fruit and vegetables
1549	*	1513	*	Roasting of nuts
1549	*	1549		Manufacture of other food products n.e.c.; except roasting of nuts
1712	*	1712		Finishing of textiles; except "while-you-wait" services
1712	*	5260	*	"While-you-wait" services, printing of textiles
2211	*	2211		Publishing of books, brochures, maps etc.
2211	*	2213	*	Publishing of sheet music
2213	*	2213	*	Publishing of recorded media
2892	*	2892		Treatment and coating of metals; except "while-you-wait" services
2892	*	5260	*	"While-you-wait" services, engraving of metals
2926		2926	*	Manufacture of machinery for textile, apparel and leather production
2929	*	2926	*	Manufacture of machines for extruding, drawing, texturing, manufacturing or cutting man-made textile fibres, materials or yarns
2929	*	2929		Manufacture of other special-purpose machinery
G		**Wholesale and retail trade; repair of motor vehicles, motorcycles and personal and household goods**		
5150	*	5151		Wholesale of computers, computer peripheral equipment and software
5150	*	5152		Wholesale of electronic parts and equipment
5150	*	5159		Wholesale of other machinery, equipment and supplies
5240	*	5240		Retail sale of second-hand goods in stores
5240	*	6592	*	Pawnshops
5260		5260	*	Repair of personal and household goods
5520		5520	*	Restaurants, bars and canteens

I			**Transport, storage and communications**
6420		6420	* Telecommunication services
6592		6592	* Other credit granting
K			**Real estate, renting and business activities**
7220	*	7221	Software publishing
7220	*	7229	Software consultancy and supply, except software publishing
7494	*	7494	* Other photographic activities
7494	*	9309	* Coin-operated photo machines
7499	*	7494	* Microfilming
7499	*	7499	Other business activities n.e.c.; except microfilming
M			**Education**
8010		8010	* Primary education
8090	*	8010	* Adult education, primary level
8021		8021	* General secondary education
8090	*	8021	* Adult education, secondary level, general
8022		8022	* Technical and vocational secondary education
8090	*	8022	* Adult education, secondary level, technical and vocational
8090	*	8090	Adult and other education; except adult education at primary and secondary level
N			**Health and social work**
8532	*	5520	"Meals on wheels"
8532	*	8532	Other social work activities without accommodation
O			**Other community, social and personal service activities**
9211		9211	* Motion picture and video production and distribution
9241		9241	* Sporting activities
9249	*	9211	* Sound recording studios
9249	*	9241	* Recreational fishing and related service activities
9249	*	9249	Other recreational activities
9309	*	6420	* Pay-telephone services
9309	*	9309	* Other service activities n.e.c.
Other			
n/a		9600	(These activities had to be partially allocated to other ISIC sections, such as agriculture, fishing, construction etc., with estimated split ratios.)
n/a		9700	(These activities are not covered in ISIC, Rev.3.)

C. Correspondence between ISIC, Rev.3.1, and ISIC, Rev.3 (condensed)

205.   This table shows only ISIC classes that are affected by the changes made in ISIC, Rev.3.1. All unlisted classes have the same scope and code in both classifications. An asterisk (*) next to the ISIC code indicates that only a part of the class is involved in this particular link.

Rev.3.1		Rev.3		Activity
A		**Agriculture, hunting and forestry**		
0112		0112	*	Growing of vegetables, horticultural specialties and nursery products, except olives
0113	*	0112	*	Growing of olives
0113	*	0113		Growing of fruit, nuts, beverage and spice crops; except olives
0113	*	0200	*	Gathering of berries or nuts
0140		0140	*	Agricultural and animal husbandry services, boarding of farm animals; except pet boarding
0200		0200	*	Forestry, logging activities; gathering of forest products, except mushroom, truffles, berries or nuts
B		**Fishing**		
0501		0500	*	Fishing
0502		0500	*	Fish farming
D		**Manufacturing**		
1513	*	1513		Processing and preserving of fruit and vegetables
1513	*	1549	*	Roasting of nuts
1549		1549	*	Manufacture of other food products n.e.c.; except roasting of nuts
1712		1712	*	Finishing of textiles
2211		2211	*	Publishing of books, brochures, maps etc.
2213	*	2211	*	Publishing of sheet music
2213	*	2213	*	Publishing of recorded media
2892		2892	*	Treatment and coating of metals; general mechanical engineering on a fee or contract basis
2926	*	2926		Manufacture of machinery for textile, apparel and leather production
2926	*	2929	*	Manufacture of machines for extruding, drawing, texturing, manufacturing or cutting man-made textile fibres, materials or yarns
2929		2929	*	Manufacture of other special-purpose machinery
G		**Wholesale and retail trade; repair of motor vehicles, motorcycles and personal and household goods**		
5151		5150	*	Wholesale of computers, computer peripheral equipment and software
5152		5150	*	Wholesale of electronic parts and equipment
5159		5150	*	Wholesale of other machinery, equipment and supplies
5240		5240	*	Retail sale of second-hand goods in stores
5260	*	1712	*	"While-you-wait" services, printing of textiles
5260	*	2892	*	"While-you-wait" services, engraving of metals
5260	*	5260		Repair of personal and household goods
5520	*	5520		Restaurants, bars and canteens
5520		8532	*	"Meals on wheels"

I	**Transport, storage and communications**			
6420	*	6420		Telecommunication services
6420	*	9309	*	Pay-telephone services
J	**Financial intermediation**			
6592	*	5240	*	Pawnshops
6592	*	6592		Other credit granting
K	**Real estate, renting and business activities**			
7221		7220	*	Software publishing
7229		7220	*	Software consultancy and supply, except software publishing
7494	*	7494	*	Other photographic activities
7494	*	7499	*	Microfilming
7499		7499	*	Other business activities n.e.c.; except microfilming
M	**Education**			
8010	*	8010		Primary education
8010	*	8090	*	Adult education, primary level
8021	*	8021		General secondary education
8021	*	8090	*	Adult education, secondary level, general
8022	*	8022		Technical and vocational secondary education
8022	*	8090	*	Adult education, secondary level, technical and vocational
8090		8090	*	Adult and other education; except adult education at primary and secondary level
N	**Health and social work**			
8532		8532	*	Other social work activities without accommodation
O	**Other community, social and personal service activities**			
9211	*	9211		Motion picture and video production and distribution
9211	*	9249	*	Sound recording studios
9241	*	9241		Sporting activities
9241	*	9249	*	Recreational fishing and related service activities
9249		9249	*	Other recreational activities
9309	*	0140	*	Pet boarding
9309	*	7494	*	Coin-operated photo machines
9309	*	9309	*	Other service activities n.e.c.
P	**Activities of private households as employers and undifferentiated production activities of private households**			
9600		n/a		(These activities had to be partially allocated to other ISIC sections, such as agriculture, fishing, construction etc., with estimated split ratios.)
9700		n/a		(These activities are not covered in ISIC, Rev.3.)

D. Correspondence between ISIC, Rev.2, and ISIC, Rev.3.1

206.   This table shows the complete correspondence between ISIC, Rev.2, and ISIC, Rev.3.1. An asterisk (*) next to the ISIC code indicates that only a part of the class is involved in this particular link.

Rev.2		Rev.3.1		Activity
	1.	**Agriculture, hunting, forestry and fishing**		
1110				**Agriculture and livestock production**
1110	*	0111		Growing of cereals and other crops n.e.c.
1110	*	0112	*	Growing of vegetables, horticultural specialties and nursery products
1110	*	0113		Growing of fruit, nuts, beverage and spice crops
1110	*	0121		Farming of cattle, sheep, goats, horses, asses, mules and hinnies; dairy farming
1110	*	0122	*	Raising domesticated or wild animals n.e.c. (e.g. swine, poultry, rabbits)
1110	*	0130		Growing of crops combined with farming of animals (mixed farming)
1110	*	0140	*	Landscape gardening
1110	*	0200	*	Tree nurseries, except forest trees
1120				**Agricultural services**
1120	*	0122	*	Poultry hatchery, silkworm raising, on a fee or contract basis
1120	*	0140	*	Agricultural and animal husbandry activities, on a fee or contract basis
1120	*	7414	*	Farm management activities
1130				**Hunting, trapping and game propagation**
1130		0150	*	Hunting, trapping and game propagation
1210				**Forestry**
1210	*	0112	*	Gathering of mushrooms, truffles
1210	*	0200	*	Forestry and related service activities
1220				**Logging**
1220		0200	*	Logging
1301				**Ocean and coastal fishing**
1301	*	0150	*	Catching of sea mammals, except whales
1301	*	0501	*	Ocean and coastal fishing
1302				**Fishing not elsewhere classified**
1302	*	0122	*	Frog farming
1302	*	0501	*	Fishing in inland waters; service activities related to fishing
1302	*	0502		Fish hatcheries, cultivated beds; service activities related to aquaculture

Rev.2		Rev.3.1		Activity
	2.	**Mining and quarrying**		
2100				**Coal mining**
2100	*	1010	*	Mining and agglomeration of hard coal
2100	*	1020	*	Mining and agglomeration of lignite
2200				**Crude petroleum and natural gas production**
2200	*	1010	*	On-site gasification of coal
2200	*	1110		Extraction of crude petroleum and natural gas
2301				**Iron ore mining**
2301		1310		Mining of iron ores
2302				**Non-ferrous ore mining**
2302	*	1200		Mining of uranium and thorium ores
2302	*	1320		Mining of non-ferrous metal ores, except uranium and thorium ores
2901				**Stone quarrying, clay and sand pits**
2901	*	1410	*	Quarrying of building or monumental stone; mining of ceramic or refractory clay, chalk, dolomite; sand and gravel
2901	*	1429	*	Mining of feldspar
2902				**Chemical and fertilizer mineral mining**
2902		1421		Mining of chemical and fertilizer minerals
2903				**Salt mining**
2903		1422		Extraction of salt
2909				**Mining and quarrying not elsewhere classified**
2909	*	1030	*	Mining and agglomeration of peat
2909	*	1410	*	Mining of gypsum, anhydrite
2909	*	1429	*	Mining and quarrying of asbestos, mica, quartz, gemstones, abrasives, asphalt and bitumen, other non-metallic minerals, n.e.c.
	3.	**Manufacturing**		
3111				**Slaughtering, preparing and preserving meat**
3111	*	1511	*	Slaughtering, preparing and preserving meat, including sausage, edible animal fats, flours and meals, by-products (hides, bones etc.)
3111	*	1549	*	Manufacture of soup containing meat
3112				**Manufacture of dairy products**
3112		1520		Manufacture of dairy products

Rev.2		Rev.3.1		Activity
3113				**Canning and preserving of fruits and vegetables**
3113	*	1513	*	Canning and preserving of fruits and vegetables (except soups)
3113	*	1549	*	Manufacture of soups of vegetables and fruit
3114				**Canning, preserving and processing of fish, crustacea and similar foods**
3114	*	1512	*	Canning, preserving and processing of fish, crustacea and similar foods (except soups)
3114	*	1549	*	Manufacture of fish and seafood soups and specialties
3115				**Manufacture of vegetable and animal oils and fats**
3115	*	1511	*	Processing of inedible oils and fats
3115	*	1512	*	Production of fishmeal
3115	*	1514		Manufacture of vegetable and animal oils and fats
3115	*	1532	*	Manufacture of meal, cake of vegetables, nuts
3116				**Grain mill products**
3116	*	1513	*	Potato flour and meal
3116	*	1531	*	Grain milling: flour, meal, cereal grains; rice milling; vegetable milling; manufacture of breakfast foods
3116	*	1532	*	Manufacture of tapioca; wet corn milling
3117				**Manufacture of bakery products**
3117	*	1541		Manufacture of bakery products (bread, pastry etc.)
3117	*	1544	*	Manufacture of macaroni, noodles, couscous and similar farinaceous products
3118				**Sugar factories and refineries**
3118		1542	*	Sugar factories and refineries
3119				**Manufacture of cocoa, chocolate and sugar confectionery**
3119	*	1513	*	Roasting of nuts
3119	*	1543	*	Manufacture of cocoa, chocolate and sugar confectionery
3121				**Manufacture of food products not elsewhere classified**
3121	*	1513	*	Processing of fruits and vegetables n.e.c. (e.g. baked beans, grape sugar, juice extracts)
3121	*	1532	*	Manufacture of starch products n.e.c.
3121	*	1542	*	Production of maple sugar, invert sugar, sugars other than cane or beet
3121	*	1543	*	Manufacture of marshmallow crème
3121	*	1544	*	Manufacture of pasta-based convenience food products
3121	*	1549	*	Manufacture of coffee and coffee substitutes, tea, spices, condiments, vinegar, yeast, egg products
3121	*	2429	*	Edible salt refining

Rev.2		Rev.3.1		Activity
3122				**Manufacture of prepared animal feeds**
3122	*	1531	*	Grain milling residues
3122	*	1533		Manufacture of prepared animal feeds
3131				**Distilling, rectifying and blending spirits**
3131		1551		Distilling, rectifying and blending of spirits; ethyl alcohol production from fermented materials
3132				**Wine industries**
3132		1552		Manufacture of wines
3133				**Malt liquors and malt**
3133		1553		Manufacture of malt liquors and malt
3134				**Soft drinks and carbonated waters industries**
3134		1554		Manufacture of soft drinks; production of mineral waters
3140				**Tobacco manufactures**
3140		1600		Manufacture of tobacco products
3211				**Spinning, weaving and finishing textiles**
3211	*	0140	*	Cotton ginning
3211	*	1711		Preparation and spinning of textile fibres; weaving of textiles
3211	*	1712		Finishing of textiles
3211	*	1729	*	Manufacture of narrow fabrics, braids, lace
3211	*	2430	*	Manufacture of synthetic filament yarns (spinning and weaving of purchased man-made fibres)
3211	*	2610	*	Manufacture of yarn of glass fibres
3211	*	5260	*	"While-you-wait" services, e.g. textile printing
3212				**Manufacture of made-up textile goods except wearing apparel**
3212	*	1721	*	Manufacture of made-up textile articles, except apparel
3212	*	2520	*	Manufacture of made-up plastics textile goods, except wearing apparel (e.g. bags, household furnishings)
3213				**Knitting mills**
3213		1730		Manufacture of knitted and crocheted fabrics and articles
3214				**Manufacture of carpets and rugs**
3214	*	1722		Manufacture of carpets and rugs
3214	*	2029	*	Manufacture of woven cane or straw floor mats
3215				**Cordage, rope and twine industries**
3215		1723		Manufacture of cordage, rope, twine and netting

Rev.2		Rev.3.1		Activity
3219				**Manufacture of textiles not elsewhere classified**
3219	*	1729	*	Manufacture of fabric for industrial use, wicks; textiles n.e.c. (e.g. felt, coated or laminated fabrics, painters' cloths)
3219	*	1820	*	Manufacture of artificial fur; horsehair
3219	*	3699	*	Manufacture of linoleum and hard-surface floor coverings
3219	*	3720	*	Recycling of textile fibres
3220				**Manufacture of wearing apparel, except footwear**
3220	*	1810	*	Manufacture of wearing apparel, except fur apparel
3220	*	1820	*	Manufacture of fur apparel, accessories, trimmings
3231				**Tanneries and leather finishing**
3231		1911		Tanning and dressing of leather
3232				**Fur dressing and dyeing industries**
3232		1820	*	Fur dressing and dyeing industries
3233				**Manufacture of products of leather and leather substitutes, except footwear and wearing apparel**
3233	*	1912	*	Manufacture of luggage, handbags and the like, saddlery and harness
3233	*	3699	*	Manufacture of whips and riding crops
3240				**Manufacture of footwear, except vulcanized or moulded rubber or plastic footwear**
3240	*	1920	*	Manufacture of footwear, except vulcanized or moulded rubber or plastics footwear
3240	*	2899	*	Manufacture of shoe clasps and buckles
3311				**Sawmills, planing and other wood mills**
3311	*	2010	*	Sawmilling and planing of wood, including by-products; manufacture of unassembled wood flooring, wooden railway sleepers; preservation of wood
3311	*	2021	*	Manufacture of veneers, sheets, plywood, laminated wood, particle board
3311	*	2022		Manufacture of builders' carpentry and joinery
3311	*	2023	*	Manufacture of coopers' products of wood
3312				**Manufacture of wooden and cane containers and small cane ware**
3312	*	2023	*	Manufacture of boxes, crates, drums, barrels, other wood containers
3312	*	2029	*	Manufacture of plaiting materials; baskets and other articles of cane, plaiting materials
3319				**Manufacture of wood and cork products not elsewhere classified**
3319	*	1920	*	Manufacture of footwear wholly of wood
3319	*	2010	*	Manufacture of wood flour, sawdust
3319	*	2029	*	Cork processing; manufacture of cork products, small wares of wood, such as tools, household utensils, ornaments, cases, wood articles n.e.c.
3319	*	3699	*	Manufacture of burial caskets

Rev.2		Rev.3.1		Activity
3320				**Manufacture of furniture and fixtures, except primarily of metal**
3320	*	1721	*	Manufacture of textile window blinds and shades
3320	*	2029	*	Manufacture of furnishings of wood, e.g. coat racks, window blinds (not standing furniture)
3320	*	3610	*	Manufacture of furniture and fixtures, except of plastics or metal
3320	*	3699	*	Manufacture of theatrical scenery and properties
3411				**Manufacture of pulp, paper and paperboard**
3411	*	2021	*	Manufacture of fibreboard, other building board
3411	*	2101	*	Manufacture of pulp, paper, paperboard
3411	*	2102	*	Manufacture of corrugated paper or paperboard
3411	*	2699	*	Manufacture of asbestos paper
3412				**Manufacture of containers and boxes of paper and paperboard**
3412	*	2102	*	Manufacture of containers and boxes of paper and paperboard
3412	*	2109	*	Manufacture of constructions of paper and paperboard, such as spools, cones, cores and bobbins
3419				**Manufacture of pulp, paper and paperboard articles not elsewhere classified**
3419	*	1920	*	Manufacture of footwear of paper
3419	*	2101	*	Manufacture of off-machine coated, glazed, gummed, laminated paper and paperboard
3419	*	2109	*	Manufacture of articles of paper and paperboard such as plates, utensils, stationery, towels, toilet articles, filter blocks
3420				**Printing, publishing and allied industries**
3420	*	2109	*	Printing or embossing of stationery and labels
3420	*	2211		Publishing of books, brochures, maps and other publications
3420	*	2212		Publishing of newspapers, journals and periodicals
3420	*	2213	*	Publishing of sheet music
3420	*	2219		Other publishing (photos, engravings, postcards, timetables, forms, posters, art reproductions etc.)
3420	*	2221	*	Printing (periodicals, books, maps, music, posters, catalogues, stamps, currency) on account of publishers, producers, government and others
3420	*	2222		Service activities related to printing (bookbinding, production of type, plates etc.)
3511				**Manufacture of basic industrial chemicals except fertilizers**
3511	*	2330		Processing of nuclear fuel
3511	*	2411		Manufacture of basic chemicals, except fertilizers and nitrogen compounds
3511	*	2412	*	Manufacture of products of the nitrogenous fertilizer industry (nitric acid, ammonia, nitrate of potassium, urea)
3511	*	2429	*	Manufacture of activated carbon; antifreeze preparations; chemical products for industrial and laboratory use

Rev.2		Rev.3.1		Activity
3512				**Manufacture of fertilizers and pesticides**
3512	*	2412	*	Manufacture of straight, mixed, compound and complex nitrogenous, phosphatic and potassic fertilizers
3512	*	2421		Manufacture of pesticides and other agrochemical products
3513				**Manufacture of synthetic resins, plastic materials and man-made fibres except glass**
3513	*	2413		Manufacture of plastics in primary forms and of synthetic rubber
3513	*	2430	*	Manufacture of man-made filament tow or staple fibres, except glass
3513	*	2519	*	Manufacture of synthetic rubber products in basic forms: sheets, rods, tubes
3513	*	2520	*	Manufacture of plastics products in basic forms: sheets, rods, tubes etc.
3521				**Manufacture of paints, varnishes and laquers**
3521		2422	*	Manufacture of paints, varnishes and lacquers
3522				**Manufacture of drugs and medicines**
3522		2423	*	Manufacture of drugs and medicines
3523				**Manufacture of soap and cleaning preparations, perfumes, cosmetics and other toilet preparations**
3523		2424	*	Manufacture of soap and cleaning preparations, perfumes, cosmetics and other toilet preparations
3529				**Manufacture of chemical products not elsewhere classified**
3529	*	2422	*	Manufacture of printer's ink
3529	*	2424	*	Manufacture of polishes for furniture, metal etc.; waxes; deodorizing preparations
3529	*	2429	*	Manufacture of writing and drawing ink; gelatine products; photochemical products, plates, films; sensitized unexposed film, unrecorded recording media
3529	*	2927	*	Manufacture of explosives and ammunition
3529	*	3699	*	Manufacture of candles, matches
3530				**Petroleum refineries**
3530		2320	*	Petroleum refineries
3540				**Manufacture of miscellaneous products of petroleum and coal**
3540	*	1010	*	Manufacture of briquettes of hard coal, at mining site or from purchased coal
3540	*	1020	*	Manufacture of briquettes of lignite, at mining site or from purchased coal
3540	*	2310		Manufacture of coke oven products
3540	*	2320	*	Manufacture of petroleum refinery products from purchased materials
3540	*	2699	*	Manufacture of asphalt products
3540	*	3699	*	Manufacture of asphalt floor tiles

Rev.2		Rev.3.1		Activity
3551				**Tyre and tube industries**
3551	*	2511		Manufacture of rubber tyres and tubes; retreading and rebuilding of rubber tyres
3551	*	2519	*	Manufacture of tube repair materials
3559				**Manufacture of rubber products not elsewhere classified**
3559	*	1920	*	Manufacture of footwear primarily of vulcanized or moulded rubber
3559	*	2429	*	Manufacture of rubber cement
3559	*	2519	*	Manufacture of finished or semi-finished products, n.e.c. of natural or synthetic rubber (e.g. industrial, pharmaceutical, apparel articles)
3559	*	3140	*	Manufacture of battery separators, containers, parts, boxes etc., of rubber
3559	*	3511	*	Manufacture of inflatable rafts (rubber)
3559	*	3512	*	Manufacture of inflatable boats (rubber)
3559	*	3694	*	Manufacture of rubber toys
3559	*	3720	*	Recycling of rubber
3560				**Manufacture of plastic products not elsewhere classified**
3560	*	1920	*	Manufacture of plastics footwear
3560	*	2429	*	Manufacture of phonograph record blanks
3560	*	2520	*	Manufacture of plastics articles n.e.c. (dinnerware, tiles, builders' parts etc.)
3560	*	3140	*	Manufacture of battery separators, containers, parts, boxes etc., of plastic
3560	*	3430	*	Manufacture of plastic grills and fenders for automobiles
3560	*	3610	*	Manufacture of plastics furniture
3560	*	3699	*	Manufacture of plastic vacuum bottles and vacuum bottle stoppers
3560	*	3720	*	Recycling of used plastic materials
3610				**Manufacture of pottery, china and earthenware**
3610		2691		Manufacture of non-structural non-refractory ceramic ware (pottery, china and earthenware)
3620				**Manufacture of glass and glass products**
3620	*	2610	*	Manufacture of glass and glass products
3620	*	3190	*	Manufacture of glass insulating fittings
3691				**Manufacture of structural clay products**
3691	*	2692	*	Manufacture of refractory clay products
3691	*	2693		Manufacture of structural non-refractory clay and ceramic products
3692				**Manufacture of cement, lime and plaster**
3692		2694		Manufacture of cement, lime and plaster
3699				**Manufacture of non-metallic mineral products not elsewhere classified**
3699	*	1030	*	Manufacture of peat briquettes (not at mine)
3699	*	2610	*	Manufacture of glass wool

Rev.2		Rev.3.1		Activity
3699	*	2692	*	Manufacture of non-clay refractory products
3699	*	2695		Manufacture of articles of concrete, cement and plaster
3699	*	2696		Cutting, shaping and finishing of stone (not at quarry)
3699	*	2699	*	Manufacture of asbestos products; friction materials; mineral insulating materials; grindstones, abrasive products; articles of mica, graphite or other mineral substances n.e.c.
3699	*	2720	*	Manufacture of cermets
3699	*	3190	*	Manufacture of graphite products
3699	*	3699	*	Manufacture of vinyl asbestos floor tiles
3710				**Iron and steel basic industries**
3710	*	2710	*	Manufacture of primary iron and steel products (excluding forging and casting operations)
3710	*	2731		Casting of iron and steel
3710	*	2891	*	Forging of iron and steel
3710	*	2892	*	Treatment and specialized operation on iron and steel, on a fee or contract basis
3710	*	3520	*	Manufacture of wheels for railway cars and locomotives
3710	*	3710	*	Recycling of non-ferrous metal waste and scrap, outside of scrapyard
3720				**Non-ferrous metal basic industries**
3720	*	2720	*	Manufacture of primary products of precious and non-ferrous metal (excluding forging and casting operations)
3720	*	2732		Casting of non-ferrous metals
3720	*	2891	*	Forging of precious and non-ferrous metals
3720	*	2892	*	Treatment and specialized operation on precious and non-ferrous metals, on a fee or contract basis
3720	*	3710	*	Recycling of non-ferrous metal waste and scrap
3811				**Manufacture of cutlery, hand tools and general hardware**
3811	*	2891	*	Blacksmithing, hand forging of metal products
3811	*	2893	*	Manufacture of metal household articles (knives, utensils etc.); hand tools for agriculture, gardening; tools used by plumbers, carpenters, other trades; locks and general hardware
3811	*	2899	*	Manufacture of hand-operated kitchen appliances
3811	*	2915	*	Manufacture of jacks, block and tackle
3811	*	2921	*	Manufacture of hand lawnmowers
3811	*	3699	*	Manufacture of vacuum containers
3812				**Manufacture of furniture and fixtures primarily of metal**
3812	*	2899	*	Manufacture of metal goods for office use (excluding furniture)
3812	*	3150	*	Manufacture of metal lamps
3812	*	3311	*	Manufacture of medical, surgical, dental furniture and fixtures
3812	*	3610	*	Manufacture of furniture and fixtures of metal

Rev.2		Rev.3.1		Activity
3813				**Manufacture of structural metal products**
3813	*	2811		Manufacture of structural metal products
3813	*	2812	*	Manufacture of metal reservoirs and tanks for storage and manufacturing use; central heating boilers
3813	*	2813	*	Manufacture of steam generators, except central heating hot water boilers
3813	*	2899	*	Manufacture of furnace casings, laundry trays, and similar sheet metal products
3813	*	2930	*	Manufacture of sheet metal range hoods, domestic type
3813	*	3420	*	Manufacture of metal plate tanks designed and equipped for carriage by one or more modes of transport (e.g. trucks)
3813	*	3511	*	Manufacture of metal sections for ships and barges
3819				**Manufacture of fabricated metal products except machinery and equipment not elsewhere classified**
3819	*	2710	*	Manufacture of pipe fittings of iron and steel
3819	*	2720	*	Manufacture of pipe fittings of non-ferrous metal; non-ferrous wire and cable from purchased rod
3819	*	2812	*	Manufacture of radiators, metal containers for compressed and liquefied gas
3819	*	2891	*	Pressing, stamping of metal products
3819	*	2892	*	Treatment and coating of metal (e.g. plating, polishing, engraving, welding), on a fee or contract basis
3819	*	2899	*	Manufacture of metal fasteners, springs, containers, wire articles, metal sanitary ware (e.g. sinks), kitchenware, safes, picture frames, headgear
3819	*	2912	*	Manufacture of plumbers' valves, brass goods
3819	*	2914	*	Manufacture of non-electrical metal furnaces, stoves, and other space heaters
3819	*	2919	*	Manufacture of domestic fuel oil filters and cartridges, portable lawn sprinklers, chill coils; and manufacture, repair and servicing of fire extinguishers
3819	*	2921	*	Manufacture of metal incubators for poultry, livestock and other agricultural purposes
3819	*	2929	*	Manufacture of metallic and metal-faced type
3819	*	2930	*	Manufacture of non-electric domestic stoves and space heaters
3819	*	3150	*	Manufacture of metal lighting equipment and parts, except for use on cycle and motor equipment
3819	*	3190	*	Manufacture of bicycle lighting equipment
3819	*	3699	*	Manufacture of hand sifting or screening apparatus
3819	*	5260	*	While-you-wait services, such as engraving of metal
3821				**Manufacture of engines and turbines**
3821		2911	*	Manufacture of engines and turbines
3822				**Manufacture of agricultural machinery and equipment**
3822	*	2912	*	Manufacture of windmills for pumping water
3822	*	2915	*	Manufacture of loaders, stackers, farm elevators etc.
3822	*	2921	*	Manufacture of agricultural and forestry machinery other than power-driven agricultural hand tools
3822	*	2922	*	Manufacture of power-driven agricultural hand tools

Rev.2		Rev.3.1		Activity
3823				**Manufacture of metal and wood working machinery**
3823	*	2893	*	Manufacture of attachments and accessories for machine tools (whether or not power-operated)
3823	*	2922	*	Manufacture of machine tools, attachments and accessories for metal and woodworking machinery (non-electric)
3823	*	2923	*	Manufacture of machinery for metallurgy
3823	*	2929	*	Manufacture of moulds for metal
3823	*	3312	*	Manufacture of machinists' measuring tools
3824				**Manufacture of special industrial machinery and equipment except metal and wood working machinery**
3824	*	2813	*	Manufacture of parts for nuclear reactors
3824	*	2912	*	Manufacture of laboratory pumps
3824	*	2914	*	Manufacture of electric bakery ovens
3824	*	2915	*	Manufacture of derricks; lifting and handling equipment for construction and mining
3824	*	2919	*	Manufacture of machinery for packing and packaging; bottling and canning; bottle cleaning; calendering
3824	*	2922	*	Manufacture of machine tools for industrial machinery other than metal- and woodworking (non-electric)
3824	*	2923	*	Manufacture of smelting and refining machinery
3824	*	2924	*	Manufacture of machinery for mining, quarrying and construction
3824	*	2925		Manufacture of special industrial machinery for food, beverage and tobacco processing
3824	*	2926	*	Manufacture of textile machinery
3824	*	2929	*	Manufacture of printing trade machinery; paper industry machinery; machines for man-made textile fibres or yarns, glass-working, tile-making
3824	*	3190	*	Manufacture of apparatus for electroplating, electrolysis, electrophoresis
3824	*	3511	*	Manufacture of floating drilling platforms, oil rigs
3825				**Manufacture of office, computing and accounting machinery**
3825	*	2919	*	Manufacture of weighing machines
3825	*	3000	*	Manufacture of office, accounting and computing machinery
3825	*	7250	*	Repair of office, computing and accounting machinery
3829				**Machinery and equipment except electrical not elsewhere classified**
3829	*	2892	*	Machine shop work: machining, tooling and fabricating including repairs
3829	*	2899	*	Manufacture of weather vanes, ship propellers and metal pallets, flexible tubing and hose
3829	*	2911	*	Manufacture of pistons and piston rings
3829	*	2912	*	Manufacture of pumps, air and gas compressors and valves
3829	*	2913		Manufacture of bearings, gears, gearing and driving elements
3829	*	2914	*	Manufacture of industrial process furnaces and ovens (non-electric)
3829	*	2915	*	Manufacture of lifting and hoisting machinery, cranes, elevators, industrial trucks, tractors, stackers; specialized parts for lifting and handling equipment

Rev.2		Rev.3.1		Activity
3829	*	2919	*	Manufacture of unit air conditioners, refrigerating equipment, fans (industrial), gas generators, fire sprinklers, centrifuges, other machinery n.e.c.
3829	*	2922	*	Manufacture of scrap shredders, fan forges and hydraulic brake equipment
3829	*	2924	*	Manufacture of material handling equipment
3829	*	2926	*	Manufacture of sewing machines; washing, laundry, dry-cleaning, pressing machines
3829	*	2927	*	Manufacture of small arms and accessories, heavy ordnance and artillery; tanks
3829	*	2929	*	Manufacture of centrifugal clothes driers
3829	*	2930	*	Manufacture of domestic cooking ranges, refrigerators, laundry machines
3829	*	3190	*	Manufacture of dishwashing machines, except household type
3829	*	3311	*	Manufacture of beauty parlour and barber sterilizers
3829	*	3420	*	Manufacture of industrial trailers; containers
3829	*	3599	*	Manufacture of hand carts, trucks and trolleys (including specialized industrial use)
3829	*	3694	*	Manufacture of mechanical and coin-operated amusement machines
3829	*	3699	*	Manufacture of amusement park equipment
3831				**Manufacture of electrical industrial machinery and apparatus**
3831	*	2922	*	Manufacture of electric welding equipment
3831	*	3110	*	Manufacture of electric motors, generators, transformers
3831	*	3120	*	Manufacture of switch gear and switchboard apparatus; electricity distribution equipment
3831	*	3190	*	Manufacture of electric ignition or starting equipment for internal combustion engines; electromagnetic clutches and brakes; electric timing, controlling and signalling devices
3831	*	3210	*	Manufacture of capacitors except fixed and variable electronic capacitors
3831	*	3520	*	Manufacture of railway motor control electrical equipment
3832				**Manufacture of radio, television and communication equipment and apparatus**
3832	*	2213	*	Publishing of recorded media
3832	*	2230	*	Reproduction of records, audio and computer tapes from master copies; reproduction of floppy disks, compact discs
3832	*	3110	*	Manufacture of radio transformers
3832	*	3120	*	Manufacture of semiconductor circuits
3832	*	3190	*	Manufacture of visual and sound signalling and traffic control apparatus
3832	*	3210	*	Manufacture of electronic valves and tubes and other electronic components including fixed and variable electronic capacitors
3832	*	3220		Manufacture of television and radio transmitters and apparatus for line telephony and line telegraphy
3832	*	3230		Manufacture of television and radio receivers, sound or video recording or reproducing apparatus and associated goods
3832	*	3311	*	Manufacture of X-ray apparatus; electrotherapeutic apparatus
3832	*	3312	*	Manufacture of radar equipment, radio remote control apparatus
3833				**Manufacture of electrical appliances and housewares**
3833		2930	*	Manufacture of electrical appliances and housewares

Rev.2		Rev.3.1		Activity
3839				**Manufacture of electrical apparatus and supplies not elsewhere classified**
3839	*	3120	*	Manufacture of switches, fuses, sockets, plugs, conductors, lightning arresters
3839	*	3130		Manufacture of insulated wire and cable
3839	*	3140	*	Manufacture of accumulators, primary cells and primary batteries
3839	*	3150	*	Manufacture of electric lamps, fixtures
3839	*	3190	*	Manufacture of motor vehicle lighting equipment; carbon and graphite electrodes; other electrical equipment n.e.c.
3841				**Ship building and repairing**
3841	*	2911	*	Manufacture of engines and turbines for marine propulsion
3841	*	2915	*	Manufacture of marine capstans, pulleys, tackle etc.
3841	*	3511	*	Building and repairing of ships (other than sport and pleasure boats) and specialized parts
3841	*	3512	*	Building and repairing of sport and pleasure boats and specialized parts
3842				**Manufacture of railroad equipment**
3842		3520	*	Manufacture of railway and tramway locomotives and rolling stock
3843				**Manufacture of motor vehicles**
3843	*	2912	*	Manufacture of pumps, compressors for motor vehicles
3843	*	3190	*	Manufacture of electric windshield wipers, defrosters
3843	*	3410		Manufacture of motor vehicles
3843	*	3420	*	Manufacture of motor vehicle bodies; trailers, semi-trailers; trailer parts
3843	*	3430	*	Manufacture of parts and accessories for motor vehicles and their engines
3843	*	3592	*	Manufacture of motorized invalid carriages
3844				**Manufacture of motorcycles and bicycles**
3844	*	3591		Manufacture of motorcycles
3844	*	3592	*	Manufacture of bicycles, bicycle parts
3845				**Manufacture of aircraft**
3845	*	3511	*	Building of hovercraft
3845	*	3530		Manufacture of aircraft and spacecraft
3849				**Manufacture of transport equipment not elsewhere classified**
3849	*	3592	*	Manufacture of invalid carriages, not motorized
3849	*	3599	*	Manufacture of hand-propelled vehicles, animal-drawn vehicles, n.e.c.
3849	*	3699	*	Manufacture of baby carriages
3851				**Manufacture of professional and scientific, and measuring and controlling equipment, not elsewhere classified**
3851	*	1729	*	Manufacture of sanitary napkins
3851	*	2423	*	Manufacture of surgical, medical dressings, sutures, bandages; cements used in dentistry

Rev.2		Rev.3.1		Activity
3851	*	2519	*	Manufacture of medical rubber hose
3851	*	2914	*	Manufacture of laboratory heating apparatus
3851	*	2919	*	Manufacture of laboratory centrifuges
3851	*	2929	*	Manufacture of special-purpose machinery n.e.c.
3851	*	3190	*	Manufacture of accelerators (cyclotrons, betatrons); mine detectors
3851	*	3311	*	Manufacture of surgical, medical, dental equipment, instruments and supplies; orthopaedic and prosthetic appliances
3851	*	3312	*	Manufacture of instruments and appliances for measuring and controlling equipment, except industrial process control equipment
3851	*	3313		Manufacture of industrial process control equipment
3852				**Manufacture of photographic and optical goods**
3852	*	3000	*	Manufacture of photocopying machines
3852	*	3311	*	Manufacture of ophthalmic instruments
3852	*	3312	*	Manufacture of scientific optical measuring instruments
3852	*	3320		Manufacture of optical instruments and photographic equipment
3853				**Manufacture of watches and clocks**
3853		3330	*	Manufacture of watches and clocks
3901				**Manufacture of jewellery and related articles**
3901	*	2892	*	Plating, engraving etc. of jewellery and silverware for the trade
3901	*	2899	*	Manufacture of precious metal plated ware
3901	*	3330	*	Manufacture of watch bands and bracelets of precious metal; jewels for watches
3901	*	3691		Manufacture of jewellery and related articles
3902				**Manufacture of musical instruments**
3902		3692	*	Manufacture of musical instruments
3903				**Manufacture of sporting and athletic goods**
3903	*	3692	*	Manufacture of whistles, call horns, signalling instruments
3903	*	3693		Manufacture of sports goods
3903	*	3694	*	Manufacture of billiard and pool tables and equipment
3909				**Manufacturing industries not elsewhere classified**
3909	*	1810	*	Manufacture of hairnets
3909	*	1912	*	Manufacture of instrument cases, except leather and precious metal
3909	*	2101	*	Manufacture of carbon paper in rolls or sheets
3909	*	2109	*	Manufacture of carbon paper, cut to size
3909	*	2221	*	Manufacture of advertising displays and novelties
3909	*	2422	*	Manufacture of artists' colours, paints
3909	*	2899	*	Manufacture of small metal articles n.e.c.

Rev.2		Rev.3.1		Activity
3909	*	2926	*	Manufacture of needles for knitting, sewing machines
3909	*	3150	*	Manufacture of electric signs
3909	*	3592	*	Manufacture of children's bicycles
3909	*	3694	*	Manufacture of toys and games n.e.c.
3909	*	3699	*	Manufacture of pens and pencils; costume jewellery; umbrellas, canes; feathers, artificial flowers; tobacco pipes; stamps; novelties; other manufactured goods n.e.c.

4. Electricity, gas and water

4101				**Electric light and power**
4101		4010		Production, transmission and distribution of electricity

4102				**Gas manufacture and distribution**
4102		4020		Manufacture of gas; distribution of gaseous fuels through mains

4103				**Steam and hot water supply**
4103		4030		Steam and hot water supply

4200				**Water works and supply**
4200		4100		Collection, purification and distribution of water

5. Construction

5000				**Construction**
5000	*	1120		Service activities incidental to oil and gas extraction excluding surveying
5000	*	4510		Site preparation (construction)
5000	*	4520	*	Building of complete constructions or parts thereof; civil engineering
5000	*	4530	*	Building installation
5000	*	4540		Building completion
5000	*	4550		Renting of construction or demolition equipment with operator
5000	*	7421	*	Project management activities for construction
5000	*	7422	*	Testing and building inspection services

6. Wholesale and retail trade and restaurants and hotels

6100				**Wholesale trade**
6100	*	3710	*	Recycling of metal waste and scrap
6100	*	3720	*	Recycling of products n.e.c.
6100	*	5010	*	Wholesale of motor vehicles, including by auction
6100	*	5030	*	Wholesale of motor vehicle parts and accessories
6100	*	5040	*	Wholesale of motorcycles and snowmobiles and related parts and accessories

Rev.2		Rev.3.1		Activity
6100	*	5110		Wholesale on a fee or contract basis
6100	*	5121		Wholesale of agricultural raw materials and live animals
6100	*	5122		Wholesale of food, beverages and tobacco
6100	*	5131		Wholesale of textiles, clothing and footwear
6100	*	5139		Wholesale of other household goods
6100	*	5141		Wholesale of solid, liquid and gaseous fuels and related products
6100	*	5142		Wholesale of metals and metal ores
6100	*	5143		Wholesale of construction materials, hardware, plumbing and heating equipment and supplies
6100	*	5149		Wholesale of other intermediate products, waste and scrap
6100	*	5151		Wholesale of computers, computer peripheral equipment and software
6100	*	5152		Wholesale of electronic parts and equipment
6100	*	5159		Wholesale of other machinery, equipment and supplies
6100	*	5190		Other wholesale
6200				**Retail trade**
6200	*	5010	*	Retail sale of motor vehicles
6200	*	5030	*	Retail sale of motor vehicle parts and accessories
6200	*	5040	*	Retail sale of motorcycles and snowmobiles and related parts and accessories
6200	*	5050		Retail sale of automotive fuel
6200	*	5211		Retail sale in non-specialized stores with food, beverages or tobacco predominating
6200	*	5219		Other retail sale in non-specialized stores
6200	*	5220		Retail sale of food, beverages and tobacco in specialized stores
6200	*	5231		Retail sale of pharmaceutical and medical goods, cosmetic and toilet articles
6200	*	5232		Retail sale of textiles, clothing, footwear and leather goods
6200	*	5233		Retail sale of household appliances, articles and equipment
6200	*	5234		Retail sale of hardware, paints and glass
6200	*	5239		Other retail sale in specialized stores
6200	*	5240		Retail sale of second-hand goods in stores
6200	*	5251		Retail sale via mail order houses
6200	*	5252		Retail sale via stalls and markets
6200	*	5259		Other non-store retail sale
6200	*	7130	*	Renting of goods to the general public for personal or household use
6310				**Restaurants, cafés and other eating and drinking places**
6310		5520	*	Restaurants, cafes and other eating and drinking places
6320				**Hotels, rooming houses, camps and other lodging places**
6320		5510	*	Hotels, rooming houses, camps and other lodging places

Rev.2		Rev.3.1		Activity

7. Transport, storage and communication

7111   **Railway transport**

7111   *   5510   *   Sleeping car operation (carried on separately)
7111   *   5520   *   Dining car operation (carried on separately)
7111   *   6010   Transport via railways
7111   *   6021   *   Urban and suburban railway transport
7111   *   6303   *   Terminals and other railway transport supporting service activities, except switching

7112   **Urban, suburban and inter-urban highway passenger transport**

7112   *   5020   *   Maintenance facilities for road transport
7112   *   6021   *   Scheduled highway passenger transport
7112   *   6303   *   Terminals; maintenance facilities for road vehicles

7113   **Other passenger land transport**

7113   *   6021   *   Other scheduled passenger land transport
7113   *   6022   Other non-scheduled passenger land transport

7114   **Freight transport by road**

7114   *   6023   Freight transport by road
7114   *   6303   *   Terminals for freight transport by road
7114   *   6412   *   Courier activities other than national post activities, by road

7115   **Pipeline transport**

7115   6030   Transport via pipelines

7116   **Supporting services to land transport**

7116   *   6301   *   Cargo handling for land transport
7116   *   6303   *   Other supporting transport activities for land transport n.e.c.
7116   *   7111   *   Renting (without operator) of land transport equipment

7121   **Ocean and coastal water transport**

7121   6110   Sea and coastal water transport

7122   **Inland water transport**

7122   *   6120   Inland water transport
7122   *   6303   *   Other supporting activities for inland water transport

7123   **Supporting services to water transport**

7123   *   6301   *   Cargo handling for water transport
7123   *   6303   *   Other supporting activities for water transport

Rev.2		Rev.3.1		Activity
7123	*	6309	*	Activities of steamship agencies
7123	*	7112		Renting of water transport equipment (without operator)
7131				**Air transport carriers**
7131	*	6210		Scheduled air transport
7131	*	6220		Non-scheduled air transport
7131	*	6412	*	Courier activities other than national post activities, by air
7132				**Supporting services to air transport**
7132	*	6301	*	Cargo handling for air transport
7132	*	6303	*	Other supporting activities for air transport
7132	*	6420	*	Radio beacon and radar station operation
7132	*	7113		Renting of air transport equipment (without operator)
7191				**Services incidental to transport**
7191	*	6303	*	Other supporting transport activities, except steamship agencies
7191	*	6304	*	Activities of travel agencies and tour operators
7191	*	6309	*	Activities of other transport agencies
7191	*	6412	*	Courier activities, with public transport
7192				**Storage and warehousing**
7192		6302		Storage and warehousing
7200				**Communication**
7200	*	6411		National post activities
7200	*	6420	*	Other telecommunications n.e.c.
7200	*	7499	*	Telephone answering activities

8. Financing, insurance, real estate and business services

Rev.2		Rev.3.1		Activity
8101				**Monetary institutions**
8101	*	6511		Central banking
8101	*	6519	*	Monetary intermediation of commercial and other banks
8102				**Other financial institutions**
8102	*	6519	*	Monetary intermediation of commercial and other banks
8102	*	6591		Financial leasing
8102	*	6592		Other credit granting
8102	*	6599	*	Financial intermediation by credit institutions other than banks n.e.c.
8102	*	6712		Security dealing activities
8102	*	6719	*	Activities auxiliary to financial intermediation n.e.c.

Rev.2		Rev.3.1		Activity
8103				**Financial services**
8103	*	6599	*	Distributing funds other than by making loans
8103	*	6711		Administration of financial markets
8103	*	6719	*	Activities auxiliary to financial intermediation n.e.c.
8200				**Insurance**
8200	*	6601		Life insurance
8200	*	6602		Pension funding
8200	*	6603		Non-life insurance
8200	*	6720		Activities auxiliary to insurance and pension funding
8310				**Real estate**
8310	*	4520	*	Real estate development
8310	*	7010		Real estate activities with own or leased property
8310	*	7020		Real estate activities on a fee or contract basis
8321				**Legal services**
8321		7411		Legal activities
8322				**Accounting, auditing and bookkeeping services**
8322		7412		Accounting, bookkeeping and auditing activities; tax consultancy
8323				**Data processing and tabulating services**
8323	*	7210		Hardware consultancy
8323	*	7221		Software publishing
8323	*	7229		Software consultancy and supply, except software publishing
8323	*	7230		Data processing
8323	*	7240		Database activities
8323	*	7290		Other computer-related activities
8324				**Engineering, architectural and technical services**
8324	*	7310	*	Research and experimental development on natural sciences and engineering
8324	*	7421	*	Architectural and engineering activities and related technical consultancy
8324	*	7422	*	Technical testing and analysis
8325				**Advertising services**
8325	*	7413		Market research and public opinion polling
8325	*	7430	*	Advertising n.e.c.
8325	*	7499	*	Mail advertising

Rev.2		Rev.3.1		Activity
8329				**Business services, except machinery and equipment rental and leasing, not elsewhere classified**
8329	*	0140	*	Activities of farm labour contractors
8329	*	7320	*	Economic research, non-commercial
8329	*	7414	*	Business and management consultancy n.e.c.
8329	*	7430	*	Publishers' representatives
8329	*	7491		Labour recruitment and provision of personnel other than farm labour contractors
8329	*	7492		Investigation and security activities
8329	*	7495		Packaging activities
8329	*	7499	*	Bill collecting, credit rating, direct mailing, photocopying and duplicating and other business activities n.e.c.
8329	*	9220		News agency activities
8329	*	9309	*	Issuing licence plates by private contractors
8330				**Machinery and equipment rental and leasing**
8330	*	7121		Renting of agricultural machinery and equipment
8330	*	7122		Renting of construction and civil engineering machinery and equipment
8330	*	7123		Renting of office machinery and and equipment (including computers)
8330	*	7129		Renting of other machinery and equipment n.e.c.
8330	*	7130	*	Renting of office furniture

9. Community, social and personal services

Rev.2		Rev.3.1		Activity
9100				**Public administration and defence**
9100	*	7511		General (overall) public service activities
9100	*	7512		Regulation of the activities of agencies that provide health care, education, cultural services and other social services, excluding social security
9100	*	7513		Regulation of and contribution to more efficient operation of business
9100	*	7514		Ancillary service activities for the government as a whole
9100	*	7521		Foreign affairs
9100	*	7522		Defence activities
9100	*	7523		Public order and safety activities
9100	*	7530		Compulsory social security activities
9200				**Sanitary and similar services**
9200	*	7493	*	Building-cleaning activities
9200	*	9000		Sewage and refuse disposal, sanitation and similar activities
9310				**Education services**
9310	*	8010		Primary education
9310	*	8021		General secondary education
9310	*	8022		Technical and vocational secondary education

Rev.2		Rev.3.1		Activity
9310	*	8030		Higher education
9310	*	8090	*	Other education n.e.c.
9310	*	8532	*	Job training and vocational rehabilitation
9310	*	9219	*	Dance instruction
9320				**Research and scientific institutes**
9320	*	7310	*	Basic and general research in the biological, medical and physical sciences
9320	*	7320	*	Research and experimental development on social sciences and humanities
9331				**Medical, dental and other health services**
9331	*	3311	*	Manufacture of prosthetic appliances, artificial teeth made to order
9331	*	8511		Hospital activities
9331	*	8512		Medical and dental practice activities
9331	*	8519		Other human health activities
9332				**Veterinary services**
9332	*	0140	*	Animal grooming and boarding, farm animals
9332	*	8520		Veterinary activities
9332	*	9309	*	Pet grooming and boarding
9340				**Welfare institutions**
9340	*	5520	*	Meals-on-wheels services
9340	*	8531		Social work with accommodation
9340	*	8532	*	Social work without accommodation
9350				**Business, professional and labour associations**
9350	*	9111		Activities of business and employers' organizations
9350	*	9112		Activities of professional organizations
9350	*	9120		Activities of trade unions
9391				**Religious organizations**
9391		9191		Activities of religious organizations
9399				**Social and related community services not elsewhere classified**
9399	*	9192		Activities of political organizations
9399	*	9199		Activities of other membership organizations n.e.c.
9411				**Motion picture production**
9411	*	2230	*	Film and video reproduction
9411	*	9211	*	Motion picture and video production
9411	*	9249	*	Casting activities, motion pictures

ISIC Rev.3.1

Rev.2		Rev.3.1		Activity
9412				**Motion picture distribution and projection**
9412	*	7130	*	Renting of videotapes
9412	*	9211	*	Motion picture and video distribution
9412	*	9212		Motion picture projection
9413				**Radio and television broadcasting**
9413	*	6420	*	Radio and television programme transmission, on a fee or contract basis
9413	*	9213		Production of radio and television programmes, whether or not combined with broadcasting
9414				**Theatrical producers and entertainment services**
9414	*	7130	*	Renting of theatrical equipment
9414	*	7499	*	Agency activities for engagements in entertainment or sport attractions
9414	*	9211	*	Sound recording studios
9414	*	9214	*	Production of theatrical presentations
9414	*	9219	*	Other entertainment activities n.e.c.
9414	*	9249	*	Casting or booking agency activities
9415				**Authors, music composers and other independent artists not elsewhere classified**
9415		9214	*	Activities by authors, music composers and other independent artists n.e.c.
9420				**Libraries, museums, botanical and zoological gardens, and other cultural services not elsewhere classified**
9420	*	9231		Library and archives activities
9420	*	9232		Museums activities and preservation of historic sites and buildings
9420	*	9233		Botanical and zoological gardens and nature reserves activities
9490				**Amusement and recreational services not elsewhere classified**
9490	*	0140	*	Training of horses and other animal specialties, excluding racing and pets
9490	*	7111	*	Renting of motorcycles
9490	*	7130	*	Renting of recreational goods n.e.c. (e.g. bicycles, saddle horses, pleasure craft, sports equipment)
9490	*	9219	*	Operation of ballrooms, discotheques, amusement parks and similar attractions
9490	*	9241		Sporting activities
9490	*	9249	*	Other amusement and recreational service activities n.e.c.
9490	*	9309	*	Training of pets
9511				**Repair of footwear and other leather goods**
9511		5260	*	Repair of personal and household goods

Rev.2		Rev.3.1		Activity
9512				**Electrical repair shops**
9512	*	4530	*	Installing electrical equipment in homes
9512	*	5260	*	Electrical repair
9513				**Repair of motor vehicles and motorcycles**
9513	*	5020	*	Maintenance and repair of motor vehicles
9513	*	5040	*	Repair of motorcycles and related parts
9514				**Watch, clock and jewellery repair**
9514		5260	*	Watch, clock and jewellery repair
9519				**Other repair shops not elsewhere classified**
9519	*	5040	*	Maintenance and repair of snowmobiles
9519	*	5260	*	Other repair n.e.c.
9519	*	7250	*	Repair of typewriters
9520				**Laundries, laundry services, and cleaning and dyeing plants**
9520	*	5260	*	Alteration and repair of made-up personal and household textiles
9520	*	9301		Washing and (dry-)cleaning of textile and fur products
9530				**Domestic services**
9530		9500		Private households with employed persons
9591				**Barber and beauty shops**
9591	*	8090	*	Activities of barber and beauty schools
9591	*	9302		Hairdressing and other beauty treatment
9592				**Photographic studios, including commercial photography**
9592		7494		Photographic activities
9599				**Personal services not elsewhere classified**
9599	*	6304	*	Tourist assistance activities n.e.c.
9599	*	7493	*	Janitorial activities
9599	*	9303		Funeral and related activities
9599	*	9309	*	Other personal service activities n.e.c.
9600				**International and other extra-territorial bodies**
9600		9900		Extra-territorial organizations and bodies
n/a		9600		Undifferentiated goods-producing activities of private households for own use
n/a		9700		Undifferentiated service-producing activities of private households for own use

E. Correspondence between ISIC, Rev.3.1, and ISIC, Rev.2

207.   This table shows the complete correspondence between ISIC, Rev.2, and ISIC, Rev.3.1. An asterisk (*) next to the ISIC code indicates that only a part of the class is involved in this particular link.

Rev.3.1		Rev.2		Activity
				A Agriculture, hunting and forestry
0111				**Growing of cereals and other crops n.e.c.**
0111		1110	*	Growing of cereals and other crops n.e.c
0112				**Growing of vegetables, horticultural specialties and nursery products**
0112	*	1110	*	Growing of vegetables, horticultural specialities, nursery products
0112	*	1210	*	Gathering of mushrooms, truffles
0113				**Growing of fruit, nuts, beverage and spice crops**
0113		1110	*	Growing of fruit, nuts, beverage and spice crops
0121				**Farming of cattle, sheep, goats, horses, asses, mules and hinnies; dairy farming**
0121		1110	*	Farming of cattle, sheep, goats, horses, asses, mules and hinnies; dairy farming
0122				**Other animal farming; production of animal products n.e.c.**
0122	*	1110	*	Raising domesticated or wild animals n.e.c. (e.g. swine, poultry, rabbits)
0122	*	1120	*	Poultry hatchery, silkworm raising, on a fee or contract basis
0122	*	1302	*	Frog farming
0130				**Growing of crops combined with farming of animals (mixed farming)**
0130		1110	*	Growing of crops combined with farming of animals (mixed farming)
0140				**Agricultural and animal husbandry service activities, except veterinary activities**
0140	*	1110	*	Landscape gardening
0140	*	1120	*	Agricultural and animal husbandry activities, on a fee or contract basis
0140	*	3211	*	Cotton ginning
0140	*	8329	*	Activities of farm labour contractors
0140	*	9332	*	Animal grooming and boarding, farm animals
0140	*	9490	*	Training of horses and other animal specialties, excluding racing and pets
0150				**Hunting, trapping and game propagation including related service activities**
0150	*	1130		Hunting, trapping and game propagation
0150	*	1301	*	Catching of sea mammals, except whales

Rev.3.1		Rev.2		Activity

B Fishing

0200   **Forestry, logging and related service activities**
0200 * 1110 * Tree nurseries, except forest trees
0200 * 1210 * Forestry and related service activities
0200 * 1220   Logging

0501   **Fishing**
0501 * 1301 * Ocean and coastal fishing
0501 * 1302 * Fishing in inland waters; service activities related to fishing

0502   **Aquaculture**
0502   1302 * Fish hatcheries, cultivated beds; service activities related to aquaculture

C Mining and quarrying

1010   **Mining and agglomeration of hard coal**
1010 * 2100 * Mining and agglomeration of hard coal
1010 * 2200 * On-site gasification of coal
1010 * 3540 * Manufacture of briquettes of hard coal, at mining site or from purchased coal

1020   **Mining and agglomeration of lignite**
1020 * 2100 * Mining and agglomeration of lignite
1020 * 3540 * Manufacture of briquettes of lignite, at mining site or from purchased coal

1030   **Extraction and agglomeration of peat**
1030 * 2909 * Mining and agglomeration of peat
1030 * 3699 * Manufacture of peat briquettes (not at mine)

1110   **Extraction of crude petroleum and natural gas**
1110   2200 * Extraction of crude petroleum and natural gas

1120   **Service activities incidental to oil and gas extraction excluding surveying**
1120   5000 * Service activities incidental to oil and gas extraction excluding surveying

1200   **Mining of uranium and thorium ores**
1200   2302 * Mining of uranium and thorium ores

1310   **Mining of iron ores**
1310   2301   Mining of iron ores

1320   **Mining of non-ferrous metal ores, except uranium and thorium ores**
1320   2302 * Mining of non-ferrous metal ores, except uranium and thorium ores

Rev.3.1		Rev.2		Activity
1410				**Quarrying of stone, sand and clay**
1410	*	2901	*	Quarrying of building or monumental stone; mining of ceramic or refractory clay, chalk, dolomite; sand and gravel
1410	*	2909	*	Mining of gypsum, anhydrite
1421				**Mining of chemical and fertilizer minerals**
1421		2902		Mining of chemical and fertilizer minerals
1422				**Extraction of salt**
1422		2903		Extraction of salt
1429				**Other mining and quarrying n.e.c.**
1429	*	2901	*	Mining of feldspar
1429	*	2909	*	Mining and quarrying of asbestos, mica, quartz, gemstones, abrasives, asphalt and bitumen, other non-metallic minerals, n.e.c.
	D	**Manufacturing**		
1511				**Production, processing and preserving of meat and meat products**
1511	*	3111	*	Slaughtering, preparing and preserving meat, including sausage, edible animal fats, flours and meals, by-products (hides, bones etc.)
1511	*	3115	*	Processing of inedible oils and fats
1512				**Processing and preserving of fish and fish products**
1512	*	3114	*	Canning, preserving and processing of fish, crustacea and similar foods (except soups)
1512	*	3115	*	Production of fish meal
1513				**Processing and preserving of fruit and vegetables**
1513	*	3113	*	Canning and preserving of fruits and vegetables (except soups)
1513	*	3116	*	Potato flour and meal
1513	*	3119	*	Roasting of nuts
1513	*	3121	*	Processing of fruits and vegetables n.e.c. (e.g. baked beans, grape sugar, juice extracts)
1514				**Manufacture of vegetable and animal oils and fats**
1514		3115	*	Manufacture of vegetable and animal oils and fats
1520				**Manufacture of dairy products**
1520		3112		Manufacture of dairy products
1531				**Manufacture of grain mill products**
1531	*	3116	*	Grain milling: flour, meal, cereal grains; rice milling; vegetable milling; manufacture of breakfast foods
1531	*	3122	*	Grain milling residues

Rev.3.1		Rev.2		Activity

1532   **Manufacture of starches and starch products**

1532	*	3115	*	Manufacture of meal, cake of vegetables, nuts
1532	*	3116	*	Manufacture of tapioca; wet corn milling
1532	*	3121	*	Manufacture of starch products n.e.c.

1533   **Manufacture of prepared animal feeds**

| 1533 | | 3122 | * | Manufacture of prepared animal feeds |

1541   **Manufacture of bakery products**

| 1541 | | 3117 | * | Manufacture of bakery products (bread, pastry etc.) |

1542   **Manufacture of sugar**

| 1542 | * | 3118 | | Sugar factories and refineries |
| 1542 | * | 3121 | * | Production of maple sugar, invert sugar, sugars other than cane or beet |

1543   **Manufacture of cocoa, chocolate and sugar confectionery**

| 1543 | * | 3119 | * | Manufacture of cocoa, chocolate and sugar confectionery |
| 1543 | * | 3121 | * | Manufacture of marshmallow crème |

1544   **Manufacture of macaroni, noodles, couscous and similar farinaceous products**

| 1544 | * | 3117 | * | Manufacture of macaroni, noodles, couscous and similar farinaceous products |
| 1544 | * | 3121 | * | Manufacture of pasta-based convenience food products |

1549   **Manufacture of other food products n.e.c.**

1549	*	3111	*	Manufacture of soup containing meat
1549	*	3113	*	Manufacture of soups of vegetables and fruit
1549	*	3114	*	Manufacture of fish and seafood soups and specialties
1549	*	3121	*	Manufacture of coffee and coffee substitutes, tea, spices, condiments, vinegar, yeast, egg products

1551   **Distilling, rectifying and blending of spirits; ethyl alcohol production from fermented materials**

| 1551 | | 3131 | | Distilling, rectifying and blending of spirits; ethyl alcohol production from fermented materials |

1552   **Manufacture of wines**

| 1552 | | 3132 | | Manufacture of wines |

1553   **Manufacture of malt liquors and malt**

| 1553 | | 3133 | | Manufacture of malt liquors and malt |

1554   **Manufacture of soft drinks; production of mineral waters**

| 1554 | | 3134 | | Manufacture of soft drinks; production of mineral waters |

Rev.3.1		Rev.2		Activity
1600				**Manufacture of tobacco products**
1600		3140		Manufacture of tobacco products
1711				**Preparation and spinning of textile fibres; weaving of textiles**
1711		3211	*	Preparation and spinning of textile fibres; weaving of textiles
1712				**Finishing of textiles**
1712		3211	*	Finishing of textiles
1721				**Manufacture of made-up textile articles, except apparel**
1721	*	3212	*	Manufacture of made-up textile articles, except apparel
1721	*	3320	*	Manufacture of textile window blinds and shades
1722				**Manufacture of carpets and rugs**
1722		3214	*	Manufacture of carpets and rugs
1723				**Manufacture of cordage, rope, twine and netting**
1723		3215		Manufacture of cordage, rope, twine and netting
1729				**Manufacture of other textiles n.e.c.**
1729	*	3211	*	Manufacture of narrow fabrics, braids, lace
1729	*	3219	*	Manufacture of fabric for industrial use, wicks; textiles n.e.c. (e.g. felt, coated or laminated fabrics, painters' cloths)
1729	*	3851	*	Manufacture of sanitary napkins
1730				**Manufacture of knitted and crocheted fabrics and articles**
1730		3213		Manufacture of knitted and crocheted fabrics and articles
1810				**Manufacture of wearing apparel, except fur apparel**
1810	*	3220	*	Manufacture of wearing apparel, except fur apparel
1810	*	3909	*	Manufacture of hairnets
1820				**Dressing and dyeing of fur; manufacture of articles of fur**
1820	*	3219	*	Manufacture of artificial fur; horsehair
1820	*	3220	*	Manufacture of fur apparel, accessories, trimmings
1820	*	3232		Fur dressing and dyeing industries
1911				**Tanning and dressing of leather**
1911		3231		Tanning and dressing of leather
1912				**Manufacture of luggage, handbags and the like, saddlery and harness**
1912	*	3233	*	Manufacture of luggage, handbags and the like, saddlery and harness
1912	*	3909	*	Manufacture of instrument cases, except leather and precious metal

Rev.3.1		Rev.2		Activity
1920				**Manufacture of footwear**
1920	*	3240	*	Manufacture of footwear, except vulcanized or moulded rubber or plastics footwear
1920	*	3319	*	Manufacture of footwear wholly of wood
1920	*	3419	*	Manufacture of footwear of paper
1920	*	3559	*	Manufacture of footwear primarily of vulcanized or moulded rubber
1920	*	3560	*	Manufacture of plastics footwear
2010				**Sawmilling and planing of wood**
2010	*	3311	*	Sawmilling and planing of wood, including by-products; manufacture of unassembled wood flooring, wooden railway sleepers; preservation of wood
2010	*	3319	*	Manufacture of wood flour, sawdust
2021				**Manufacture of veneer sheets; manufacture of plywood, laminboard, particle board and other panels and boards**
2021	*	3311	*	Manufacture of veneers, sheets, plywood, laminated wood, particle board
2021	*	3411	*	Manufacture of fibreboard, other building board
2022				**Manufacture of builders' carpentry and joinery**
2022		3311	*	Manufacture of builders' carpentry and joinery
2023				**Manufacture of wooden containers**
2023	*	3311	*	Manufacture of coopers' products of wood
2023	*	3312	*	Manufacture of boxes, crates, drums, barrels, other wood containers
2029				**Manufacture of other products of wood; manufacture of articles of cork, straw and plaiting materials**
2029	*	3214	*	Manufacture of woven cane or straw floor mats
2029	*	3312	*	Manufacture of plaiting materials; baskets and other articles of cane, plaiting materials
2029	*	3319	*	Cork processing; manufacture of cork products, small wares of wood, such as tools, household utensils, ornaments, cases, wood articles, n.e.c.
2029	*	3320	*	Manufacture of furnishings of wood, e.g. coat racks, window blinds (not standing furniture)
2101				**Manufacture of pulp, paper and paperboard**
2101	*	3411	*	Manufacture of pulp, paper, paperboard
2101	*	3419	*	Manufacture of off-machine coated, glazed, gummed, laminated paper and paperboard
2101	*	3909	*	Manufacture of carbon paper in rolls or sheets
2102				**Manufacture of corrugated paper and paperboard and of containers of paper and paperboard**
2102	*	3411	*	Manufacture of corrugated paper or paperboard
2102	*	3412	*	Manufacture of containers and boxes of paper and paperboard

Rev.3.1		Rev.2		Activity
2109				**Manufacture of other articles of paper and paperboard**
2109	*	3412	*	Manufacture of constructions of paper and paperboard, such as spools, cones, cores and bobbins
2109	*	3419	*	Manufacture of articles of paper and paperboard such as plates, utensils, stationery, towels, toilet articles, filter blocks
2109	*	3420	*	Printing or embossing of stationery and labels
2109	*	3909	*	Manufacture of carbon paper, cut to size
2211				**Publishing of books, brochures and other publications**
2211		3420	*	Publishing of books, brochures, maps and other publications
2212				**Publishing of newspapers, journals and periodicals**
2212		3420	*	Publishing of newspapers, journals and periodicals
2213				**Publishing of music**
2213	*	3420	*	Publishing of sheet music
2213	*	3832	*	Publishing of recorded media
2219				**Other publishing**
2219		3420	*	Other publishing (photos, engravings, postcards, timetables, forms, posters, art reproductions etc.)
2221				**Printing**
2221	*	3420	*	Printing (periodicals, books, maps, music, posters, catalogues, stamps, currency) on account of publishers, producers, government, others
2221	*	3909	*	Manufacture of advertising displays and novelties
2222				**Service activities related to printing**
2222		3420	*	Service activities related to printing (bookbinding, production of type, plates etc.)
2230				**Reproduction of recorded media**
2230	*	3832	*	Reproduction of records, audio and computer tapes from master copies; reproduction of floppy disks, compact discs
2230	*	9411	*	Film and video reproduction
2310				**Manufacture of coke oven products**
2310		3540	*	Manufacture of coke oven products
2320				**Manufacture of refined petroleum products**
2320	*	3530		Petroleum refineries
2320	*	3540	*	Manufacture of petroleum refinery products from purchased materials
2330				**Processing of nuclear fuel**
2330		3511	*	Processing of nuclear fuel

Rev.3.1		Rev.2		Activity
2411				**Manufacture of basic chemicals, except fertilizers and nitrogen compounds**
2411		3511	*	Manufacture of basic chemicals, except fertilizers and nitrogen compounds
2412				**Manufacture of fertilizers and nitrogen compounds**
2412	*	3511	*	Manufacture of products of the nitrogenous fertilizer industry (nitric acid, ammonia, nitrate of potassium, urea)
2412	*	3512	*	Manufacture of straight, mixed, compound and complex nitrogenous, phosphatic and potassic fertilizers
2413				**Manufacture of plastics in primary forms and of synthetic rubber**
2413		3513	*	Manufacture of plastics in primary forms and of synthetic rubber
2421				**Manufacture of pesticides and other agrochemical products**
2421		3512	*	Manufacture of pesticides and other agrochemical products
2422				**Manufacture of paints, varnishes and similar coatings, printing ink and mastics**
2422	*	3521		Manufacture of paints, varnishes and lacquers
2422	*	3529	*	Manufacture of printer's ink
2422	*	3909	*	Manufacture of artists' colours, paints
2423				**Manufacture of pharmaceuticals, medicinal chemicals and botanical products**
2423	*	3522		Manufacture of drugs and medicines
2423	*	3851	*	Manufacture of surgical, medical dressings, sutures, bandages; cements used in dentistry
2424				**Manufacture of soap and detergents, cleaning and polishing preparations, perfumes and toilet preparations**
2424	*	3523		Manufacture of soap and cleaning preparations, perfumes, cosmetics and other toilet preparations
2424	*	3529	*	Manufacture of polishes for furniture, metal etc.; waxes; deodorizing preparations
2429				**Manufacture of other chemical products n.e.c.**
2429	*	3121	*	Edible salt refining
2429	*	3511	*	Manufacture of activated carbon; antifreeze preparations; chemical products for industrial and laboratory use
2429	*	3529	*	Manufacture of writing and drawing ink; gelatine products; photochemical products, plates, films; sensitized unexposed film, unrecorded recording media
2429	*	3559	*	Manufacture of rubber cement
2429	*	3560	*	Manufacture of phonograph record blanks
2430				**Manufacture of man-made fibres**
2430	*	3211	*	Manufacture of synthetic filament yarns (spinning and weaving of purchased man-made fibres)
2430	*	3513	*	Manufacture of man-made filament tow or staple fibres, except glass

ISIC Rev.3.1

Rev.3.1		Rev.2		Activity
2511				**Manufacture of rubber tyres and tubes; retreading and rebuilding of rubber tyres**
2511		3551	*	Manufacture of rubber tyres and tubes; retreading and rebuilding of rubber tyres
2519				**Manufacture of other rubber products**
2519	*	3513	*	Manufacture of synthetic rubber products in basic forms: sheets, rods, tubes etc.
2519	*	3551	*	Manufacture of tube repair materials
2519	*	3559	*	Manufacture of finished or semi-finished products, n.e.c. of natural or synthetic rubber (e.g. industrial, pharmaceutical, apparel articles)
2519	*	3851	*	Manufacture of medical rubber hose
2520				**Manufacture of plastics products**
2520	*	3212	*	Manufacture of made-up plastics textile goods, except wearing apparel (e.g. bags, household furnishings)
2520	*	3513	*	Manufacture of plastics products in basic forms: sheets, rods, tubes etc.
2520	*	3560	*	Manufacture of plastics articles n.e.c. (dinnerware, tiles, builders' parts etc.)
2610				**Manufacture of glass and glass products**
2610	*	3211	*	Manufacture of yarn of glass fibres
2610	*	3620	*	Manufacture of glass and glass products
2610	*	3699	*	Manufacture of glass wool
2691				**Manufacture of non-structural non-refractory ceramic ware**
2691		3610		Manufacture of non-structural non-refractory ceramic ware (pottery, china and earthenware)
2692				**Manufacture of refractory ceramic products**
2692	*	3691	*	Manufacture of refractory clay products
2692	*	3699	*	Manufacture of non-clay refractory products
2693				**Manufacture of structural non-refractory clay and ceramic products**
2693		3691	*	Manufacture of structural non-refractory clay and ceramic products
2694				**Manufacture of cement, lime and plaster**
2694		3692		Manufacture of cement, lime and plaster
2695				**Manufacture of articles of concrete, cement and plaster**
2695		3699	*	Manufacture of articles of concrete, cement and plaster
2696				**Cutting, shaping and finishing of stone**
2696		3699	*	Cutting, shaping and finishing of stone (not at quarry)
2699				**Manufacture of other non-metallic mineral products n.e.c.**
2699	*	3411	*	Manufacture of asbestos paper

Rev.3.1		Rev.2		Activity
2699	*	3540	*	Manufacture of asphalt products
2699	*	3699	*	Manufacture of asbestos products; friction materials; mineral insulating materials; grindstones, abrasive products; articles of mica, graphite or other mineral substances n.e.c.
2710				**Manufacture of basic iron and steel**
2710	*	3710	*	Manufacture of primary iron and steel products (except forging and casting operations)
2710	*	3819	*	Manufacture of pipe fittings of iron and steel
2720				**Manufacture of basic precious and non-ferrous metals**
2720	*	3699	*	Manufacture of cermets
2720	*	3720	*	Manufacture of primary products of precious and non-ferrous metal (excluding forging and casting operations)
2720	*	3819	*	Manufacture of pipe fittings of non-ferrous metal; non-ferrous wire and cable from purchased rod
2731				**Casting of iron and steel**
2731		3710	*	Casting of iron and steel
2732				**Casting of non-ferrous metals**
2732		3720	*	Casting of non-ferrous metals
2811				**Manufacture of structural metal products**
2811		3813	*	Manufacture of structural metal products
2812				**Manufacture of tanks, reservoirs and containers of metal**
2812	*	3813	*	Manufacture of metal reservoirs and tanks for storage and manufacturing use; central heating boilers
2812	*	3819	*	Manufacture of radiators, metal containers for compressed and liquefied gas
2813				**Manufacture of steam generators, except central heating hot water boilers**
2813	*	3813	*	Manufacture of steam generators, except central heating hot water boilers
2813	*	3824	*	Manufacture of parts for nuclear reactors
2891				**Forging, pressing, stamping and roll-forming of metal; powder metallurgy**
2891	*	3710	*	Forging of iron and steel
2891	*	3720	*	Forging of precious and non-ferrous metals
2891	*	3811	*	Blacksmithing, hand forging of metal products
2891	*	3819	*	Pressing, stamping of metal products
2892				**Treatment and coating of metals; general mechanical engineering on a fee or contract basis**
2892	*	3710	*	Treatment and specialized operation on iron and steel, on a fee or contract basis
2892	*	3720	*	Treatment and specialized operation on precious and non-ferrous metals, on a fee or contract basis

Rev.3.1		Rev.2		Activity
2892	*	3819	*	Treatment and coating of metal (e.g. plating, polishing, engraving, welding), on a fee or contract basis
2892	*	3829	*	Machine shop work: machining, tooling and fabricating including repairs
2892	*	3901	*	Plating, engraving etc. of jewellery and silverware for the trade
2893				**Manufacture of cutlery, hand tools and general hardware**
2893	*	3811	*	Manufacture of metal household articles (knives, utensils etc.); hand tools for agriculture, gardening; tools used by plumbers, carpenters, other trades; locks and general hardware
2893	*	3823	*	Manufacture of attachments and accessories for machine tools (whether or not power-operated)
2899				**Manufacture of other fabricated metal products n.e.c.**
2899	*	3240	*	Manufacture of shoe clasps and buckles
2899	*	3811	*	Manufacture of hand-operated kitchen appliances
2899	*	3812	*	Manufacture of metal goods for office use (excluding furniture)
2899	*	3813	*	Manufacture of furnace casings, laundry trays, and similar sheet metal products
2899	*	3819	*	Manufacture of metal fasteners, springs, containers, wire articles, metal sanitary ware (e.g. sinks), kitchenware, safes, picture frames, headgear
2899	*	3829	*	Manufacture of weathervanes, ship propellers and metal pallets, flexible tubing and hose
2899	*	3901	*	Manufacture of precious metal plated ware
2899	*	3909	*	Manufacture of small metal articles n.e.c.
2911				**Manufacture of engines and turbines, except aircraft, vehicle and cycle engines**
2911	*	3821		Manufacture of engines and turbines
2911	*	3829	*	Manufacture of pistons and piston rings
2911	*	3841	*	Manufacture of engines and turbines for marine propulsion
2912				**Manufacture of pumps, compressors, taps and valves**
2912	*	3819	*	Manufacture of plumbers' valves, brass goods
2912	*	3822	*	Manufacture of windmills for pumping water
2912	*	3824	*	Manufacture of laboratory pumps
2912	*	3829	*	Manufacture of pumps, air and gas compressors and valves
2912	*	3843	*	Manufacture of pumps, compressors for motor vehicles
2913				**Manufacture of bearings, gears, gearing and driving elements**
2913		3829	*	Manufacture of bearings, gears, gearing and driving elements
2914				**Manufacture of ovens, furnaces and furnace burners**
2914	*	3819	*	Manufacture of non-electrical metal furnaces, stoves, and other space heaters
2914	*	3824	*	Manufacture of electric bakery ovens
2914	*	3829	*	Manufacture of industrial process furnaces and ovens (non-electric)
2914	*	3851	*	Manufacture of laboratory heating apparatus

Rev.3.1		Rev.2		Activity

2915   **Manufacture of lifting and handling equipment**

2915	*	3811	*	Manufacture of jacks, block and tackle
2915	*	3822	*	Manufacture of loaders, stackers, farm elevators etc.
2915	*	3824	*	Manufacture of derricks; lifting and handling equipment for construction and mining
2915	*	3829	*	Manufacture of lifting and hoisting machinery, cranes, elevators, industrial trucks, tractors, stackers; specialized parts for lifting and handling equipment
2915	*	3841	*	Manufacture of marine capstans, pulleys, tackle etc.

2919   **Manufacture of other general-purpose machinery**

2919	*	3819	*	Manufacture of domestic fuel oil filters and cartridges, portable lawn sprinklers, chill coils; and manufacture, repair and servicing of fire extinguishers
2919	*	3824	*	Manufacture of machinery for packing and packaging; bottling and canning; bottle cleaning; calendering
2919	*	3825	*	Manufacture of weighing machines
2919	*	3829	*	Manufacture of unit air conditioners, refrigerating equipment, fans (industrial), gas generators, fire sprinklers, centrifuges, other machinery n.e.c.
2919	*	3851	*	Manufacture of laboratory centrifuges

2921   **Manufacture of agricultural and forestry machinery**

2921	*	3811	*	Manufacture of hand lawnmowers
2921	*	3819	*	Manufacture of metal incubators for poultry, livestock and other agricultural purposes
2921	*	3822	*	Manufacture of agricultural and forestry machinery other than power-driven agricultural hand tools

2922   **Manufacture of machine tools**

2922	*	3822	*	Manufacture of power-driven agricultural hand tools
2922	*	3823	*	Manufacture of machine tools, attachments and accessories for metal and woodworking machinery (non-electric)
2922	*	3824	*	Manufacture of machine tools for industrial machinery other than metal and woodworking (non-electric)
2922	*	3829	*	Manufacture of scrap shredders, fan forges and hydraulic brake equipment
2922	*	3831	*	Manufacture of electric welding equipment

2923   **Manufacture of machinery for metallurgy**

| 2923 | * | 3823 | * | Manufacture of machinery for metallurgy |
| 2923 | * | 3824 | * | Manufacture of smelting and refining machinery |

2924   **Manufacture of machinery for mining, quarrying and construction**

| 2924 | * | 3824 | * | Manufacture of machinery for mining, quarrying and construction |
| 2924 | * | 3829 | * | Manufacture of material handling equipment |

2925   **Manufacture of machinery for food, beverage and tobacco processing**

| 2925 | | 3824 | * | Manufacture of special industrial machinery for food, beverage and tobacco processing |

Rev.3.1		Rev.2		Activity
2926				**Manufacture of machinery for textile, apparel and leather production**
2926	*	3824	*	Manufacture of textile machinery
2926	*	3829	*	Manufacture of sewing machines; washing, laundry, dry-cleaning, pressing machines
2926	*	3909	*	Manufacture of needles for knitting, sewing machines
2927				**Manufacture of weapons and ammunition**
2927	*	3529	*	Manufacture of explosives and ammunition
2927	*	3829	*	Manufacture of small arms and accessories, heavy ordnance and artillery; tanks
2929				**Manufacture of other special-purpose machinery**
2929	*	3819	*	Manufacture of metallic and metal-faced type
2929	*	3823	*	Manufacture of moulds for metal
2929	*	3824	*	Manufacture of printing trade machinery; paper industry machinery; machines for man-made textile fibres or yarns, glass-working, tile-making
2929	*	3829	*	Manufacture of centrifugal clothes driers
2929	*	3851	*	Manufacture of special-purpose machinery n.e.c.
2930				**Manufacture of domestic appliances n.e.c.**
2930	*	3813	*	Manufacture of sheet metal range hoods, domestic type
2930	*	3819	*	Manufacture of non-electric domestic stoves and space heaters
2930	*	3829	*	Manufacture of domestic cooking ranges, refrigerators, laundry machines
2930	*	3833		Manufacture of electrical appliances and housewares
3000				**Manufacture of office, accounting and computing machinery**
3000	*	3825	*	Manufacture of office, accounting and computing machinery
3000	*	3852	*	Manufacture of photocopying machines
3110				**Manufacture of electric motors, generators and transformers**
3110	*	3831	*	Manufacture of electric motors, generators, transformers
3110	*	3832	*	Manufacture of radio transformers
3120				**Manufacture of electricity distribution and control apparatus**
3120	*	3831	*	Manufacture of switch gear and switchboard apparatus; electricity distribution equipment
3120	*	3832	*	Manufacture of semiconductor circuits
3120	*	3839	*	Manufacture of switches, fuses, sockets, plugs, conductors, lightning arresters
3130				**Manufacture of insulated wire and cable**
3130		3839	*	Manufacture of insulated wire and cable
3140				**Manufacture of accumulators, primary cells and primary batteries**
3140	*	3559	*	Manufacture of battery separators, containers, parts, boxes etc., of rubber

Rev.3.1		Rev.2		Activity
3140	*	3560	*	Manufacture of battery separators, containers, parts, boxes etc., of plastic
3140	*	3839	*	Manufacture of accumulators, primary cells and primary batteries
3150				**Manufacture of electric lamps and lighting equipment**
3150	*	3812	*	Manufacture of metal lamps
3150	*	3819	*	Manufacture of metal lighting equipment and parts, except for use on cycle and motor equipment
3150	*	3839	*	Manufacture of electric lamps, fixtures
3150	*	3909	*	Manufacture of electric signs
3190				**Manufacture of other electrical equipment n.e.c.**
3190	*	3620	*	Manufacture of glass insulating fittings
3190	*	3699	*	Manufacture of graphite products
3190	*	3819	*	Manufacture of bicycle lighting equipment
3190	*	3824	*	Manufacture of apparatus for electroplating, electrolysis, electrophoresis
3190	*	3829	*	Manufacture of dishwashing machines, except household type
3190	*	3831	*	Manufacture of electric ignition or starting equipment for internal combustion engines; electromagnetic clutches and brakes; electric timing, controlling and signalling devices
3190	*	3832	*	Manufacture of visual and sound signalling and traffic control apparatus
3190	*	3839	*	Manufacture of motor vehicle lighting equipment; carbon and graphite electrodes; other electrical equipment n.e.c.
3190	*	3843	*	Manufacture of electric windshield wipers, defrosters
3190	*	3851	*	Manufacture of accelerators (cyclotrons, betatrons); mine detectors
3210				**Manufacture of electronic valves and tubes and other electronic components**
3210	*	3831	*	Manufacture of capacitors except fixed and variable electronic capacitors
3210	*	3832	*	Manufacture of electronic valves and tubes and other electronic components including fixed and variable electronic capacitors
3220				**Manufacture of television and radio transmitters and apparatus for line telephony and line telegraphy**
3220		3832	*	Manufacture of television and radio transmitters and apparatus for line telephony and line telegraphy
3230				**Manufacture of television and radio receivers, sound or video recording or reproducing apparatus, and associated goods**
3230		3832	*	Manufacture of television and radio receivers, sound or video recording or reproducing apparatus and associated goods
3311				**Manufacture of medical and surgical equipment and orthopaedic appliances**
3311	*	3812	*	Manufacture of medical, surgical, dental furniture and fixtures
3311	*	3829	*	Manufacture of beauty parlour and barber sterilizers
3311	*	3832	*	Manufacture of X-ray apparatus; electrotherapeutic apparatus

Rev.3.1		Rev.2		Activity
3311	*	3851	*	Manufacture of surgical, medical, dental equipment, instruments and supplies; orthopaedic and prosthetic appliances
3311	*	3852	*	Manufacture of ophthalmic instruments
3311	*	9331	*	Manufacture of prosthetic appliances, artificial teeth made to order
3312				**Manufacture of instruments and appliances for measuring, checking, testing, navigating and other purposes, except industrial process control equipment**
3312	*	3823	*	Manufacture of machinists' measuring tools
3312	*	3832	*	Manufacture of radar equipment, radio remote control apparatus
3312	*	3851	*	Manufacture of instruments and appliances for measuring and controlling equipment, except industrial process control equipment
3312	*	3852	*	Manufacture of scientific optical measuring instruments
3313				**Manufacture of industrial process control equipment**
3313		3851	*	Manufacture of industrial process control equipment
3320				**Manufacture of optical instruments and photographic equipment**
3320		3852	*	Manufacture of optical instruments and photographic equipment
3330				**Manufacture of watches and clocks**
3330	*	3853		Manufacture of watches and clocks
3330	*	3901	*	Manufacture of watch bands and bracelets of precious metal; jewels for watches
3410				**Manufacture of motor vehicles**
3410		3843	*	Manufacture of motor vehicles
3420				**Manufacture of bodies (coachwork) for motor vehicles; manufacture of trailers and semi-trailers**
3420	*	3813	*	Manufacture of metal plate tanks designed and equipped for carriage by one or more modes of transport (e.g. trucks)
3420	*	3829	*	Manufacture of industrial trailers; containers
3420	*	3843	*	Manufacture of motor vehicle bodies; trailers, semi-trailers; trailer parts
3430				**Manufacture of parts and accessories for motor vehicles and their engines**
3430	*	3560	*	Manufacture of plastic grills and fenders for automobiles
3430	*	3843	*	Manufacture of parts and accessories for motor vehicles and their engines
3511				**Building and repairing of ships**
3511	*	3559	*	Manufacture of inflatable rafts (rubber)
3511	*	3813	*	Manufacture of metal sections for ships and barges
3511	*	3824	*	Manufacture of floating drilling platforms, oil rigs
3511	*	3841	*	Building and repairing of ships (other than sport and pleasure boats) and specialized parts
3511	*	3845	*	Building of hovercraft

Rev.3.1		Rev.2		Activity
3512				**Building and repairing of pleasure and sporting boats**
3512	*	3559	*	Manufacture of inflatable boats (rubber)
3512	*	3841	*	Building and repairing of sport and pleasure boats and specialized parts
3520				**Manufacture of railway and tramway locomotives and rolling stock**
3520	*	3710	*	Manufacture of wheels for railway cars and locomotives
3520	*	3831	*	Manufacture of railway motor control electrical equipment
3520	*	3842		Manufacture of railway and tramway locomotives and rolling stock
3530				**Manufacture of aircraft and spacecraft**
3530		3845	*	Manufacture of aircraft and spacecraft
3591				**Manufacture of motorcycles**
3591		3844	*	Manufacture of motorcycles
3592				**Manufacture of bicycles and invalid carriages**
3592	*	3843	*	Manufacture of motorized invalid carriages
3592	*	3844	*	Manufacture of bicycles, bicycle parts
3592	*	3849	*	Manufacture of invalid carriages, not motorized
3592	*	3909	*	Manufacture of children's bicycles
3599				**Manufacture of other transport equipment n.e.c.**
3599	*	3829	*	Manufacture of hand carts, trucks and trolleys (including specialized industrial use)
3599	*	3849	*	Manufacture of hand-propelled vehicles, animal-drawn vehicles, n.e.c.
3610				**Manufacture of furniture**
3610	*	3320	*	Manufacture of furniture and fixtures, except of plastics or metal
3610	*	3560	*	Manufacture of plastics furniture
3610	*	3812	*	Manufacture of furniture and fixtures of metal
3691				**Manufacture of jewellery and related articles**
3691		3901	*	Manufacture of jewellery and related articles
3692				**Manufacture of musical instruments**
3692	*	3902		Manufacture of musical instruments
3692	*	3903	*	Manufacture of whistles, call horns, signalling instruments
3693				**Manufacture of sports goods**
3693		3903	*	Manufacture of sports goods
3694				**Manufacture of games and toys**
3694	*	3559	*	Manufacture of rubber toys
3694	*	3829	*	Manufacture of mechanical and coin-operated amusement machines

Rev.3.1		Rev.2		Activity
3694	*	3903	*	Manufacture of billiard and pool tables and equipment
3694	*	3909	*	Manufacture of toys and games n.e.c.
3699				**Other manufacturing n.e.c.**
3699	*	3219	*	Manufacture of linoleum and hard-surface floor coverings
3699	*	3233	*	Manufacture of whips and riding crops
3699	*	3319	*	Manufacture of burial caskets
3699	*	3320	*	Manufacture of theatrical scenery and properties
3699	*	3529	*	Manufacture of candles, matches
3699	*	3540	*	Manufacture of asphalt floor tiles
3699	*	3560	*	Manufacture of plastic vacuum bottles and vacuum bottle stoppers
3699	*	3699	*	Manufacture of vinyl asbestos floor tiles
3699	*	3811	*	Manufacture of vacuum containers
3699	*	3819	*	Manufacture of hand sifting or screening apparatus
3699	*	3829	*	Manufacture of amusement park equipment
3699	*	3849	*	Manufacture of baby carriages
3699	*	3909	*	Manufacture of pens and pencils; costume jewellery; umbrellas, canes; feathers, artificial flowers; tobacco pipes; stamps; novelties; other manufactured goods n.e.c.
3710				**Recycling of metal waste and scrap**
3710	*	3710	*	Recycling of non-ferrous metal waste and scrap, outside of scrapyard
3710	*	3720	*	Recycling of non-ferrous metal waste and scrap
3710	*	6100	*	Recycling of metal waste and scrap
3720				**Recycling of non-metal waste and scrap**
3720	*	3219	*	Recycling of textile fibres
3720	*	3559	*	Recycling of rubber
3720	*	3560	*	Recycling of used plastic materials
3720	*	6100	*	Recycling of products n.e.c.
	E			**Electricity, gas and water supply**
4010				**Production, transmission and distribution of electricity**
4010		4101		Production, transmission and distribution of electricity
4020				**Manufacture of gas; distribution of gaseous fuels through mains**
4020		4102		Manufacture of gas; distribution of gaseous fuels through mains
4030				**Steam and hot water supply**
4030		4103		Steam and hot water supply
4100				**Collection, purification and distribution of water**
4100		4200		Collection, purification and distribution of water

Rev.3.1		Rev.2		Activity

F Construction

4510 **Site preparation**
4510 5000 * Site preparation (construction)

4520 **Building of complete constructions or parts thereof; civil engineering**
4520 * 5000 * Building of complete constructions or parts thereof; civil engineering
4520 * 8310 * Real estate development

4530 **Building installation**
4530 * 5000 * Building installation
4530 * 9512 * Installing electrical equipment in homes

4540 **Building completion**
4540 5000 * Building completion

4550 **Renting of construction or demolition equipment with operator**
4550 5000 * Renting of construction or demolition equipment with operator

G Wholesale and retail trade; repair of motor vehicles, motorcycles and personal and household goods

5010 **Sale of motor vehicles**
5010 * 6100 * Wholesale of motor vehicles, including by auction
5010 * 6200 * Retail sale of motor vehicles

5020 **Maintenance and repair of motor vehicles**
5020 * 7112 * Maintenance facilities for road transport
5020 * 9513 * Maintenance and repair of motor vehicles

5030 **Sale of motor vehicle parts and accessories**
5030 * 6100 * Wholesale of motor vehicle parts and accessories
5030 * 6200 * Retail sale of motor vehicle parts and accessories

5040 **Sale, maintenance and repair of motorcycles and related parts and accessories**
5040 * 6100 * Wholesale of motorcycles and snowmobiles and related parts and accessories
5040 * 6200 * Retail sale of motorcycles and snowmobiles and related parts and accessories
5040 * 9513 * Repair of motorcycles and related parts
5040 * 9519 * Maintenance and repair of snowmobiles

5050 **Retail sale of automotive fuel**
5050 6200 * Retail sale of automotive fuel

Rev.3.1	Rev.2		Activity
5110			**Wholesale on a fee or contract basis**
5110	6100	*	Wholesale on a fee or contract basis
5121			**Wholesale of agricultural raw materials and live animals**
5121	6100	*	Wholesale of agricultural raw materials and live animals
5122			**Wholesale of food, beverages and tobacco**
5122	6100	*	Wholesale of food, beverages and tobacco
5131			**Wholesale of textiles, clothing and footwear**
5131	6100	*	Wholesale of textiles, clothing and footwear
5139			**Wholesale of other household goods**
5139	6100	*	Wholesale of other household goods
5141			**Wholesale of solid, liquid and gaseous fuels and related products**
5141	6100	*	Wholesale of solid, liquid and gaseous fuels and related products
5142			**Wholesale of metals and metal ores**
5142	6100	*	Wholesale of metals and metal ores
5143			**Wholesale of construction materials, hardware, plumbing and heating equipment and supplies**
5143	6100	*	Wholesale of construction materials, hardware, plumbing and heating equipment and supplies
5149			**Wholesale of other intermediate products, waste and scrap**
5149	6100	*	Wholesale of other intermediate products, waste and scrap
5151			**Wholesale of computers, computer peripheral equipment and software**
5151	6100	*	Wholesale of computers, computer peripheral equipment and software
5152			**Wholesale of electronic parts and equipment**
5152	6100	*	Wholesale of electronic parts and equipment
5159			**Wholesale of other machinery, equipment and supplies**
5159	6100	*	Wholesale of other machinery, equipment and supplies
5190			**Other wholesale**
5190	6100	*	Other wholesale
5211			**Retail sale in non-specialized stores with food, beverages or tobacco predominating**
5211	6200	*	Retail sale in non-specialized stores with food, beverages or tobacco predominating

Rev.3.1		Rev.2		Activity
5219				**Other retail sale in non-specialized stores**
5219		6200	*	Other retail sale in non-specialized stores
5220				**Retail sale of food, beverages and tobacco in specialized stores**
5220		6200	*	Retail sale of food, beverages and tobacco in specialized stores
5231				**Retail sale of pharmaceutical and medical goods, cosmetic and toilet articles**
5231		6200	*	Retail sale of pharmaceutical and medical goods, cosmetic and toilet articles
5232				**Retail sale of textiles, clothing, footwear and leather goods**
5232		6200	*	Retail sale of textiles, clothing, footwear and leather goods
5233				**Retail sale of household appliances, articles and equipment**
5233		6200	*	Retail sale of household appliances, articles and equipment
5234				**Retail sale of hardware, paints and glass**
5234		6200	*	Retail sale of hardware, paints and glass
5239				**Other retail sale in specialized stores**
5239		6200	*	Other retail sale in specialized stores
5240				**Retail sale of second-hand goods in stores**
5240		6200	*	Retail sale of second-hand goods in stores
5251				**Retail sale via mail order houses**
5251		6200	*	Retail sale via mail order houses
5252				**Retail sale via stalls and markets**
5252		6200	*	Retail sale via stalls and markets
5259				**Other non-store retail sale**
5259		6200	*	Other non-store retail sale
5260				**Repair of personal and household goods**
5260	*	3211	*	"While-you-wait" services, e.g. textile printing
5260	*	3819	*	While-you-wait services, such as engraving of metal
5260	*	9511		Repair of personal and household goods
5260	*	9512	*	Electrical repair
5260	*	9514		Watch, clock and jewellery repair
5260	*	9519	*	Other repair n.e.c.
5260	*	9520	*	Alteration and repair of made-up personal and household textiles

Rev.3.1		Rev.2		Activity
	H	**Hotels and restaurants**		
5510				**Hotels; camping sites and other provision of short-stay accommodation**
5510	*	6320		Hotels, rooming houses, camps and other lodging places
5510	*	7111	*	Sleeping car operation (carried on separately)
5520				**Restaurants, bars and canteens**
5520	*	6310		Restaurants, cafes and other eating and drinking places
5520	*	7111	*	Dining car operation (carried on separately)
5520	*	9340	*	Meals-on-wheels services
	I	**Transport, storage and communications**		
6010				**Transport via railways**
6010		7111	*	Transport via railways
6021				**Other scheduled passenger land transport**
6021	*	7111	*	Urban and suburban railway transport
6021	*	7112	*	Scheduled highway passenger transport
6021	*	7113	*	Other scheduled passenger land transport
6022				**Other non-scheduled passenger land transport**
6022		7113	*	Other non-scheduled passenger land transport
6023				**Freight transport by road**
6023		7114	*	Freight transport by road
6030				**Transport via pipelines**
6030		7115		Transport via pipelines
6110				**Sea and coastal water transport**
6110		7121		Sea and coastal water transport
6120				**Inland water transport**
6120		7122	*	Inland water transport
6210				**Scheduled air transport**
6210		7131	*	Scheduled air transport
6220				**Non-scheduled air transport**
6220		7131	*	Non-scheduled air transport
6301				**Cargo handling**
6301	*	7116	*	Cargo handling for land transport

Rev.3.1		Rev.2		Activity
6301	*	7123	*	Cargo handling for water transport
6301	*	7132	*	Cargo handling for air transport
6302				**Storage and warehousing**
6302		7192		Storage and warehousing
6303				**Other supporting transport activities**
6303	*	7111	*	Terminals and other railway transport supporting service activities, except switching
6303	*	7112	*	Terminals; maintenance facilities for road vehicles
6303	*	7114	*	Terminals for freight transport by road
6303	*	7116	*	Other supporting transport activities for land transport n.e.c.
6303	*	7122	*	Other supporting activities for inland water transport
6303	*	7123	*	Other supporting activities for water transport
6303	*	7132	*	Other supporting activities for air transport
6303	*	7191	*	Other supporting transport activities, except steamship agencies
6304				**Activities of travel agencies and tour operators; tourist assistance activities n.e.c.**
6304	*	7191	*	Activities of travel agencies and tour operators
6304	*	9599	*	Tourist assistance activities n.e.c.
6309				**Activities of other transport agencies**
6309	*	7123	*	Activities of steamship agencies
6309	*	7191	*	Activities of other transport agencies
6411				**National post activities**
6411		7200	*	National post activities
6412				**Courier activities other than national post activities**
6412	*	7114	*	Courier activities other than national post activities, by road
6412	*	7131	*	Courier activities other than national post activities, by air
6412	*	7191	*	Courier activities, with public transport
6420				**Telecommunications**
6420	*	7132	*	Radio beacon and radar station operation
6420	*	7200	*	Other telecommunications n.e.c.
6420	*	9413	*	Radio and television programme transmission, on a fee or contract basis
	J			**Financial intermediation**
6511				**Central banking**
6511		8101	*	Central banking

Rev.3.1		Rev.2		Activity
6519				**Other monetary intermediation**
6519	*	8101	*	Monetary intermediation of commercial and other banks
6519	*	8102	*	Monetary intermediation of commercial and other banks
6591				**Financial leasing**
6591		8102	*	Financial leasing
6592				**Other credit granting**
6592		8102	*	Other credit granting
6599				**Other financial intermediation n.e.c.**
6599	*	8102	*	Financial intermediation by credit institutions other than banks n.e.c.
6599	*	8103	*	Distributing funds other than by making loans
6601				**Life insurance**
6601		8200	*	Life insurance
6602				**Pension funding**
6602		8200	*	Pension funding
6603				**Non-life insurance**
6603		8200	*	Non-life insurance
6711				**Administration of financial markets**
6711		8103	*	Administration of financial markets
6712				**Security dealing activities**
6712		8102	*	Security dealing activities
6719				**Activities auxiliary to financial intermediation n.e.c.**
6719	*	8102	*	Activities auxiliary to financial intermediation n.e.c.
6719	*	8103	*	Activities auxiliary to financial intermediation n.e.c.
6720				**Activities auxiliary to insurance and pension funding**
6720		8200	*	Activities auxiliary to insurance and pension funding
	K			**Real estate, renting and business activities**
7010				**Real estate activities with own or leased property**
7010		8310	*	Real estate activities with own or leased property
7020				**Real estate activities on a fee or contract basis**
7020		8310	*	Real estate activities on a fee or contract basis

Rev.3.1		Rev.2		Activity
7111				**Renting of land transport equipment**
7111	*	7116	*	Renting (without operator) of land transport equipment
7111	*	9490	*	Renting of motorcycles
7112				**Renting of water transport equipment**
7112		7123	*	Renting of water transport equipment (without operator)
7113				**Renting of air transport equipment**
7113		7132	*	Renting of air transport equipment (without operator)
7121				**Renting of agricultural machinery and equipment**
7121		8330	*	Renting of agricultural machinery and equipment
7122				**Renting of construction and civil engineering machinery and equipment**
7122		8330	*	Renting of construction and civil engineering machinery and equipment
7123				**Renting of office machinery and equipment (including computers)**
7123		8330	*	Renting of office machinery and and equipment (including computers)
7129				**Renting of other machinery and equipment n.e.c.**
7129		8330	*	Renting of other machinery and equipment n.e.c.
7130				**Renting of personal and household goods n.e.c.**
7130	*	6200	*	Renting of goods to the general public for personal or household use
7130	*	8330	*	Renting of office furniture
7130	*	9412	*	Renting of video tapes
7130	*	9414	*	Renting of theatrical equipment
7130	*	9490	*	Renting of recreational goods n.e.c. (e.g. bicycles, saddle horses, pleasure craft, sports equipment)
7210				**Hardware consultancy**
7210		8323	*	Hardware consultancy
7221				**Software publishing**
7221		8323	*	Software publishing
7229				**Other software consultancy and supply**
7229		8323	*	Software consultancy and supply, except software publishing
7230				**Data processing**
7230		8323	*	Data processing
7240				**Database activities and online distribution of electronic content**
7240		8323	*	Database activities

Rev.3.1		Rev.2		Activity
7250				**Maintenance and repair of office, accounting and computing machinery**
7250	*	3825	*	Repair of office, computing and accounting machinery
7250	*	9519	*	Repair of typewriters
7290				**Other computer-related activities**
7290		8323	*	Other computer-related activities
7310				**Research and experimental development on natural sciences and engineering (NSE)**
7310	*	8324	*	Research and experimental development on natural sciences and engineering
7310	*	9320	*	Basic and general research in the biological, medical and physical sciences
7320				**Research and experimental development on social sciences and humanities (SSH)**
7320	*	8329	*	Economic research, non-commercial
7320	*	9320	*	Research and experimental development on social sciences and humanities
7411				**Legal activities**
7411		8321		Legal activities
7412				**Accounting, bookkeeping and auditing activities; tax consultancy**
7412		8322		Accounting, bookkeeping and auditing activities; tax consultancy
7413				**Market research and public opinion polling**
7413		8325	*	Market research and public opinion polling
7414				**Business and management consultancy activities**
7414	*	1120	*	Farm management activities
7414	*	8329	*	Business and management consultancy n.e.c.
7421				**Architectural and engineering activities and related technical consultancy**
7421	*	5000	*	Project management activities for construction
7421	*	8324	*	Architectural and engineering activities and related technical consultancy
7422				**Technical testing and analysis**
7422	*	5000	*	Testing and building inspection services
7422	*	8324	*	Technical testing and analysis
7430				**Advertising**
7430	*	8325	*	Advertising, n.e.c.
7430	*	8329	*	Publishers' representatives

Rev.3.1		Rev.2		Activity

7491   **Labour recruitment and provision of personnel**

7491   8329   *   Labour recruitment and provision of personnel other than farm labour contractors

7492   **Investigation and security activities**

7492   8329   *   Investigation and security activities

7493   **Building-cleaning and industrial-cleaning activities**

7493   *   9200   *   Building-cleaning activities

7493   *   9599   *   Janitorial activities

7494   **Photographic activities**

7494   9592   Photographic activities

7495   **Packaging activities**

7495   8329   *   Packaging activities

7499   **Other business activities n.e.c.**

7499   *   7200   *   Telephone answering activities

7499   *   8325   *   Mail advertising

7499   *   8329   *   Bill collecting, credit rating, direct mailing, photocopying and duplicating and other business activities n.e.c.

7499   *   9414   *   Agency activities for engagements in entertainment or sport attractions

    L   **Public administration and defence; compulsory social security**

7511   **General (overall) public service activities**

7511   9100   *   General (overall) public service activities

7512   **Regulation of the activities of agencies that provide health care, education, cultural services and other social services, excluding social security**

7512   9100   *   Regulation of the activities of agencies that provide health care, education, cultural services and other social services, excluding social security

7513   **Regulation of and contribution to more efficient operation of business**

7513   9100   *   Regulation of and contribution to more efficient operation of business

7514   **Supporting service activities for the government as a whole**

7514   9100   *   Ancillary service activities for the government as a whole

7521   **Foreign affairs**

7521   9100   *   Foreign affairs

Rev.3.1		Rev.2		Activity

7522 **Defence activities**
7522 9100 * Defence activities

7523 **Public order and safety activities**
7523 9100 * Public order and safety activities

7530 **Compulsory social security activities**
7530 9100 * Compulsory social security activities

M Education

8010 **Primary education**
8010 9310 * Primary education

8021 **General secondary education**
8021 9310 * General secondary education

8022 **Technical and vocational secondary education**
8022 9310 * Technical and vocational secondary education

8030 **Higher education**
8030 9310 * Higher education

8090 **Other education**
8090 * 9310 * Other education n.e.c.
8090 * 9591 * Activities of barber and beauty schools

N Health and social work

8511 **Hospital activities**
8511 9331 * Hospital activities

8512 **Medical and dental practice activities**
8512 9331 * Medical and dental practice activities

8519 **Other human health activities**
8519 9331 * Other human health activities

8520 **Veterinary activities**
8520 9332 * Veterinary activities

8531 **Social work activities with accommodation**
8531 9340 * Social work with accommodation

Rev.3.1		Rev.2		Activity
8532				**Social work activities without accommodation**
8532	*	9310	*	Job training and vocational rehabilitation
8532	*	9340	*	Social work without accommodation
	O			**Other community, social and personal service activities**
9000				**Sewage and refuse disposal, sanitation and similar activities**
9000		9200	*	Sewage and refuse disposal, sanitation and similar activities
9111				**Activities of business and employers organizations**
9111		9350	*	Activities of business and employers organizations
9112				**Activities of professional organizations**
9112		9350	*	Activities of professional organizations
9120				**Activities of trade unions**
9120		9350	*	Activities of trade unions
9191				**Activities of religious organizations**
9191		9391		Activities of religious organizations
9192				**Activities of political organizations**
9192		9399	*	Activities of political organizations
9199				**Activities of other membership organizations n.e.c.**
9199		9399	*	Activities of other membership organizations n.e.c.
9211				**Motion picture and video production and distribution**
9211	*	9411	*	Motion picture and video production
9211	*	9412	*	Motion picture and video distribution
9211	*	9414	*	Sound recording studios
9212				**Motion picture projection**
9212		9412	*	Motion picture projection
9213				**Radio and television activities**
9213		9413	*	Production of radio and television programmes, whether or not combined with broadcasting
9214				**Dramatic arts, music and other arts activities**
9214	*	9414	*	Production of theatrical presentations
9214	*	9415		Activities by authors, music composers and other independent artists n.e.c.

Rev.3.1		Rev.2		Activity
9219				**Other entertainment activities n.e.c.**
9219	*	9310	*	Dance instruction
9219	*	9414	*	Other entertainment activities n.e.c.
9219	*	9490	*	Operation of ballrooms, discotheques, amusement parks and similar attractions
9220				**News agency activities**
9220		8329	*	News agency activities
9231				**Library and archives activities**
9231		9420	*	Library and archives activities
9232				**Museums activities and preservation of historic sites and buildings**
9232		9420	*	Museums activities and preservation of historic sites and buildings
9233				**Botanical and zoological gardens and nature reserves activities**
9233		9420	*	Botanical and zoological gardens and nature reserves activities
9241				**Sporting activities**
9241		9490	*	Sporting activities
9249				**Other recreational activities**
9249	*	9411	*	Casting activities, motion pictures
9249	*	9414	*	Casting or booking agency activities
9249	*	9490	*	Other amusement and recreational service activities n.e.c.
9301				**Washing and (dry-)cleaning of textile and fur products**
9301		9520	*	Washing and (dry-)cleaning of textile and fur products
9302				**Hairdressing and other beauty treatment**
9302		9591	*	Hairdressing and other beauty treatment
9303				**Funeral and related activities**
9303		9599	*	Funeral and related activities
9309				**Other service activities n.e.c.**
9309	*	8329	*	Issuing licence plates by private contractors
9309	*	9332	*	Pet grooming and boarding
9309	*	9490	*	Training of pets
9309	*	9599	*	Other personal service activities n.e.c.

Rev.3.1	Rev.2	Activity
	P	**Activities of private households as employers and undifferentiated production activities of private households**
9500		**Activities of private households as employers of domestic staff**
9500	9530	Private households with employed persons
9600		**Undifferentiated goods-producing activities of private households for own use**
9600	n/a	Undifferentiated goods-producing activities of private households for own use
9700		**Undifferentiated service-producing activities of private households for own use**
9700	n/a	Undifferentiated service-producing activities of private households for own use
	Q	**Extraterritorial organizations and bodies**
9900		**Extraterritorial organizations and bodies**
9900	9600	Extraterritorial organizations and bodies